Library Juice Concentrate

Library Juice Concentrate

Edited by Rory Litwin

Library Juice Press, LLC
Duluth, Minnesota

Published in 2006

Printed on acid-free paper

ISBN 978-0-9778617-3-6

Library Juice Press
PO Box 3320
Duluth, MN 55803
http://libraryjuicepress.com/

For Elizabeth Cobey

Contents

Acknowlegments

I owe debts of gratitude to individuals who offered moral support and advice over the years that I have been producing *Library Juice*. They are simply too many to name. However, Kathleen de la Peña McCook and Mark Rosenzweig deserve to be singled out for thanks. Conversations with Mark through the years that I published the web-zine and blog were inspiring and energizing and helped me clarify my thinking. Mark is a remarkable person, and his friendship has been tremendously rewarding to me as a writer and as a person. Kathleen's faith in me and her belief in the importance of *Library Juice* as a contribution to librarianship have been a great support. Additionally, her long career as an academic on the library scene has made her uniquely valuable as an advisor to me in editing this book and, especially, in moving forward with Library Juice Press. Without the help of Mark and Kathleen and others friends over the years, this book would not have been published.

Preface

Library Juice Concentrate:
A Book for *die Jahrtausendwende*

Kathleen de la Peña McCook

Library Juice Concentrate is a millennial touchstone for librarianship. The essays, interviews, and discussions in *Library Juice Concentrate* were published in Rory Litwin's webzine, *Library Juice*, between 1998-2005. The topics are of utmost concern to librarians at the start of the 21st century, but the initial format of these essays as postings on the worldwide web is emblematic of the transformed and transformative nature of librarianship at this time. Rory Litwin has characterized himself as an avid user of social networking Web 2.0 types of sites, but also as a frequent communicator with librarians of the baby-boom generation. He is "something of a bridge between two generational cultures in librarianship" (p.71).

In the mid-1990s many librarians, especially new graduates, adopted Internet technologies and web-based services with great enthusiasm. Many programs that educated librarians changed their names to become "Information Schools" or "I-schools," and a generation of people who work in libraries, for the most part, lost connection to the shared history and philosophy of librarianship. People still took jobs in libraries, but their skill set—in general—was increasingly removed from a connection to the scholars and philosophers of librarianship who through writing and service had developed one of humanity's most trusted professions.

When I wrote the paper, "Using Ockham's Razor" for the American Library Association Congress on Professional Education in 1998 I realized that "librarianship" was being abandoned by a large part of the LIS professorate and the students that filled our classes were more focused on the web than print collections or archives. I began reading *Library Juice* in 1999. I found my way to it when I read Litwin's essay, "Cease and Desist," in the mailed to my house paper copy of the *SRRT Newsletter* of December 1998. I remember thinking what a good grasp Litwin had of social change issues. I realized I could subscribe to *Library Juice* online, and I did. *Library Juice* was just what I needed to begin to lead me through the growing online discussions among new librarians that didn't take place in print-on-paper.

Looking back to the initial issues of *Library Juice* I realize that I responded to the publication because Litwin grasped the traditions and history of librarianship so well and commented upon them with intelligence and insight in an online format. He demonstrated promise for rapprochement between the old and new librarianship. I should point out that the essays in *Library Daylight: Tracings of Modern Librarianship, 1874-1922*, a companion volume to *Library Juice Concentrate*, also appeared online as part of the webzine and contributed to my confidence in Litwin as a thoughtful individual who looked to the past for knowledge and the future as a convergence of the old and the new. So much of the material posted in various library blogs at this same period assumed the world had just begun, which, naturally, did not inspire the same level of interest in someone who had journeyed from keypunch cards to the Internet. In fact, it seemed ironic to me that so many writing about libraries at the turn of the millennium were willing to disregard the thousands of years of library traditions. Litwin's work demonstrated that there was a cadre of librarians who saw the profession as a continuum. The fact that he used the (then) new format of the web to explore timeless issues underscored that librarianship was, indeed, a continuum and not a dead end.

I had been Chair of the American Library Association Office for Literacy and Outreach Services in 1997 and worked to get greater attention to the ALA Policy 61 (Library Services to Poor People). Some of this effort was rewarded in the spring of 2000. When asked to be guest editor for American Libraries I chose the theme "Ending the Isolation of Poor People." I took a big step from print to blog with this issue and sent a note about the "Ending the Isolation of Poor People" theme to Rory Litwin, which he published in *Library Juice* 3(6). He included a link to the Social Responsibilities Hunger, Homelessness and Poverty Task Force (HHPTF). *Library Juice* made me see the power of linkage. People read the articles in the magazine and didn't connect to SRRT HHPTF—but if they read the note in *Library Juice* they made the connection. This was a Eureka moment for me in seeing how blogs could move us ahead from passivity to action. It was June, 2000. I recognize that in a few years someone will read this and wonder how this could seem amazing, but this is part of the importance of *Library Juice*.

Library Juice existed at the dawn of the online experience and it was a central resource for the transition. Libraries cataloged *Library Juice* as an online serial. More library blogs appeared in the first years of the millennium but *Library Juice* continued to be iconic. Litwin included essays by library activists such as Mark Rosenzweig, Ann Sparanese, and Chuck

D'Adamo. He edited listserv discussions on topics such as the Better Salaries Initiative. He interviewed key "nextgen" figures such as Jessamyn West. He organized items on Cuban libraries. *Library Juice* also included trenchant and thought-provoking quotations, websites of the week and reading lists.

The essays and other artifacts from the webzine that appear in this volume stand on their own as thoughtful contributions to the practices of librarianship in the 21st century. But it must be remembered that they had their first life in an electronic format that has become an important component in the way librarians began to communicate at the turn of the millennium. With the publication of *Library Juice Concentrate* Rory Litwin has captured the spirit of a time that began in great hope with the Clinton-Gore optimism for a new century with widely available information for all people and ended in a time of great despair with the oppressive regime of Bush-Cheney and the structure of the USAPATRIOT Act and CIPA.

In the pages of *Library Juice Concentrate* we find thoughtful deliberations on politics, democracy, human rights, commercialization of information, intellectual freedom, anarchism, and Cuba. We see how the instantaneous capacity to post information can create a new level of discussion shared among far more people than ever before. *Library Juice Concentrate* captures a tectonic shift in the development of librarianship.

Kathleen de la Peña McCook Is Distinguished University Professor, University of South Florida, School of Library and Information Science in Tampa.

Editor's Introduction

Library Juice was a web-based electronic serial that dealt with issues at the intersection of libraries and society, generally from a left-wing perspective, often from a philosophical point of view and often with humor. I published *Library Juice* from January, 1998 through September of 2005, turning out issues of 15,000 words or so on a weekly and then a biweekly basis. A few months after ceasing publication of the online serial, I resumed it as a blog, which continues today, albeit with far less content in a given month.

This book is one of many potential anthologies of material from *Library Juice*, and represents decisions that I hope were the right ones. Some readers may notice the absence of certain features or elements that they liked: none of those interesting listserv discussion threads are present; a number of popular essays are not here; and some of the fiery radicalism and irreverent humor that made a splash in the earlier days are missing. Among my reasons for putting the book together as I have are copyright and privacy concerns; the ephemeral, current-events orientation of much of what originally went into the e-zine; my sense of what works in a book versus what works in an online publication; and a sensibility that has changed a bit since the late 90s. The things that I decided were most important to include were the articles that invited readers to think a little bit more deeply, or at least a little differently, about questions in librarianship that are typically given ready-made but inconsequential and poorly thought-out answers. In addition to those pieces I threw in a few lighter elements, a decision that I think keeps the book faithful to the old *Library Juice*.

The first section of the book, titled "Foundation Building," contains five short articles by me and a sixth by Mark Rosenzweig, all dealing with some aspect of the philosophical foundations of the profession. The first, "The Library Juice Manifesto," is a declaration of the "library spirit" that moved *Library Juice*, and aims to communicate the ideas that originally inspired me, as well as to provide a simple and clear basis on which to hold together a progressive vision for the profession. Next, "Neutrality, Objectivity, and the Political Center" is my attempt to unravel persistent questions about the tension between neutrality and activist social ethics in librarianship. This essay provides one conceptual solution that I think both protects professional neutrality as a value and respects and supports the right and responsibility of librarians to respond to known reality as moral beings. Following that is "Classic and Neo-Information," a brief, slightly cheeky essay that draws an important distinction between two fundamentally different ways in which the word "information" is used by librarians, pointing out the consequences of our conflation of the two separate meanings behind this central piece of our vocabulary. Our treatment of "information" in the sense of bits and bytes according to the ethics of "information" in the sense of facts relevant to an issue or problem has implications for practice that should be examined. The next three articles are from the later period of *Library Juice*, in its blog phase of 2006, and they are concerned, each in a different way, with certain existential issues that have arisen in society and in librarianship as a result of technological change. "Why Our Relevence Lies in Not Being Information Professionals" is inspired by the writings of Sven Birkerts, Neil Postman, Theodore Roszak, and Dan Schiller. The aim of this essay is to establish a humanistic understanding of what it is that librarians offer that is unique. "Questioning the Techie Mission," the next piece, identifies a technological ideology that circulates through the profession, and raises questions as to its source and its ultimate end. "Print Virtue and the Ontology of the Bo-ring," the next of these essays, pertains to the effects of technological change on our modes of learning, communicating, and thinking. This article is a response to popular ideas about "the millenial" generation and how academic libraries should change in order to serve them, and is informed by the writings of Walter Ong and Marshall McLuhan. Finishing this section is Mark Rosenzweig's expression of a philosophical foundation for the profession as a whole, based on service directed toward the goal of human autonomy, which he calls "an implicit project of all humankind." The title of this essay is "Aspects of a Humanist Approach to Librarianship... A Contribution to a Philosophical Foundation." I recommend this essay to anyone who suffers from nagging questions about whether her work as a librarian has any meaning; it shows, in a deep sense, why our work matters, and offers renewal and reconnection to those for whom librarianship may have become just a job.

The second section, "Librarianship: Professional Issues," has three essays, an interview, and an email debate dealing with more everyday, down-to-earth professional matters. The email debate, the first item in the section, is over the question of librarians' salaries, and begins with my unpopular assertion that the campaign to improve our pay is based on myths and colored by an attraction to the role of the victim. Next, and somewhat related, is my brief essay titled "Undone by Flattery," which criticizes our tendency, as a profession, to flatter ourselves, and to reward celebrities and dignitaries who insincerely flatter us. Next is my response to Google's December 13, 2004 announcement of their massive library book scanning project, which I published in *Library Juice* a few days later: "On Google's Monetization of Libraries." This essay touches on critical questions of continuing relevance which are for the most part avoided or ignored in our discussions of this mammoth project. It is because these questions, (which have for the most part also been raised by others at other times) are the key ones, and go to the heart of what librarianship has become, that they tend to be avoided. Next in this group is a 2006 item from the *Library Juice* blog that looks at the Library 2.0 phenomenon in relation to the core value of patron privacy, titled, logically, "The Central Problem of Library 2.0: Privacy." This brief essay makes a rather simple point, that at the heart of many proposed Library 2.0 services is the sharing of personal information, and that in combination with library services this is problematic. Finishing the section is an interview with Barbara Tillett, who has served in the Library of Congress for many years as the chief of their Cataloging Policy and Support Office. Many in the library left first encountered her name as the villain character in Sanford Berman's tales of cataloging heroism; that is, as the personification of the bureaucratic obstacle to Mr. Berman's valiant pursuit of subject heading reform. I interviewed Ms. Tillett about subject heading reform and other issues, out of an interest in presenting the other side to this story, and found the interview informative and interesting.

Section three, "Intellectual Freedom and Media Independence," pairs two concepts that are linked by analysis in one of the essays. The four articles in this section are by four different authors. The first, "Four Popular Errors About Free Speech… An Attack on Complacency and Dissociation," is my challenge to readers to look a little bit more deeply into some of the ideas we have received about intellectual freedom. Our longstanding strength with respect to this core value as a profession, as proud as it should make us of our tradition and our practice, has the unfortunate effect of making intellectual freedom a closed question, one to which we already know the answers, perhaps without thinking. This essay argues that some of our common assumptions about intellectual freedom are in fact false. The next essay is Tami Oliphant's thorough explanation of the importance of alternative media in a society that is dominated by market forces. She makes it clear that market effects on publishing are an intellectual freedom issue, and active collection of alternative publications is necessary for the full support of intellectual freedom in society. Following that is Chuck D'Adamo's well-informed history of the alternative press, "Some Alternative

Press History," which serves to connect this book to its political roots. Finishing the section is Doug Horne's article, "Information-Seeking During Wartime: Reconsidering the Role of the Library in Increasing User Self-Sufficiency." This article explores the way the internet expanded access to information about war and conflict during the second Gulf War, and asks some questions about what librarians can learn from these observations.

Section four is "Librarians: Culture and Identity." For some reason that I have not yet been able to understand, the generation of librarians that entered the profession as the internet was just booming made it a priority in their web publishing to celebrate and to worry about their cultural identity as librarians. Concerns about image have always been with us, but not with the intensity, excitement or playfulness that young librarians exhibited in the late 1990s and into the 2000s. I engaged in this to an extent and responded to it, and the three items in this section are examples. The first item, titled "A Librarian's Confession," is a brief self-disclosure in which I offer what I hope is an antidote to attempts to refigure librarians as various species of rock'n'rollers in an effort to promote the idea that libraries and librarians are something entirely new in the electronic era. I argue that the public image of librarians has strength, and that the stereotype is mostly a good one and tends to describe us better than some young librarians acknowledge. After that is an essay that might attract objections to its placement in this section: "A Critique of Anarchist Librarianship." It is my view that self-described anarchist librarians are engaging in an identity game more than they are engaging in actual politics. This essay is my attempt to show that anarchist librarianship is, despite the objections of those who claim to practice it, an oxymoron. The last item in this section is somewhat related to that: an interview with internet maven Jessamyn West in which she gives a defense of her idea of anarchist librarianship and discusses her politics and values.

Section five could have been ommitted without harming the book from the reader's point of view; the book would still have seemed cohesive and complete to the reader. This section, titled "Cuba," is about the Cuban "independent library movement," or rather, the response from the library left to that political campaign. I have included this section primarily for historical reasons. In my view, this issue has changed the character of the library left drastically, as it has sparked the emergence of serious differences between people who had previously considered themselves warm friends and comrades (a split that reflected similar political faultlines that emerged within the left after the terrorist attacks of September 11th, 2001). Those in the library left who have stayed in the fight to defend Cuba against this very sophisticated PR campaign have paid a certain price to do it. I want our reasons to be remembered. The articles in this section, though it may be possible to find them in other places as well, are included here as a contribution to our memory of this issue and the fight that has surrounded it. These articles include Rhonda Neugebauer's report from a 2000 educational visit to Cuba, Ann Sparanese's report on Cuba to the ALA International Relations Committee's Latin American and Caribbean Subcommittee, and Larry Oberg's "The Status of Gays in Cuba: Myth and Reality."

Section six, "Various and Sundry Readings," is a collection of the kind of things that originally put the "juice" in *Library Juice*. The first item, a collection of "Library Limericks" by Carol Reid, is actually previously unpublished. It is included in this book to represent a thread of humor in *Library Juice* that lacks useable examples from back issues, while offering something new. The next item, "Some Meditations on Those Amusing Searches," takes a look at some gems dug out of the Libr.org server logs over a period of a year or so. It categorizes and analyzes some of the bizarre and embarrassing web searches that led users to pages on Libr.org in that time period. The next item, "Selected Quotes for the Week," is a digest of some of the best examples from a regular feature of *Library Juice,* in which I shared a thought provoking, inspiring, or aggravating quotation at the beginning of each week's issue. This collection of quotes is rich with ideas. "Suggested Paper Topics," the next item, is simply a collection of original paper topics that have the potential to engage library school students in some interesting issues and enlightening research. The section, and the book, finishes with a reading list for progressive librarians.

Many of the essays included here have been partially rewritten for publication in the book.

It is my hope that this book reaches a thoughtful audience of veteran and new librarians. I hope that it encourages younger librarians, especially, to approach professional questions with confidence, originality, and attention to the intellectual and political struggles of the past.

Rory Litwin
Duluth, MN
November, 2006

Section One:
Foundation Building

The Library Juice Manifesto

By Rory Litwin
Originally published in *Library Juice* 4:35, October 3, 2001

Libraries are special because they are at once communitarian, libertarian, and models for sustainability.

They are communitarian in the economic sense because they are built on solidarity. A community pools its resources in order to share them.

Libraries are libertarian in the social/intellectual sense (civil libertarian) because of the ethic of intellectual freedom, which says that all ideas should be included and nothing censored.

This combination of economic communitarianism and social/intellectual libertarianism creates the ideal support system for a democratic society, because the library provides everyone with access to ideas and provides access to every idea.

In addition, libraries are models for sustainable systems. By following the "borrow, don't buy" ethic, libraries provide an alternative to consumerism, an alternative to environmentally unsound overproduction and spiritually unsound overconsumption.

And libraries are further exciting because they need to be changed. They tend to leave out alternative or street-level materials; there is presently a tendency toward privatization of services and functions (with attendant barriers to access); libraries and library organizations need their decision-making processes democratized; access to local community information in libraries needs to be improved; in general, libraries tend to depart routinely from their founding principles as they struggle for a handhold in the environment of an increasingly neoliberal political economy and an increasingly reactionary social climate. We need to advance the Library Paradigm of information organization, preservation and access, to freshly propagate the idea of the library in society in terms of its underlying principles.

Notwithstanding their imperfections, libraries serve as a rare example of beautiful ideals actually functioning successfully in the world. This means that libraries should serve as a model for other institutions and endeavors. We need to spread the Library Spirit across society and teach it, as a model for positive change beyond the walls of libraries and throughout all contexts of information, communication, and learning. This is the Library Paradigm, and we can make it grow.

Neutrality, Objectivity, and the Political Center

By Rory Litwin
Published in *Library Juice* 4:7, February 28, 2001
Republished in this revised version in *Progressive Librarian* No. 21, Winter 2003

A discussion on the topic of "web site evaluation" from a bibliographic instruction listserv a couple of years ago made me think about the common confusion between neutrality, objectivity, and the political center. Neutrality, in our professional ethics, means being unbiased in our work and separating it from our personal viewpoints. Objectivity, whether we say we believe in it or not, is something we expect in factual information, and evaluate various resources based on our perception of its degree of presence or absence in them. The political center is that balance point in society on individual issues or in political identities, where the mainstream feels that "both sides of the issue" have been properly considered, policies are at their least controversial, and competing power interests are at an equilibrium. This essay will attempt to elucidate the confusion that exists between neutrality, objectivity, and the political center and show its relevance to our discourse about reference service, book selection, bibliographic instruction, and our professional role as librarians.

First, neutrality. The idea of neutrality springs from a truly important value—to respect the minds of our patrons, to let them think for themselves. However, this idea sometimes goes beyond the simple recognition of the patron's autonomy and says that we can do something undesirable: remove ourselves from our individual perspectives and suspend our personal, and perhaps even professional, judgment about information sources and information needs. While it is possible to present a wide range of materials to a patron that include opinions that we personally disagree with, it is not possible to represent these information sources entirely neutrally when we talk about them. We characterize them in certain ways, however subtly, that reflect our own feelings. This is inescapable. In collection development, too, we cannot help but be influenced by our own opinions about what is most important or credible, even though we can select materials that we disagree with. Where we do not follow our own opinions, we follow someone else's (which, sometimes, is appropriate). There is no getting around having opinions if we are authentic beings. And this leads to the most unfortunate problem regarding the idea of neutrality in librarianship: the belief by some librarians, in history and today, that the ethic of neutrality should discourage us from taking positions on social issues, either as a profession or as individuals. To be "neutral" on social issues is to pretend that ones life and ones mind is in a separate sphere from the world as it is affected by the issue in question. There is no escape from our connection to the rest of society and our ultimate involvement in every issue that affects it. And, there is nothing in the demand to respect our patrons' right to think for themselves that should preclude us from taking a stand, as individuals who are parts of a profession with a certain role in society and certain values, where it matters. When we do chose to be "neutral" on an issue, to pretend that we don't have an opinion or that it doesn't count (because as librarians it is not our "role" to have opinions), we are effectively supporting the existing balance of power. And that is, in effect, a significant position to take, and one that ought to be justified explicitly if it is to be chosen, and not hidden behind a phony understanding of an important ethic.

And then there is objectivity. As the question of the possibility of objectivity has been debated to death both near and far, I believe certain things have become clear. It is possible to use standards for what counts as objectivity that make objectivity impossible to achieve. This accomplishes nothing but the loss of a good word. In fact, we use the word "objectivity" all the time. The question is, what does it stand for when it is used properly? What is objectivity? Are we as librarians clear on its meaning?

In my view, objective information is simply information that is verifiable by any other person with their sensory and reasoning faculties intact. If you say I that have a blue aura, that is not objective information; it can't be verified. If I say that the WTO, through a secretive, undemocratic process, is rewriting the laws of sovereign states, including our own, and getting rid of important environmental and labor laws and regulations that were created through nominally democratic processes, that is objective information. It can be verified by examining the WTO's own internal rules, and their agreements and how they have been enforced in courts of law around the world (all information which is publicly available). Similarly, if a death-row inmate who claims to be innocent has his claim verified by a DNA test, it is the objectivity of that information which gives it its power in society. Objective information is what we can know to be factually true. Now, depending on our point of view, we can use different words when we talk about the objective facts. For example, I might talk about an Israeli occupation of Palestinian territory, and you might use other words to describe the situation (less justifiably, in my opinion), even if we have access to the same objective, factual information. Ultimately, we can't communicate about facts without lending our own point of view to our representation. However, there is something in factual information that is independent of our personal perspective. Objective information, if it is not distorted by its representation to the point that it says something very different, has a way of advocating for itself, as a result of calling human values into play. What this means is that sound opinions are founded on objective information and objective information will lead authentic beings to adopt opinions and act on them, according to their understanding of their interests. Accordingly, we are making a mistake if we regard information sources that express opinions as less than objective. They may in fact be more objective, in any given instance, than an information source that appears "unbiased" or "neutral," particularly if the existing balance of power requires misinformation in order to be justified. (If you want examples of how the mainstream media commonly propagates misinformation, or inaccurate representations of fact, in the interest of existing powers, read some of the articles on the website for Fairness and Accuracy in Reporting and their quarterly magazine, *EXTRA!*, at http://www.fair.org/. Two books that do something similar for popular versions of American history include *A People's History of the United States* by Howard Zinn, and *Lies My Teacher Told Me: Everything Your American History Textbook Got Wrong*, by James Loewen.)

A side note: The popular notion of objectivity has been damaged by the philosophical viewpoint known as "positivism" (which, while it remains the dominant way of thinking in the human sciences, has been increasingly challenged throughout the last few decades), and aspects of its historical antecedent, the Humean Empiricist tradition. According to Positivism, only statements that can be verified by science as either true or false have an actual meaning, and such statements, known as propositions, can never contain an attribution or judgment of value (goodness, badness, right or wrong). Therefore, according to this view, science, which is our path to the truth, can only tell us what "is," never what "ought" to be. It is because of positivism and the older, Humean tradition (which was the source of the general distinction between facts and values) that statements that advocate anything are so often seen as less than objective. Various philosophical currents, allowing for various different ways of understanding factual truth and its relationship to values and interpretation, have sprung up and grown up alongside positivism, borne out of a dissatisfaction with its hermetic separation of the thinking mind from lived reality. Some of these have weaknesses in terms of providing a foundation for knowledge in any kind of objective sense, but others, including Frederic Jameson's critique of Post-Modernism and Roy Bhaskar's Critical Realism provide high degrees of knowability for independently-existing reality.

In terms of librarianship, my feeling is that the concept of objectivity is often misused in teaching information literacy and in bibliography and collection development. Often, in instructional materials that teach students how to evaluate information resources, the concept of objectivity is often contrasted with "bias" or "advocacy." This is potentially misleading. Taken simplistically, in practice this understanding sometimes treats "objectivity" as a reason to support mainstream information sources, because these centrist sources are able to affect a tone of neutrality and balance on contentious issues (as if neutrality and balance are the same as objectivity). But these sources do represent a particular point of view and particular interests, and "balance" is in the eye of the beholder. One way that information sources affect an "unbiased" tone is by not challenging the existing balance of power, and therefore not giving the appearance of advocating anything. But the existing balance of power does favor certain interests over others, interests that are certainly advocated by such "unbiased" materials. (Indeed, the existing balance of power is what it is in large part because of the influence of these supposedly "objective" sources of information.)

The way that a debate is framed in an information source is an important but often unrecognized aspect of rhetoric. The ability to recognize the framing of a news story, for example, is part of what is known as media literacy, and should be an everyday part of information literacy teaching. For example, are the sources quoted mostly industry and government sources and representatives of industry-supported think tanks? Are people from the community used as sources? How are the different sources and their interests characterized by the reporter? If we apply the principles of media literacy to mainstream sources, their appearance of objectivity becomes questionable and their neutrality is exposed as an invisible advocacy.

Finally, the political center. Of course, centrism isn't touted as a professional value or consciously sought out in reference sources. But having a bias toward the political center is often mistaken for objectivity, and the effect of "neutrality," as it is usually understood, is to support the interests of the political center, the existing balance of power. The political center can exert a strong attraction for conformists, because of its promise of acceptability. This social sense of acceptability can be a substitute for critical thought, because it offers answers that are approved in advance. While it is true that within subgroups the phenomenon of conformity can lead to politically varying beliefs, and that no ideology has a monopoly on independent thought, there is a definite, erroneous sense that the truth is to be found at the average of what various people believe, that the truth must be "somewhere in the middle." this comes partly from a graphical representation of a political spectrum that ranges from one side to another on a horizontal plane, and an accompanying metaphor of the scales of justice. But this is not necessarily the most accurate representation of the political field. The political field is the field of competing interests in society, competing power interests. In a class-based society (such as any mass society now in existence, in one way or another), a more accurate representation of politics might be vertical—the power elite at the top (who claim the profits of the people's work and determine what that work will be) and the people further down (who create the profits but don't see them or exert control over the nature of their own work or its uses). Serious theories along these lines are complicated, but the basic idea of a vertical differentiation is sound, and while it is commonly understood in a certain sense, it is seldom applied to public discourse about specific issues. Nevertheless, in a nominally democratic society like ours, the people use politics to have some control over what happens, and to improve their situation by degrees without changing the basic, class-based state of affairs. The resulting, ever-shifting balance of power is what is commonly understood as the "political center."

The political center should not be mistaken for objectivity, though it often is. And it should not be supported by our interpretation of professional neutrality, as it often is. We should understand "objectivity" as referring to whatever is verifiably true apart from what anyone might believe, without an implication that to be objective means to lack a point of view or an opinion. We should certainly be on the lookout for that bias that says that centrist ideas are more objective. We should respect the call for professional neutrality insofar as it amounts to offering our patrons full respect for their right to think for themselves, and we should be happy to present to them information sources with which we personally disagree. We should not be unsatisfied if they reach conclusions that are different from our own, as long as we have provided them with good information and offered realistic, well-founded caveats. But neutrality as it is often understood, meaning that in our professional lives we will be absolutely uninfluenced by personal opinions, is impossible. And where it is taken to mean that we should refrain from taking positions on social issues either personally or as a profession, the idea of neutrality is a definite evil, because it supports the existing balance of power, and does it invisibly, in cases where caring individuals, armed with objective information, likely would not.

Postscript:

When I posted a previous version of this essay to LISnews.com, one critical reader, Bob Watson, responded, "That's all very fine, but what one does also has an imbedded nature due to the institution in which one works. The institution has values of its own." This is surely an important part of the picture, to which I can only respond by pointing out that it is the people who act within institutions that give the institutions their values. While it is undeniable that our freedom within institutions is limited, there are times when we should take personal risks—great or small—in order to exercise a greater degree of that freedom and commit ourselves to a moral purpose. Adolf Eichman wrote in his memoirs (still unpublished), "Now that I look back, I realize that a life predicated on being obedient is a very comfortable life indeed. Living in such a way reduces to a minimum one's own need to think." That is an extreme statement to juxtapose with an issue like collection development decision-making or information literacy instruction in an institutional setting, but the principle applies.

Classic and Neo-Information

By Rory Litwin
Originally published in *Library Juice* 4:16, May 2, 2001
Republished in this revised version in *Information for Social Change*
No. 13, Summer 2001

You've undoubtedly noticed that the pace of cultural change has given rise to new uses to the word "classic": classic rock, Classic Coke, classic cars. When new things replace old things, the new things usually lack something that we didn't appreciate before it was missing. What is missing from the new then gives a new value to the old thing that can be indicated with the word "classic." (The word "retro," by contrast, is trivializing.) I think that this is sometimes more than simple nostalgia; it is part of how our culture is dealing with the fact that change, or even what is commonly thought of as "progress," is not exactly the same thing as improvement. (This is true even if you don't prefer classic rock).

This editorial is concerned with the way a new concept of information, which I will call neo-information, has replaced the old, which I will call classic information. Understanding this conceptual change is essential for understanding the "information age." It is also important in thinking about the role of libraries in an "information society."

Classic information is knowledge about facts or events or the communication of that knowledge. Libraries provide classic information in the sense that they provide access to reference materials and the facts contained therein. Classic information, is, in a sense, that which is "about" reality. Long before the information age, libraries provided the classic information that is contained in almanacs, directories, dictionaries, etc. Libraries also provided access to literature, but literature was not information or something that information could contain; it was a different category. Classic information is a much more limited concept than neo-information.

What I call neo-information is the concept of information created by Shannon and Weaver, and is the accidental development that, in my opinion, gives their work its social significance. Shannon and Weaver created a special definition of information for use in their theory—it became that which could be carried by a signal in the process of electronic communication. Electronic signals now primarily carry images and sounds; thus, images and sounds are now also information (neo-information).

Neo-information is also "that which is about reality", but in a new way: in the sense that it is form abstracted from substance or that which gives order and pattern to physical matter. Thus, your DNA contains the information that gives order to the protein molecules that make up your body. The TV signal contains the information that gives order to the electrons that hit the phosphorescent screen. There are machines, used by engineers to create models, that take three-dimensional maps or designs created on computers and turn them into three-dimensional objects. And, a TCP/IP stream might contain the information that makes up Sartre's Nausea, thus making literature a subset of neo-information.

In a sense, neo-information is just overgrown classic information: nothing more than very extensive knowledge (whether in someone's mind or only in a device) of facts and events—the facts and events that make up reality. But in becoming so ubiquitous it has become something new as well. Perhaps the main feature of the contemporary age is the way in which the images and information with which we are surrounded have become our reality. Where Jean Baudrillard speaks of simulacra, he could just as easily speak of neo-information (or the mediated world we create through our use of neo-information). Where information was originally "about" reality, in the age of neo-information it has become the substance of "reality" itself.

This characteristic of neo-information is what reveals the value of classic information. Where neo-information creates a new reality that is dependent upon it for existence, classic information is dependent on the real world which it is "about" and privileges that reality. Classic information, therefore, has the potential of maintaining our connection to the real world and authentic existence, while neo-information offers a connection to itself via images.

Today, classic information and neo-information exist side by side under the same name ("information"), and that is the source of a problem, in that neo-information borrows from the moral authority of classic information. Classic information is related to truth telling, investigative journalism, critical reflection and sworn testimony; the practices which bind us to reality as a group. Thus we have the moral weight of the saying, "information wants to be free" and the traditional values of librarianship (equity of access to information, intellectual freedom). Because it falls under the same title of "information," neo-information borrows from the value of classic information and uses it to support its own form of non-connection to reality.

This is evidenced in legal protection for the crappiest corporate entertainment, commercial billboards, and the other junk that makes up our mental environment, and their presence in libraries.

Drawing a distinction between classic information and neo-information is important for thinking about library services in the information age. In an age where the majority of our experience throughout the day is taken up by "information," how can we begin to think about the future of an institution we understand as being based on "information provision?" With information so ubiquitous, how can we have any claim to being "information professionals" any more than a graphic artist who uses Photoshop or a television producer is an "information professional?"

The answer is to conceive of information as it relates to libraries in terms of classic information and not neo-information.

Shannon and Weaver have been nothing if not a source of confusion for our profession.

Why Our Relevance Lies in Not Being "Information Professionals"

By Rory Litwin
Originally published in *Library Juice* 8:7, April 22, 2005

As librarians, the turn of the century has found us in an awkwardly grandiose and insecure position. On the one hand, we belong to humble institutions representing the hearth and home of the public sphere; thought of warmly but never feared (except by those suspicious of what offenses might lie in our collections). On the other hand, we point to something called "information" as the defining subject of our professional expertise, saying that we are and always have been the world's "information professionals," in a strategic claim to a special connection to "information" as the new defining matrix of the postmodern world as a whole. Perhaps it is out of envy for professions that carry a higher voltage in the information society that we do this. More likely, however, it is a bid for a perception of relevancy in a new era that has left many of us feeling outmoded.

Our relevance, I will argue, is only at risk to the extent that we identify ourselves with such an all-encompassingly abstract and at the same time technological concept as the new concept of "information." Our relevance into the future is securely present in the old word "librarian" and within aspects of librarianship that predate the modern library movement, with all of its efficiencies and scale. This is because the transformation of facts, narrative, interpretation, discourse, analysis, summary and ouevre, as well as sophistic rhetoric and outright disinformation, into something called "content" has created a steadily growing need for professionals with a specific role in relation to information: that of interpretively locating and recontextualizing it; in other words, matching the reader to the right book (or article or page or dataset, etc.; but perhaps usually the right book) and putting it in context for him.

By focusing on the technical sides of efficient librarianship, that is, the science of information organization, and neglecting the question of how knowledge of subjects, knowledge of publishing, knowledge of intellectual history, and knowledge of humanity itself ("information seekers") fits into professional practice, library educators have created a vision of librarianship that seems to melt into general qualities of information literacy possessed increasingly in abundance by non-"information professionals." If what librarians do is navigate and build information structures with technical proficiency then the question of our relevancy will naturally arise, because that function is already part of the nature of work and play for a generation of middle-class youth who do not necessarily think they need libraries. If, on the other hand, librarians are known to connect people to the depth of texts, that is, if we, through our knowledge of subjects and of people (as well as knowledge of information systems) provide reading that is so on-target that users will actually spend time reading it, engaging with it, reflecting upon it and understanding it, then our relevance in the information age will be assured.

The key to our relevance is to think of what we have to offer that our users generally lack. In the now-remote past what users lacked was access to and understanding of information systems, even from a user's perspective. Now this access and understanding is commonplace. What we now have to offer that is commonly lacking is the sense of the differentiation within what is generally thought of, revealingly, as "content." We have the ability to place knowledge and discourse in its proper context in order to help users make sense of it and to lend ideas their deserved coherency. In the postmodern situation, ideas have become suspect, facts easily fall into disrepute by virtue of their claim to facthood, authorship and subjectivity have been deconstructed, discourse fragmented, texts liquified into a flow of "text," and the world emptied of meaning; all appears to be undifferentiated "content," every byte exchangeable for every other byte. What critics of postmodernist ideas tend to miss, however, is that this historical situation has its roots in material (technological and economic) developments, not in the bad imagination of certain French thinkers (or whomever). Attacking champions of ideas that express the contemporary situation doesn't change the contemporary situation, does not bring back what has been lost. What we should think about when we think about the postmodern situation is not only what has been lost (and what has been gained) but what needs have newly emerged in society because of it, and how we can meet those needs. It seems to me that there cannot be an endemic loss of depth and meaning without a concommitant emergence of a new need for depth and a new need for an orienting connection to history. Librarians (and not "information professionals") are, in certain contexts at least, in a position to meet that need.

Information: what it was and what it is

In the "information age," we use the word "information" in two ways: in a simpler, older sense, and in a new, expanded sense whose historical roots are understandable, if partially distinct. A century ago, "information" was certainly something that books might hold, but books could hold other things as well, like stories, analysis, interpretation, arguments, and opinion, in the same way that someone could tell you some information that you needed to know but not every verbal utterance could be understood as providing information. In the old sense of information, the word essentially meant "potentially usable facts." So, the position, speed and heading of a gunboat was information, as was a friend's telephone number, but stories, opinions, and songs were not. We still sometimes use the word in this way (especially with regard to reference materials) and our new use of the word, as well, is colored and conditioned by features of this older use.

"Information" now means, of course, anything that can be transmitted by electronic signal and rendered meaningful to the senses by some device. Facts are still information, but so are texts of all kinds, movies, music, and the signals that control machines. "Information," in the post-metaphysical information age (marked in part by the deconstruction of the subject), can also be thought of as the totality of non-physical substance. This is a far cry from the older meaning of information, but we often use the word without knowing in which sense we are using it. Hence, ideals that have their roots in human relations concerning information-in-the-older-sense—e.g. facts that are relevant to the governance of society—are in danger of losing their wide acceptance due to their misapplication to relations concerning "information" in the newer, larger sense (e.g. positing a "right to information" where the information we're talking about is an entertainment product).

The development of this new meaning of the word "information" has its roots in early information theory in the first half of the 20th Century. Electronic engineers and mathematicians such as Ralph Hartley and Claude Shannon were theorizing the transmission of information (information in the old sense, originally) across electronic circuits for military purposes. In the interest of maximal efficiency, they developed a theory of information whereby it can be quantified into bits (unwittingly paving the way for its more complete commodification). Their work led to the word "information" being used for anything that was transmitted over a wire, despite telephone and telegraph communication having been in use for many decades without being considered "information technology." Initially it was information in the old sense that they were concerned about transmitting—logistical and strategic information, primarily. But as their work led to the development of more and more complex and capacious computer systems, lengthy texts, digitized music and movies could be transmitted digitally as bits, and the word "information" was at the ready to describe these systems of communication.

One not-very-obvious result of this change is that our way of thinking about the things that are now considered information but once were not (such as narrative, analysis, interpretation, opinion, and entertainment) has become somewhat conditioned by our way of thinking about information in the older sense. Information in the sense of "usable facts" has certain qualities. It comes in discrete, small units; it is consumed as simply and quickly as it is received; it is immediately comprehensible; it does not have depth; it is functional and directly related to action; it all has the same relation to truth (simply either accurate or inaccurate, knowable only by comparison to other known facts); and it is objective—seemingly the "view from nowhere"—rather than subjective and situated in a particular life or community. We now tend to think of anything called "information" according to these attributes, contributing to our new tendency to consume cultural material quickly and without much attention to its depth or provenance, and with more energy invested into its acquisition or consumption than to its comprehension in context.

In light of this, librarians' self-conception as "information professionals" can begin to be seen to have certain implications. According to the inherited earlier meaning of "information," it leads us to see ourselves—in all of our activities—in the light of a primary role as dispensers of potentially useful facts, regardless of the type of information we are working with. This results in an outlook on the information we are mediating (be it facts, narrative, analysis, opinion, entertainment, or whatever) that is not inclined to attend to its depth, provenance, comprehension or meaning for an individual life, but rather tends to treat it in discrete units of a neutral, objective character, to be consumed as quickly as they are received.

According to the newer definition of "information," our self-conception as "information professionals" also leads us to see ourselves as channelers of electronic information flows. To the extent that these information flows are considered according to their form as "information," or bytes, they are undifferentiated and only potentially meaningful. It is only when it ceases to be "information," that all-encompassing non-physical substance, that it can become differentiated into facts, narrative, analysis, interpretation, songs, jokes, etcetera; recorded communication with a provenance and a context.

Accordingly, it is only when we cease to be "information professionals" (and return to being librarians) that we will see ourselves and be seen as having a role in the interpretation, contextualization and use of information, not merely in its channeling.

Containers and content

"So you are saying that librarians are content people," an information-ager might respond, using a rather new expression.

The new definition of information has led to the currency of the word "content" to distinguish that part of information that means something from the part that contains or carries it, or its medium of transmission. If you try to imagine how to talk about the things that fall under the term "content" (e.g. narrative, factual compendia, analysis, etc.) using another word, you will find that it is difficult; and yet a few years ago we were not using the word "content" in this way at all. We did talk about books and articles, as well as discourse, scholarship, communication and published work, but none of these have quite the same meaning. It is worth noting that "content" is grammatically "of" something—i.e. electronic information systems, when it is used in terms of information—while "discourse," "scholarship," "communication" and "published work" are terms that indirectly invoke not technology but the context of communal intellectual activity. So even if you say "I am an information professional, but not like a computer programmer, because I am a content person," you are referring to your field of engagement from the point of view of a technological rather than an intellectual order.

This has two important implications. The first has to do with the effect upon human life of our adaptation to the technological worldview (something the late Neil Postman referred to as "Technopoly" in his book of that title). The progressive integration of machines into the fabric of our lives changes the way that human beings think and live, according to an instrumental logic of efficiency. This is a process that has been under way for centuries and probably isn't going to be reversed by anything short of a cataclysm, but it is worth being conscious of it as we think about human needs and our role in society as librarians or "information professionals."

The second implication of the conception of our field of activity as "content" is that it is an orientation to recorded discourse and communication that lends itself to the commodification of words and ideas, because "content" has a new attribute of quantifiability and a new suitability to systems of digital commerce. While it is true that books have always been bought and sold, the sphere of scholarship and shared intellectual activity has existed with a degree of independence from the marketplace that is now being eroded. There are a number of factors involved, but the transformation of ideas, narrative, analysis, song, discourse, fact and non-fact into "content" is a chief one. So whenever possible we should avoid referring to ourselves as "content people" or to our sphere of activity as the "content" of information systems.

A practical example

The foregoing has been rather abstract. I would like to present an example of one way that this problem manifests itself in libraries, specifically academic libraries serving undergraduates.

Over the past ten years vendors have begun selling more and more digital content to academic libraries, mainly collections of scholarly journal articles, sometimes aggregated in wide-ranging databases and sometimes by collection or individual journal subscription. We have also begun to see some electronic books—usually scanned versions of books originally published in print—become accessible directly from online catalogs in web browsers. There is an attractive convenience factor to information that is deliverable "right to your dorm room" or accessible without getting up from the computer, and manageable on one's hard drive after download. This convenience factor affects aspects of reference service, especially such things as virtual reference, where there is a bias in favor of information resources that are deliverable via the web. Further, as physical collections grow to the point of challenging the availability of space in library buildings, an additional incentive to shift to electronic resources emerges.

As long as librarians are providing readings based on good interpretations of user needs, contextualizing them properly and offering interpretations as needed, helping to guide library users in their use of information, and as long as the medium of communication doesn't itself distract the reader from the process of reflection and comprehension (which it can), then format by itself is not a problem. But it may be that, gradually, librarians' adoption of electronic formats has in fact interfered with our mode of service.

One thing that is rather easy to forget in the course of providing reference service if pressures exist that run counter remembering it is that the nature of the information contained in scholarly journals is usually quite different from that contained in books, primarily in that journal articles mostly communicate current research on very narrow topics in a way that requires a real knowledge and a familiarity with the language and conceptual universe of their disciplines, while books tend to offer more comprehensive treatments of topics (even though they may be narrow topics treated in sigificant depth) in a way that provides at least some introductory orientation to the matters at hand.

I find that academic librarians very often lead undergraduates doing rather broadly-focused research projects to these databases of scholarly journal articles at a point where little of what they contain will be of any use, simply because the vastness and power of these databases, and the quality of the information they contain, is so impressive, and because they are so convenient to use.

There are electronic books in the catalog as well, but relatively few. Part of the reason that electronic books designed for use in web browsers have not become a major category of academic library service the way digitized scholarly journals have is that the format is unfriendly to them. One can print out a 15 page journal article quickly and without difficulty, or even read it on a monitor relatively painlessly, but a 200 page book is grossly inconvenient to use in electronic form given the current state of technology. Often, even if a book is exactly what an undergraduate student working on a simple research project needs, they won't immediately be directed to it, because of the preference for apparently-convenient browser-based content. And if they are directed to an e-book, say, in a virtual reference setting, they are not likely to make much use of it due to the cumbersome format.

What this is an example of is how librarians have begun to be affected by the undifferentiated nature of "information" and "content," where we should above all be providing that differentiation for users, counseling them about what type of article or book or discussion we are showing them, and providing some sense of its place and its role in human discourse. This doesn't necessarily mean that we should avoid digital content, but there may be times when it takes an extra moment and an extra thought in order to break a pattern of bias in favor of electronic resources, where presently available electronic resources are inadequate for a specific real need. We should avoid reinforcing an orientation to information as an undifferentiated surface to be navigated (and work to diagnose it in ourselves), and instead engender an orientation to intellectual activity as a source of meaning, depth, connection to history and one's sense of place in the universe.

"Librarians" versus "information professionals"

My argument is about the significance of language in how culture is shaped. The terms "information," "information professional," and "content" are problematic for librarians because of the new, technologized relationship to the human record that they invoke. Because our adaptation to this new language results in our ultimate imitation of technologies that users have become adapted to themselves, the new orientation to our work that they imply is the real source of our threatened irrelevance, not the technology itself. In other words, we are only in danger of being replaced by technology if what we do is the same as what technology does. "Information professionals," I try to argue, approach information from a technological standpoint and in so doing create their own irrelevance. Within the very long history librarianship, however, are practices and roles for which the postmodern situation would seem to be creating a new need. Specifically—and I believe this function is implicit in the word "librarian"—we offer access to the depth and to the connection to history that is implicit in the human cultural record. We do it through our knowledge of information systems, yes, but no less than that, through our knowledge of subjects and our knowledge of people.

The word "wisdom" might be vulnerable to various forms of postmodern dismissal, but it represents both an enduring human reality and an enduring human need. It attaches itself easily to person of a librarian, if indirectly and in the background, but seems decidedly out-of-context in relation to an "information professional." Our relevance is attached to our ability to serve the human being in his or her subtextual quest for wisdom—not by "being the wise counsel," but by providing access to the human record in a way that recalls the importance of provenance, depth, reflection, and comprehension in context. This provision of context and invitation to depth, I would argue, is the key to the continued relevance of librarians in the 21st century.

Further Reading:

Sven Birkerts, *The Gutenberg Elegies* (Faber and Faber, 1994)

Neil Postman, *Technopoly: The Surrender of Culture to Technology* (Knopf, 1992)

Theodore Roszak, *The Cult of Information* (University of California Press, 1986)

Dan Schiller, "How to Think About Information," in *The Political Economy of Information*, Vincent Mosco and Janet Wasko, eds. (University of Wisconsin Press, 1988)

Questioning the Techie Mission

By Rory Litwin
Originally published in *Library Juice* (blog), March 27, 2006

Now that I've officially had my blog for almost month, I can reflect a little bit. Things might still change, but I have to confess that at the moment I feel somewhat outside the mainstream of library blogging culture. My blog entries aren't getting a lot of links to them and I don't feel much a part of the library blogging "conversation." It might be because I've presented myself from the beginning as not wholeheartedly into the blogging thing. But I think there is a bigger reason, and that is that most library bloggers write a lot about tech topics, and I don't.

In fact, there is almost a presumption among library bloggers that "we" are mostly techie librarians with an overriding interest and concern with bringing state-of-the-art technologies and 2.0-ish web services into our libraries. Most library bloggers, it seems to me, are advocates of technology in libraries, and often practically missionaries. I question the value in being advocates or missionaries for technology, and question the assumptions behind that posture. Technology advances strongly and securely enough without the help of technology advocates, and as librarians there are more important ends to pursue (often with technology as part of the means, but always with explicit reasoning).

A common theme on library blogs is Why Don't They "Get It?" The "they" here means usually older, not-so-techie librarians, and "getting it" means "understanding how information technology can change everything and already has changed everything for everyone and how it is the new and overriding mode of communication for libraries—right now." There are some presumptions behind this theme, and the are:

- That the techie librarians who make up the readership of these blogs represent young librarianship per se. This is probably not so accurate, because there are both lots of middle-aged techie librarians and lots of younger non-techie librarians.
- That these techie librarians generally represent the mass of new, younger library users and potential users, who are equally techie and greater in number than out-of-date librarians realize. This is probably less accurate still.

- That library users and potential library users are generally underserved at present because of the slowness of libraries' adoption of new technologies. This is an assumption that can be questioned objectively, and may turn out to be true, but hasn't yet really been tested. It is assumed irrationally.
- That aside from any attention we might pay to our users' demand or lack of demand for the newest technologies in our provision of library services (and in fact we pay little attention to this, at least not in an objective way), such technologies and all of their effects are automatically good. Technology is a cause to fight for, us against them. This is an assumption that many techie librarians make at a deep level, leading to a fervent zeal that seems very curious to those of us who fail to see its basis.

Library bloggers (and I recognize that there are loads of exceptions) tend to have those presumptions in common, and those presumptions make up a lot of the existing library blogging culture. This has certain significant results:

- Library blogging culture, because of the commonality of technology promotion, feels alienating to librarians who don't share that mission at any level (even if they are otherwise happy users and accepters of technology and sometimes see technology as a useful means to explicit ends).
- Because of the dominance of the library blogosphere by tech promoters, the assumptions behind the tech-promotional mission of many librarians are unlikely to be questioned within their own culture.
- The unquestioning enthusiasm for new technologies blinds some librarians to the complex and significant, and sometimes negative, social effects that these technologies can have, making nuanced and balanced decisionmaking within institutions more difficult.
- Technology promotion is ultimately the promotion of products offered by major vendors, which leads to an increasing power shift in our institutions away from librarians and toward corporate players. These corporate players have put continuous effort into driving our decisions over the years and replacing our work with their own, and have real success in recent decades, ultimately changing the nature of libraries for the worse by compromising our purpose and public-interest character.
- The focus on the promotion of technology as an end in itself can distract techie librarians' attention away from the educational mission

of libraries, so that as they learn more about technical tools, they learn less about the subtleties of interpreting and responding to user needs, and less about the bibliographic (electronic resources included) knowledge of subjects that's needed to be a good reference librarian.

There has been little examination, that I am aware of, of technophilia as an ideology. It is an ideology, and a very strange one. As an ideology it is a lens through which things are are rendered according to a set of values in the act of seeing. But unlike the ideologies of Right and Left, these values don't spring from any idea of what is essential to humanity, but from something else: a prioritization of the process of controlling and reshaping the world through the use of ever more complex tools, and of our own adaptation to that artificial world and to those tools. As ideologies go, seen at its root, it is rather perverse.

It would be saying too much to say that library bloggers hold to a perverse ideology of technology, and it wouldn't be true. I'm sure most techie library bloggers don't consider themselves as treating technology as an end in itself, but believe they see it strictly as a means: in their practice of librarianship they keep in mind the real ends of the enrichment, enlightenment and empowerment of their patrons. At the same time, however, I think that there are definite assumptions involved in the technology advocacy posture, and there isn't necessarily anything supporting those assumptions. In other words, the techie mission is irrational: there would be less emphasis on technology within the library blogosphere if the bloggers involved were more objective about technology.

That is what I "get." I wonder how many other librarians in my generation and younger agree? It is really rather hard to tell.

Print Virtue and the Ontology of the Bo-ring

By Rory Litwin
Originally published in *Library Juice* (blog), May 15, 2006

Here's a riddle: What does the musical interval of a fifth have to do with discussions of multiple literacies, the millenials, and Marshall McLuhan's predicted decline of print literacy and the corresponding rise of a more multi-sensory way of being, thinking, and judging?

Answer: play the high note and followed by the low note of the interval of a fifth and it says something that the written word alone can't convey: "Bo-ring," spoken as a one-word argument against an idea or a statement whose expression fails to hold the attention of a thoroughly modern person. "Bo-ring," in the age of print culture's decline, is the new "stupid."

If you say a person's argument is unsound or falls apart because of some unconsidered factor, well, you may be right and you may be wrong, but either way you're going to have to explain yourself using greater detail and subtlety than the original expression, and a rebuttal to your argument will have to go further still into that detail and subtlety, thus demanding progressively more and more of your audience's span of attention and ability to concentrate. This is simply the nature of investigations which have literal truth as their goal, and follow from a strong interest that some people have in "getting it exactly right." That interest in "getting it right," in knowing the truth, is still a virtue today, but will perhaps not be such a virtue in the future, and probably already isn't for a lot of people. The character of investigation into truth and of truth's expression as we know it from the context of written, rational discourse derives, as Marshall McLuhan and Walter Ong showed, from centuries of print literacy and is correspondingly shaped by the nature of the printed word as a medium of communication. Thus, print culture has a shaping effect not only in the way that people learn things (as advocates of multiple-learning styles like to talk about) but on the kinds of truth, in a very deep sense, that people learn and generate.

We can be somewhat specific about what print literacy is good for. Print literacy is good for engendering an intellectual separation between oneself and the world, so that one is able to make independent judgments and form abstract understandings, of things, people, events, ideas, arguments, etc., by applying to them the standards of an individual mind full of the operations of logic, insight, questions, prior knowledge, and abstract moral principles. This individualistic, intellectual separation and independent judgment is an important virtue in our culture and is sometimes called "critical thinking," in its broadest sense. This critical thinking allows us to be far more rational in our decision-making and in our everyday judgments than we would otherwise be, and much less likely to be manipulated by others. Those for whom critical thinking in this broad sense is a paramount virtue (and I am one of those people) usually think that most other people don't have enough of it. To these rational individuals, in the beginning of the 21st century, many people are frequently saying, "Bo-ring!"

To say, "Bo-ring," is, in effect, to say that there is something more important to be considered than an idea's relation to the truth. It may even be to demonstrate a comparative lack of interest in what is the truth. "What could be less virtuous than that," we critical thinkers wonder of people who say that we are "Bo-ring."

New categories of virtue may be emerging in the era of print culture's decline. A critical thinker might identify the new, non-boring virtue as "entertainment value," since that is what seems to be most valued by those who find long passages of text, or lectures without slides, too boring to tolerate, and who always prefer more sensory stimulation and less intellectual content. Those who can better articulate the new, multi-sensory virtue from its own perspective might talk about it in another way, making reference to things like Grace, connectedness, "keeping it real," life-energy, flow, Being-Here-Now, or not being paranoid. (Certainly, too much intellectual separation between oneself and the world can be pathological and dangerous to those who lack the strength to maintain that human connection, though history's greatest intellectual heroes have embodied that separation in extreme degrees.)

Whatever the opposite of boring really is, if it is a virtue of the information age, many people clearly would rather be called stupid than boring. (This is a fact that I wish Al Gore and John Kerry had understood, in all of its implications.)

I am very attached to the print literacy that is in decline, to the value of the skills of concentration that were once taught as part of a young person's development into an adult, but are now regarded merely as a personality trait of language-oriented learners. Print literacy and the critical thinking skills that go with it are the underpinnings of a rationally-deliberating, democratic society (to the extent that any such thing has ever existed). I strongly believe that the discussion about learning styles, though it has some basis in real psychological differences, is mostly a cover for a broad, society-wide de-prioritization of print literacy in favor of communication media that are a) more fun, b) more sensory, c) more interactive, d) less subject to questioning and accountability with reference to rational standards of truth, and e) more capable of manipulating people, for both commercial and political ends. I am also aware that my own beliefs about this matter are conditioned by the historical culture of print literacy in the West, and may ultimately not be connected to anything truly universal. I just wish that more people saw the unique value of print literacy and were not under the delusion that media are content-neutral, and saw the breadth and historic implications of the contemporary shift in McLuhanesque terms. The contemporary shift is not simply an extension of the values of educational democracy into our society of experiential, visual, and auditory as well as language-oriented learners, and it is not simply an accomodation to the new generation of learners reared on video games, as though the What of their learning is not being changed by the How of their learning. It is a shift that for honest educators and librarians raises questions that go much deeper than questions about format, but actually concern matters of pedagogy and values at the deepest level, that make us ask, what are we here for as educators in the first place?

I think we need to ask those most basic questions about pedagogy and the What of learning as a part of our approach to the "hot" questions our profession is facing at the moment, having to do with formats, the millenials, the web, networked information, Library 2.0, and the rest. So, to librarians who are interested in these questions I am recommending some Marshall McLuhan and Walter Ong as important complicators as well as illuminators.

Aspects of a Humanist Approach to Librarianship... A Contribution to a Philosophical Foundation

By Mark Rosenzweig
Originally published in *Library Juice* 6:15, July 17, 2003

True human autonomy, arguably the goal of human development to which we, as humanists, are committed, is never achievable, meaningful or desirable, alone, in isolation, that is, without a concrete, collective context— without others and their 'otherness', as well as their similarity.

It is the opposite of bare independence (although it requires, or entails, the exercise of independence in the sense of independence of the 'immediate'), of so called 'American individualism'. It is, more precisely, the opposite of action or inaction in an atomized universe, no matter how 'free' it seems.

Human autonomy is not a given, as 'individualism' pretends to be. It is not a 'state of nature'.

This goal of autonomy of which I speak, this possibility, is a profoundly social goal, an historic goal. For it to maintain momentum it has to be chosen and re-chosen over and again, in new circumstances, not only by individuals but by the collectivities they form and re-form in history.

Critics of progress say that its proponents are determinists. The goal of human autonomy is the negation of thoroughgoing determinism. All creatures, after all, are creatures of choices of this or that, x or y. For humanity, however, choice becomes elevated above mere 'behavior' to 'meaning', both through its possibility of free exercise and the recognition that all choices are not possible at all times, but that we, nonetheless, are not constrained within or limited to choices of either/or. This is the possible autonomy which, when enabled, is the realm of the choices beyond either/or.

An implicit project of all humankind, for all humankind, it is realized through the struggle of hominids to be, after all, more fully human, an impulse kept alive through all the history of blood and violence, unnecessary suffering, injustice and domination, that we drag behind us either as the useless burden of ignorance or the useful if more painful burden of self-knowledge.

It is the recognition of ourselves and the other as us-as-nature; us-and-nature, and our-nature-as-humanized, recognized as the shared meaning of who we are necessary for assuring a better future, as something to be cultivated.

You ask what is the implied goal of human autonomy, a goal to which we can aspire as a social-ethical imperative? It is what Marx meant when, in defining the good society, he said it was ultimately the possible emergence of the set of social arrangements which are such that the free development of each is the condition for the free development of all. Could there be a better creed for librarianship and the goal it shares with all truly humanistic pursuits?

Autonomy is possible, perhaps paradoxically, only through deepening human interconnectedness—active 'global' interconnectedness today—synchronic and diachronic, of all who exist together and all who have ever existed. It is history and co-existence. It is past and future meeting in the now. It is, above all human consciousness, the self-motivating search for knowledge, the irrepressible instinct, not just for survival, but for something far beyond mere survival.

It is well, though, to remember that this is not a predetermined evolutionary process. We do not yet, especially in our truly global society, share the same past, see the same future or live the same now, and after all, that may not ever be, or may not ever be realized under conditions fully conducive to global human development. It remains to be seen. There is no 'inevitability'.

But we can say that human autonomy alone will allow us to appreciate natural diversity and cultural plurality and group and individual difference, character and person, and to synthesize them in understanding, rather than be overwhelmed by it, oblivious to it, rejecting of it, destructive of it.

Human culture in its totality, including human knowledge, recorded and unrecorded, impossible for any one person or collective to comprehend in its diversity of interpretations and viewpoints, is the record of the struggle for human autonomy, its successes and failures, its triumphs and disasters, its truths and its lies, its glories and genius and its tragedies and follies. The shelves of the libraries of the world, full of contradictory and hostile views, of their interpretations, of the transcribed dialogues of the contests of interpretations, of the return to interpretation and, hopefully, dialogue at a higher level, are not repositories of truth or wisdom, but the tool to reach truth and wisdom, to follow the basic Socratic quest: "Know thyself!" . The librarian is not the arbiter of truth, but the facilitator of dialogue and interpretation, and of returning to dialogue and interpretation at a higher level.

It is the historicity made possible by the freedom of human autonomy and later the knowledge of historicity which is the humanists' always repeated, yet ever-new, message, which makes possible the ability to constitute an horizon of the 'new', of that which has not yet existed, which always contains the prospect, if not the promise, of liberation from the constraints which bind us in relations of domination of one by the other, relations which are the mark of unfreedom, of self-subjection, of mutual degradation, of limitation and imprisonment in meaninglessness.

The nihilism of, for instance, fascism (or crude collectivism as an end in itself) is the negation of the goal of human autonomy as a social project. The basis for the dialogical is destroyed, the foundations of the plurality of interpretations meeting each other productively is made impossible. There can be no real humanities, certainly no true librarianship under fascism.

The evolution of autonomy historically in culture is recorded in the quintessentially human activity of the creation, at first unconsciously then consciously, of artifacts and the collection, at first casually then systematically, of information—by individuals and institutions—not just as experienced and disappearing, transient, but as 'captured', preserved and recorded, therefore selected and interpreted, and, not just for one's own purposes, but for others' experience and purposes as well. No deepening communication is possible without communicants allowed, encouraged, to be open to hearing, to seeing, the voices and images, the traces, of the transmissible past, to being open to the otherness, too, of co-communicants' alternative views. And do we not know that there is no communication of even so-called information/data which is not already without meaning and interpretation, a merely abstract transfer or exchange? Every communication is a transaction, which is transforming of its content and (potentially) transformative of its communicants. It is always a reciprocal process or it is not communication.

Further, there is the collection of artifacts and texts and the creation of new information and records. And further, the collection of information about those artifacts, and of artifacts about that information.

Finally, in the anthropology of shared meaning there is the dialogue of the interpretations themselves, the acts of imagination based on the internalization and symbolic manipulation, conscious and unconscious, of the appropriated conversation of the world, at its best in respect and awe for its totality and complexity and suggestiveness.

These all, in turn, form the basis for the more-than-merely-immediate dialogue between people and cultures and their histories—shared and different, overlapping and separate—and, as well, the not-just-obviously-practical and instrumental interpretation by peoples and cultures of their artifacts and texts but also the shared, humanizing appropriation of their meanings just for their own sake, for the sake 'merely' of human, collective self-affirmation and happiness.

At first, face to face dialogue, then interior, imaginary dialogue and interpretation of the other in relation to one's self, then dialogue at distance in time and space, and social dialogue and interpretation of the-self-in-the-world-with-others: this is the complex basis for a common practice which is neither extraordinary nor merely routine, but is, nonetheless, emancipatory practice, of the common practice underlying mutuality in pursuit of seemingly simple goals, simple yet unrealized, which are 'liberatory' goals, or even of ends pursued for play and pleasure, so often permitted only to the elite, for humanizing each other in social communion.

I assert here that besides the satisfaction of basic needs—and, more darkly, despite the terrible things we historically have thought and, atavistically, still think we must do to better satisfy and secure them for ourselves revealed by a review of history—wars, enslavement, degradation, treachery, deceptions, thievery, torture, murder, rape, despoilment, exploitation—there is a parallel, if asynchronous history (not altogether independent, one might add, realistically) of 'humanization' in each epoch, marked by the enlargement of the capacities for empathy, based deeply in biology, and also just as powerfully in the potential expansion of the quest for mutual understanding, based deeply in given forms of social organization which provide for the possible creative, constructive cultivation of knowledge, understanding and self-understanding necessary to give birth to higher forms of organization,interaction and ultimately, collective action for human betterment.

The goal is not as 'utopian' as critics are so quick to point out. "Utopian" has become an epithet in today's political discourse. I prefer to believe, along with the late Herbert Marcuse that: "It is the task and duty of the intellectual to recall and preserve historical possibilities which seem to have become utopian possibilities." If we in the professions and in librarianship in particular consider ourselves in a modest, sociological way to be intellectuals, his reminder could not be more apropos.

For what is the 'utopia' we propose we can help bring about? What is 'the good society' we propose?

As Marx modestly put it, the good society is one arranged in such a way in which the possibility of the full and free development of one is the precondition for the full and free development of all. This seems very much within the universe of the possible and within the intellectual orbit of our profession.

If you care to look, human autonomy itself in the light of reason reveals the sometimes hazy horizon of humankind's strivings. True, reason does not, of course, and cannot and probably should not exist without unreason. Unreason is the shadow which reason casts. It cannot be abolished anymore than we can abolish our own physical shadow. Its darkness too often overcomes the world and reason seems to be, in fact, the shadow of unreason, and, because of its nature, its servant. When reason becomes the servant of the irrational there is much to fear. Everything is at stake.

Humankind's more worthy tasks are daunting because their ultimate realization, always taking place just beyond the shadow of unreason, presuppose commitment to the continued striving towards cultivating that which makes them possible in the first place: the assertion of the possibility of universal and perpetual peace among peoples and nations, of the possibility, the choice of prosperity without waste which we can produce and share justly, of the social justice which knows no distinctions of sex, race or class, of the respect for nature, which is our nature, but not just ours.

Yet it is is not unreason which is the sole obstacle, not ignorance or error. It is apathy, it is lack of will, it is fear, it is cowardice, it is selfishness, it is conformism, it is timidity, it is cynicism. These are the forces that eat away at the foundations of the few institutions which attempt to assure the preservation of humanity's history when faced with the calculative imperatives of purely economic reason.

Reason alone cannot assure the preservation of what has been hard fought for, or assure progress or a better future. There is no reason without emotion, nor without passion, at least not which is not suspect. No disinterested, disembodied reason. That is a myth at best, a lie at worst.

The evil of unreason is not emotion, but the rather cold and bureaucratic idea (sometimes pursued with maniacal intensity and fervor, to be sure) that reason is purely instrumental and it is instrumental possibilities which determine what is do-able and therefore worth doing.

Immanuel Kant said: "Enlightenment is man's release from self-incurred tutelage. Tutelage [rote learning, instruction in custom] is justified only by humankind's inability to make use of understanding without direction from others, that is, with true autonomy. It is self-incurred because—or when—its cause lies not in a lack of reason but in lack of resolution or courage to use it without direction.

"*Sapere aude*"—Dare to know! "have courage to use your own reason"—that is the motto of enlightenment, says Kant.

If libraries were to proclaim their social mission in an inscription over their door they could not do much better than to proclaim "*Sapere Aude*."

For, as the great socialist Karl Kautsky said early last century, "the only real security for social well-being is the free exercise of people's minds."

Creating the conditions for that is the collective project to which librarianship makes a modest yet irreplaceable contribution. It will only continue to do so, however, if it probes its humanistic roots for its constitutive purpose and rediscovers its commitment to enlightenment and human autonomy.

Mark Rosenzweig
July 4, 2003

Section Two:
Librarianship: Professional Issues

Critical Discussion of the Better Salaries Initiative of Mitch Freedman's ALA Presidency

Originally published in *Library Juice* 6:25, November 27, 2003

The following is part of a discussion about librarians' salaries and the Better Salaries Initiative of ALA President Mitch Freedman that took place in May of 2003, between myself and members the Better Salaries Task Force, including Yvonne Farley, Carol Brey, Joan Godard, Margaret Myers, Mark Hudson and Luis Acosta. I made contact with this group following conversations with Jenna Freedman about the initiative. - Rory Litwin

Subject: Re: salaries criticism
Date: Thu, 29 May 2003 22:40:42-0700
From: Rory Litwin
To: [discussants]

Hello Yvonne, Margaret, Carol, Joan, Mary, Mark, and Luis (and Jenna).

Jenna has told you that I was planning on writing an article critical of the better salaries initiative. After talking to her about it and thinking about it on my own I decided that it wouldn't serve much of a purpose. I'm not sure how offensive my ideas would be to the library community if I published them—I tend to think that a lot of people would agree with me—but I don't see much point in attacking the initiative, now that it is underway and potentially a success. After all, if the initiative succeeds and my own salary goes up as a result, I am probably not going to complain. More importantly, if a grossly underpaid librarian sees their salary go up, that would be a good outcome. I wouldn't try to deny that.

As I understand it, after Jenna gave you the news that I was not going to write the article after all, there was still some curiosity in this group about what I had been planning to say. I'll try to write it down coherently here, avoiding polemics as much as I can. You might have responses that will open my eyes. If we all agree that it would be a positive thing, we could end up publishing the collected thread in an upcoming *Library Juice*—but only if we all agree it is a positive thing.

——

My first issue with the initiative is its portrayal of librarians as low-paid as a group. The idea that librarians are low-paid is absolutely essential in turning the effort to raise our salaries into a social-justice issue, one that can get librarians angry (or angry again, if they were politically active in the late 60's and early 70's and have grown complacent since, and want to recover a sense of moral purpose). While I think there are librarians in poor parts of the country who are poorly paid by the middle class standards of the average librarian (in the United States or Europe), the average librarian in the US is actually in an upper income bracket for the country. This is contrary to conventional wisdom, which says that we are working almost for free because it is an altruistic profession (which I think it is, despite the pretty good pay—I will get to that later). I am basing my assertion on the ALA Salaries Survey, Census figures on mean and median individual income, and the Bureau of Labor Statistics article "Rankings of full-time occupations, by earnings, 2000," which is available on the web.

According to this article, librarians rank 95th out of 427 occupations surveyed, with an average rate of pay $23.76 per hour. This figure has a relative standard error of 3.8%, on the low end for the survey. Librarians rank just above "Chief executives and general administrators, public administration" at 96th, "Supervisors, extractive occupations" at 97th, "Public relations specialists" at 98th, "Tile setters, hard and soft," at 99th, and "Underwriters" at 100th. Computer programmers are 104th, and Architects are 103rd. Accountants, mentioned in the Tookit as a group we would like to be paid as well as, rank 122nd, at $21.51/hr. Making a little more than librarians are "Urban planners" at 92nd, and "Editors and reporters" at 86th, making $24.81/hr. Athletes are 65th, at $28.13/hr, and Elementary School Teachers are way up at 59th, at $28.86/hr (for a nine month year—their annual pay depends on what they do for money the other three months). This is a very interesting report that shows a certain gap between the image that various occupations have versus the pay that people in those occupations get. I think the motivation behind the salaries initiative, the feeling that we are undervalued, is more based on a sense of a lack of respect for librarians in society than a real lack of pay for any but the most poorly paid librarians.

The argument I've just made that librarians are actually well-paid compared to other occupations doesn't take into account the requirement of a masters degree. Now, some would say that it's classist to assert that a someone with a masters degree deserves more money than someone who doesn't have one, if they both work as hard (or if they are otherwise just as deserving). I won't make that argument, because I think it's not at all convincing these days, not even to me—but I will point out that it's an argument. Others would say that just because our job requires a Masters degree doesn't mean that it is more complex, requires more knowledge or is more difficult, and certainly doesn't mean that it is more physically dangerous or entails greater legal liabilities. And when I think back on the Masters program I attended and a lot of the library work I've done I'm inclined to listen to this. (Everyone wants the world to know how difficult, complex, knowledge-based, etc. their own occupation is. Comparable worth studies such as Anne Turner's in California (Anne M. Turner, "California Makes the Case for Pay Equity," *Library Journal,* vol.127 no.17, October 15, 2002) have a fatal flaw if they claim to objectively compare the worth of different jobs by using members of just one of the the occupations being compared to judge which occupations are comparable.)

But let's accept for the sake of argument that the pay of librarians should be compared to the pay of other occupations which require a masters degree, and that librarians are being paid markedly less than comparable workers. The salaries initiative says that this is a gender-based inequity, that librarians are being paid less because they are mostly women, whose work is undervalued because of sexism. This could be true, and would definitely amount to a social justice issue in that case (though not one that is likely to cause a mass movement). I personally believe that this is not the real reason librarians are paid less. I could be wrong, and I don't think there is much social science evidence coming down either way on the question, but it seems to me that women are often in lower paid occupations because they are more willing to enter altruistic professions—that is, professions where there is a strong motivation for doing the work that is not economic, and where the work itself doesn't end up generating money that can pay high salaries (like engineering or law). Whether married or not, I think women are less socialized to be breadwinners, and are probably more socialized to be of help to society.

Librarianship, at least the way we like to understand it today, has a definite "social good" aspect. The role of libraries and librarians in maintaining (or trying to build) the conditions of democracy and to preserve and provide access to culture and to empower people is frequently talked about, but seldom in the context of a discussion where it is essential to say that we have to stop thinking of librarianship as an altruistic profession. I think librarianship IS an altruistic profession. It seems to me that the downside of the salaries initiative is that it might succeed in getting librarians to stop thinking of this as an altruistic profession, where our motivation really does come from certain values that are higher than the value of more money. I think it is simply inaccurate to think that much more money can be generated or redirected to us without compromising those values, especially considering what we are already paid. The reason for this is that educating the people for democracy and preserving and providing access to culture are not activities that make business sense, but will be done by people as long as people think it's important to do them (despite salaries in the inequitable low-mid 40's).

I should probably tell you a little bit more about where I'm coming from, if this is seeming a little strange. I have pretty much a middle class background, but grew up having less than most of the people around me. As I grew up I was first aware of having less than other people, and then later became aware that I was pretty affluent by the standards of the US, and began to feel guilty. Later I learned about the affluence of Americans by global standards, including Americans barely making what is considered a "living wage." (The global poverty level is considered to be $1 a day, meaning someone making $2 a day is not considered to be living in poverty if they're in a really poor country.) The affluence of North Americans and to an extent Europeans (including the working class) has caused global warming, polluted the ocean, air and land and has radically changed the ecosystem, destroying tens of thousands of species. Unhappiness in the Global South is caused not by what we understand as poverty, but by inequality (i.e. gross affluence). Our response to this is development efforts designed to give them the same type of affluence that we have, but on a scale of billions and billions of people. It seems obvious that the environment is already straining under the pressure of existing affluence; creating that much more seems to me a kind of suicide by gluttony. It also seems clear that our affluence hasn't created happiness for us so much as it has created a large market for Zoloft and similar drugs.

That's my general perspective. Now let me take you back to that time in my life when I was chosing a career. I struggled between my desire to be a moral person and my desire to consume more than I need. I made a compromise by choosing a profession that has turned out to be much better paying than I originally thought it was when I signed up. The (I thought) low pay was one of the reasons I chose the profession—I understood that working in an altruistic profession really is its own reward. I felt good about the fact that as a librarian I would be giving (by my work) more than I would be taking (by consuming).

Besides learning that the pay is more than I ever expected (and my pay is around average), I found out on the job that the profession has other rewards that are paid lip service but are never made a part of the calculus of compensation, as I think they rightfully should be. I'm talking about the fact that as librarians we enjoy what are probably the best working conditions of any profession in existence. This is in terms of the relative lack of stress, the intellectual stimulation, the satisfaction of helping and working for a better society, the degree of control over our work, and the professional community that we enjoy. To me, this is well worth the differential between what I make and what an engineer or a lawyer makes.

So what about the librarians at the low end of the wage scale, working in West Virginia or western Pennsylvania? I personally think it might be a good idea to have a campaign specifically for the most poorly-paid librarians. A union drive and negotiations based on prevailing wage could be a real help for librarians working in poor communities. But I think—I don't really know this, but it's my general sense—I think the fact that these are poor communities is more of a factor in the librarians' low pay than a relative lack of respect for librarians in these communities. That is, it seems to me that most everyone in these communities is underpaid relative to people in the rest of the country, because these communities are poor, which means it's not clear where the money would come from to pay their librarians more; keeping the libraries open seems to be a more immediate challenge (as it is even in moderately affluent areas that have come on hard times lately). Federal funding could balance things out, to a degree, but local governments might not want the strings attached, and getting that funding would be a tremendous political challenge, maybe not even realistic to think about.

Those are most of the ideas that I had planned to work into the article. Most would have been more fleshed out.

It's what I think, but I'm open to correction and am willing to see things in another way if I'm missing major parts of the picture, so I hope you will send me your thoughts on what I've written. As I said earlier, I think that there are probably a lot of people in the profession who share my views, so the answers you come up with could be useful.

Respectfully,

Rory Litwin

Re: salaries criticism
Date: Sat, 31 May 2003 01:49:56-0400
From: Mark Hudson
To: [discussants]

Speaking as a committed supporter of the better salaries initiative, I nevertheless believe that Rory has highlighted some important contradictions in the initiative as it has developed over the past couple of years. Specifically, his contention that "The idea that librarians are low-paid is absolutely essential in turning the effort to raise our salaries into a social-justice issue" resonates very strongly with concerns I've raised before in discussions with other supporters of the campaign.

In the early days of the Moneytalks list, I expressed extreme skepticism about the data on the salaries of beginning librarians contained in the annual ALA salary study, and about the rather uncritical use of that data in the Toolkit produced by the Better Salaries Task Force, which I otherwise consider to be a very useful document for those of us who support the initiative. The ALA salary study for that year, if I recall correctly, concluded that the average salary of a beginning MLS-degreed librarian was about $34,000 a year. It arrived at this figure using what I argued was an extremely questionable methodology. A questionnaire was sent to somewhere around a thousand library directors, of which I think about a half to two-thirds responded. (I don't remember the exact number, but it isn't crucial to my criticism of the methodology of the study.) The problem with the methodology, as I saw it and continue to see it, was that the directors were asked to provide salary information only for full-time, MLS-degreed librarians. But in the public libraries in the part of the country where I live, probably at least half of the MLS-degreed library positions are less than full-time and pay between $8 and $11 an hour. And I've seen job ads and heard stories from public librarians in other parts of country that indicate this problem isn't confined to just one or two areas (contrary to what Rory suggests). So, as I see it, it's not only that the $34,000 average beginning librarian figure arrived at by the ALA study is absurdly inflated. What's worse, the study essentially refuses to even recognize the existence of a large number of very poorly-paid librarians. Although I realize there's probably little if any available statistical data on these librarians, I've never understood why an initiative that seeks to show that librarians are grossly underpaid would base itself on information that completely ignores the most grossly underpaid librarians among us. Surely the statisticians at ALA could find some way to incorporate part-time and hourly-waged librarians into their salary studies.

So I'm somewhat sympathetic to Rory's idea of "a campaign specifically for the most poorly-paid librarians." I think that would be preferable to a campaign that begins with the premise that librarians are grossly underpaid because they only start out at $34,000 a year. But what I think would be even better is an initiative that represents the interests of ALL librarians by recognizing not only the salary disparities between librarians and other occupations requiring similar skills, education and responsibilities, but also the disparities WITHIN the profession—i.e. between relatively well-paid and grossly underpaid librarians, between academic and public librarians, between librarians in large, relatively well-funded urban systems and those in smaller libraries with poor local funding bases. Such an initiative would also represent the interests of paraprofessional library workers, many of whom don't even receive a living wage—let alone $34,000 a year.

I think to a large extent the better salaries initiative has tried to incorporate these concerns. The resolution drafted by several of us on the Moneytalks list calling for a "Fair Pay for Librarians and Library Workers Week" (I'm not sure if that's the exact title) and introduced in Council at Midwinter this past January struck a very good balance between the idea of "fair pay" based on skills, education and responsibilities and the concept of a "living wage" for the most poorly-paid librarians and library workers. Interestingly, it did so over the objections of a few (but only a few) Moneytalkers who didn't think the concept of a living wage was relevant to our campaign. If I recall correctly, some of these were the same people who had earlier dismissed my concerns about part-time and hourly-waged librarians. I remember one person even suggested that focusing attention on librarians at the low end of the wage scale might have the unintended effect of reducing the salaries of those already in the $30-40,000 range!

But I still think the better salaries initiative could do more to make it clear that we want to represent all librarians and library workers, from the relatively well-paid to the grossly underpaid. We could start by getting the statisticians at ALA to do a salary study that includes data on the part-time and hourly-waged, and that also looks at health insurance, paid time off and other benefits of employment.

I've never thought of the better salaries initiative as an end in itself, but only as a means to an end. In other words, I've never believed that the initiative could in and of itself bring about better salaries for librarians and library workers. Ultimately I think that can only come about through widespread union organization and a social justice movement in coalition with other social justice movements that increase our collective power and thereby force funders, policymakers and administrators to start treating us fairly and paying us all what we're worth. The purpose of the better salaries campaign in ALA, it seems to me, is to increase awareness and expectations in the profession to the point where librarians and library workers will ON THEIR OWN start building the organizations and movement that are needed to do that.

The issue of library salaries is a political issue—an issue of social spending priorities—as much as an economic one. So I don't agree that "turning the effort to raise our salaries into a social-justice issue" simply means portraying librarians as "low-paid as a group." It means demonstrating the injustice of library salaries in disparate sectors of the profession—along with the necessity of strong, well-funded libraries for expanding democracy and preserving culture—and then building the solidarity and movement needed to achieve justice for all. And although I take seriously Rory's concern about the salaries initiative "getting librarians to stop thinking of this as an altruistic profession", I don't believe that's going to happen as long as the campaign is based on values of solidarity and social justice.

- Mark Hudson

Re: salaries criticism
Date: Fri, 06 Jun 2003 11:54:16-0400
From: "Luis Acosta"
To: [discussants]
Dear Rory,

Thank you for your e-mail of May 30 to some of us in the better salaries initiative. As is often the case with your writing, your comments raise important and thought-provoking issues. Here are some of my own personal reactions.

The most important part of your comments pertain to your concern that the salaries movement "might succeed in getting librarians to stop thinking of this as an altruistic profession," and so the initiative might do harm to the role of libraries in preserving or building democratic culture. I want to make sure you are aware that all of us active in the salaries movement agree with you that the bottom line is preserving the democratic ideals of our profession. It is precisely the need to preserve these values that motivates us to fight for better salaries for librarians.

What is the relationship between preserving the democratic values of librarianship and improving salaries for librarians? The key is that a sufficient number of people need to be recruited into the profession to keep this librarianship enterprise going. I'm sure you are aware of the studies that show that an inadequate number of people are entering library schools to replace the people who are scheduled to retire. Our profession's failure to recruit sufficient new entry demonstrates that compensation is inadequate to attract sufficient people.

This was a point I made in an article I wrote that appeared in the Spring 2003 issue of *Law Library Lights*, the newsletter of the Law Librarians' Society of Washington, D.C. Because this issue has not yet been placed on line, I'll quote several paragraphs from my article:

> Complacency toward the inadequate compensation members of our profession receive is unwarranted. The librarian profession is experiencing a crisis in recruitment. Demographic data reveal that there is inadequate entry of new librarians to replace those who will become eligible for retirement in coming years. Numerous studies, such as those by Prof. James Matarazzo of the library school at Simmons College, show that an

insufficient number of entrants to the profession will be available to replace those who will retire. [See, e.g., James M. Matarazzo, Library Human Resources: the Y2K Plus 10 Challenge, 26 *J. Acad. Librshp.* 223 (2000).]

A central reason for insufficient entry into the profession is that compensation levels are inadequate to provide incentives to incur the significant costs of education necessary for such entry. Persons considering librarianship as a career have to weigh the expected salary they will receive against the costs they will have to incur to obtain a master's degree. The economic gains from education in librarianship are far lower than those of other professions requiring similar levels of education. Because the economic rewards are insufficient, not enough people are entering the profession. Thus it will not do to simply "get over the fact that we are not sufficiently valued," as Prof. Berring counsels, because our profession will become increasingly more marginalized if we fail to make library careers more attractive financially.

Under traditional economic theory, all things being equal, the coming shortage of librarians should tend to result in salary improvements as demand begins to exceed supply. But the example of another profession, nursing, demonstrates that labor markets for professions requiring significant training do not easily correct themselves to smooth over supply-demand imbalances. The U.S. Department of Health and Human Services has found that in the year 2000 the total supply of registered nurses nationwide was 6% below the nationwide demand, and it projects this shortage to worsen to 29% by 2020. [U.S. Department of Health and Human Services, Health Resources and Services Administration, National Center for Health Workforce Analysis, Projected Supply, Demand, and Shortages of Registered Nurses, 2000-2020 (July 2002), http://bhpr.hrsa.gov/healthworkforce/rnproject/report.htm.]   Not coincidentally, nursing, like librarianship, traditionally has been a predominantly female profession that has experienced corresponding pay inequities relative to other professions requiring similar levels of education.

Moreover, as librarian retirements increase, employers who do not understand the value of skilled librarians may begin to replace them with non-librarians, or simply not bother to replace them at all. (After all, who needs a librarian when you have Google?) When labor shortages in nursing result in nurses being overworked, patients die—a tragic but numerically measurable phenomenon. But when librarians are gone, the effect of inefficient distribution of information and knowledge is much harder to measure.

Given the challenge to the very survival of the profession of librarianship, it is essential that we continue our efforts across the law librarian profession to improve our economic circumstances.

My stilted prose in the article goes on and on, but you get the idea. Anyway, my fear is that when this pending shortage begins to manifest itself in earnest, the response by organizations that currently employ librarians will not be to raise salaries (and thereby help attract new supply) but rather to simply dispense with the requirement that librarian positions be filled with people who have been trained in MLS programs. This prospect bothers me, because I believe MLS programs are an important part of preserving the democratic values of our profession. MLS programs socialize people into thinking about, and more often than not agreeing, with these democratic ideals. The salary problem has caused a recruitment crisis, which in turn could lead to a crisis of maintaining the professional ideals of librarianship. If this analysis is right, then the salary movement, rather than threatening what you call the altruistic nature of this profession, could be the savior of these values.

Turning to some of your other points, in your comments you say that "I personally believe that [gender-based inequity] is not the real reason librarians are paid less." You then observe that "women are often in lower paid professions because they are more willing to enter altruistic professions." I'm not sure whether you are positing a causal link here, but it is not correct that gender inequity cannot co-exist with women choosing to enter altruistic professions. You state that "I don't think there is much social science evidence coming down either way . . . ." In fact, there is a massive amount of scholarship dealing with these very questions in the fields of women's studies and feminist political economy. The fact of women tending to enter altruistic professions is simply a matter of women's history in industrialized societies. During the late 19th Century, as women began to leave the private, domestic sphere and moved into the public sphere of commodified labor, their opportunities were limited largely to various "caring" professions, like teaching, nursing, social work, and librarianship. Women have tended to occupy what you call altruistic professions (what feminist economists call "care work," "caring labor" or "emotional labor") not on an entirely voluntary basis, and not because of some essentially nurturing nature. Women working in paid labor began to have a choice as to whether the work was "altruistic" only fairly recently. You may wish to consult the scholarship of folks like Nancy Folbre and Carol Baines, for example, on this historical development.

It is very significant to the well-being of these "altruistic" professions, including librarianship, that society can no longer count on exploiting the selflessness of women to work in these jobs at inequitable pay. Over the last three or four decades it has become much easier for women to enter other, better paying professions. This may contribute to the recruitment crisis I mentioned above. But this doesn't mean that gender-based inequity has gone away. And the solution is not to ignore pay inequity, but to ensure that librarians and other people in altruistic professions are compensated at levels that reflect the necessary level of investment in education for entry into these professions.

Feminist scholars have also addressed concerns like yours over whether paying more equitably in the caring professions will contaminate the altruistic nature of these professions. See, e.g., Julie A. Nelson, "Of Markets and Martyrs: Is it OK to Pay Well For Care?," in *Feminist Economics*, Vol. 5 (No. 3) (1999), at pages 43-59. Nelson's article addresses the same sort of questions you raise: "Is it appropriate to apply 'market values' to caring work? Does demanding higher money payment just buy into masculinist norms of markets and commodification? Aren't we somehow assured of a higher level of 'real' caring, if the workers chose this work, when they could have made more money elsewhere? . . . . Meanwhile, what about the neoclassical economic theory of compensating wage differentials, according to which low-paid care workers are fully compensated but simply choose to take a portion of their pay in warm feelings instead of cash?" Nelson analyzes these questions finds that there is little reason to fear that higher wages for caring workers will damage the cause of altruistic work. This analysis could be applied to your specific concern that librarians in particular might stop thinking about librarianship as an altruistic profession if we succeed in improving salaries.

You mention comparable worth and remark about possible flaws in comparative worth studies. While comparable worth is not an exact science, its inexactitude does not invalidate the principle that one should strive for pay equity between the sexes. With or without comparable worth, there is no objective, value-free science to setting compensation, so attacking comparable worth as non-objective is beside the point. The wage structure in modern industrial society is a social construct. Large organizations typically have administrative mechanisms for setting wages; they do not leave wage-setting purely to the market (which would be impossible in a mature capitalist society). The prevailing wage structures between professions reflect values inherited from decades ago, prior to when feminism started advocating for comparable worth, as to what types of economic activity were deemed more valuable than others. Those determinations incorporated the prevailing sexist assumptions of that time period (which sexist assumptions still exist, although maybe in less obvious forms). Comparable worth is an effort to correct shortcomings in the way wage structures within organizations are determined to eliminate the sexist assumptions that are built into them. While there certainly are methodological difficulties, the importance of the policy of eliminating gender-based inequities make it worthwhile to try to work these difficulties out.

You question whether librarians are in fact poorly paid, citing the data in the BLS report that ranks occupations by hourly wage. While I was surprised by the data in this report, I'm not sure if that data tells the whole story. I see that the total "mean annual hours" for librarians comes in at 1,773, which accounts for librarians' relatively high per-hour wage. As you note, elementary school teachers rank even higher (their "mean annual hours" is 1,423, which accounts for their high hourly wage). Now, most of the librarians I know (obviously not a good sample) work 40 hours a week. Evidently there are enough librarians in educational settings, such as school librarians, that the annual mean hours for librarians as a whole is relatively low. If one goes to other BLS data, one sees much greater disparities between earnings of people in professions like librarianship versus other professions. (For example, in the 2000 National Occupational Employment and Wage Estimates, at http://www.bls.gov/oes/2000/oes_nat.htm , computer programmers were estimated to made on average $60,970 a year, with a "mean hourly" rate of $29.31 an hour, while librarians were estimated to have made on average $42,730 a year, or a $20.54 "mean hourly" rate.) This data assumes everyone works 2080 hours per year, which of course is not correct, but the differences in the data makes me curious how the total number of hours is calculated in the National Compensation Survey; I wonder what would happen if you just used data from folks who do work 40 hours a week, for example. (If I figure out what's going on here I'll send another e-mail.)

You make the statement that "as librarians we enjoy what are probably the best working conditions of any profession in existence. This is in terms of the relative lack of stress, the intellectual stimulation, the satisfaction of helping [etc.]." I know that it is common for librarians to tell themselves this, and most of the time I tend to agree with it. However, it occurred to me the other day that there is quite a bit of emotional labor associated with my job as I was assisting a paranoid schizophrenic woman who thought she had been hypnotized and abused by the FBI and was convinced that Johnny Cochran had represented her in the early stages of a lawsuit that ultimately went to the U.S. Supreme Court. This sort of thing happens not infequently to me at my job. I think it's hard work.

On the question whether the glory of librarianship justifies the low salaries, forgive me for questioning whether we live in the best of all possible worlds. I myself worked as a lawyer for over a decade, and while most of the time I am glad I switched careers and became a librarian, I sometimes wonder, as I sit in my cubicle, whether my working conditions are so much better that it compensates for earning less than half of what I used to make. (Of course, my job at the Law Library of Congress makes me better off than a lot of other librarians.) I guess under the economists' concept of "revealed preference," it must be true that the differential is worth it to me since I have continued to work as a librarian and not as a lawyer. I must confess, however, that I sometimes think bad thoughts.

You note correctly that Americans are relatively affluent compared to others in the world. While this is true, it does not alter the fact that librarians should be paid equitably relative to other similar professions in America, so that an adequate number of people will invest in the education necessary to enter the profession. You also note that Americans' affluence hasn't collectively increased our subjective happiness. That point appears to be correct and borne out by the social science literature. Supposedly the people of Bhutan have the highest score on the Gross Domestic Happiness index. Again, however, the question of pay equity is a matter of equity in the overall wage structure in American professions. Notwithstanding Americans' relative lack of overall happiness, it is necessary to reward people for investing in the education necessary to choose librarianship over other careers, and therefore pay equity is an appropriate policy goal.

Rory, your personal story about how you chose librarianship because you wanted to be in a profession that affirmed your altruistic values by paying you less money is probably not a good basis for setting a professional association's position on the compensation its members should receive. I understand where you're coming from, and there is a segment of the population that considers less money to be better than more. Joni Mitchell sang about this sensibility in her 1975 song "The Boho Dance," on her album "The Hissing of Summer Lawns," although Joni indicated she comes out in favor of more money over less. If we could count on a sufficient number of people to favor less money to more, we maybe wouldn't need to worry about pay inequity, but I don't think most people agree with you on this point, Rory. (Bear in mind that some people have children, aging parents, and other dependents to take care of, and it is harder for them to luxuriate in sublime and exquisite poverty.)

Lastly, you conclude by suggesting that perhaps instead of a big, nationwide salary campaign, it might be better to focus solely on the problems of poorer areas, like West Virginia. However, I would not assume that inadequate pay for librarians is limited to poor areas. I recall recently seeing, for example, a very low salary for a county law library position in Palm Beach County, Florida. Plus, in affluent locations it cost more to live, and so a higher salary in a more affluent area may not necessarily translate into more buying power. If we were forced to start picking and choosing our fights rather than going with a nationwide campaign, I would suggest focusing on those jurisdictions where there is no legislation or policy favoring pay equity. Of course, that would narrow the task down only a bit, because only a handful of states that have pay equity on the books, and anyway, even where pay equity is an express policy of the jurisdiction, the implementation of pay equity is hardly self-executing. On balance, I think a nationwide campaign is entirely appropriate. (I'm not saying a campaign on the federal level; that would be futile in the current political environment. I mean that I don't think we can just limit the activism to a handful of poor states, like you suggest.)

I believe that the better salaries initiative is a perfectly appropriate and proper activity for a professional association to engage in. I think that it is a perfectly reasonable goal for librarians in the U.S. to strive to accomplish what was accomplished in New South Wales, Australia, where, after a court battle over pay equity, government librarians received a pay increase of around 24% (if I'm recalling correctly). That seems to me like a good result, and if we could somehow magically replicate that here I think that would be a good thing.

Yours in the struggle,

Luis
Luis M. Acosta
Legal Reference Librarian
Law Library of Congress
101 Independence Ave., S.E.
Washington, D.C. 20540-3120
202-707-9131
fax: 202-707-3585
laco@loc.gov

All views expressed herein are mine, and not the official
position of my employer.

Re: "better salaries criticism" thread
Date: Thu, 17 Jul 2003 10:35:02-0400
From: "Margaret Myers"
To: [discussants]

I did not add anything earlier to the several discussions in May and June re:
better salaries. At the time, I had other commitments and felt that the
various statements required a much more thoughtful, lengthy response than
just sending a quick email. I have recently reread the statements from Rory,
Mark, and Luis and think that all three of you have raised many valid points
for discussion.

Hopefully, the new APA salaries committee (which is taking over from the
presidential task force on better salaries) can review further some of the
questions and comments that you made. In the final report of the task force,
the Research and Resources Working Group made several
recommendations for further action that address some of the issues you
discussed. These include: further analysis of library compensation data to
evaluate trends, suggest additional research, and review for possible use in
educating public officials. In addition to comparisons of library workers with
other occupations, the working group recommended more exploration of
the variations in salaries and benefits within the library community,
including such factors as geographical area, type of library, level of staff,
position responsibilities, part-time wages, gender, etc. It also recommended

that APA consider more assistance in gaining equitable compensation for those at the lower-end of salary ranges.

Additional recommendations include: 1) review of library job evaluation and classification studies and analysis of factors considered in library jobs to determine their impact on salaries; 2) closer communication with the U.S. Bureau of Labor Statistics regarding library worker data collection (to better understand the various sampling procedures and definitions for their various surveys); 3) review of existing staffing standards in various states and their impact on staff salaries; and 4) dialog with researchers looking at the value of library services to include more data on how library workers provide added value in developing and delivering these services.

Much work remains to be done on all fronts; nationally, regionally, statewide, and locally. Because of the wide variations in jurisdictional structures and who controls library job classifications and salaries, it can't all be done by ALA-APA. APA can provide tools, guidance, and visibility, but much has to be done within individual jurisdictions in cooperation with the public officials/administrators responsible for those jurisdictions (e.g., community, campus, corporate, school district, etc.).

I am not going to try and address the individual points raised by Rory and Mark, because I feel that Luis has said many of the things I'd like to say, although much better than I could verbalize. I agree with the comments he has made. Most of the other people on this small distribution list will be active in the continuing better salaries efforts through APA; I'm sure they will carry forward many of these concerns, but if you choose to publish the earlier statements in *Library Juice* or Moneytalks, they would probably generate more viewpoints. Thanks for adding to the overall dialog on salary issues.

Undone by Flattery

By Rory Litwin
Originally published in *Library Juice* 7:25, December 3, 2004

"The most advantageous negotiations are those one conducts with human vanity, for one often obtains very substantial things from it while giving very little of substance in return."
- de Toqueville

The surest sign of the insecurity of the library profession is not our worried or angry responses to negative stereotypes that pop up in the media from time to time, but our unquenchable thirst for flattery from outside the profession. When we are addressed at conferences or spoken about in the media by celebrities, by business leaders, technologists or academics, flattery is *de riguer*, and they understand this intuitively. The first thing out of their mouths is a sweet nothing about how the neighborhood librarian is responsible for all their success, or how we are going to bring about a revolution, or how we secretly control the universe, or how we are super-cutting-edge technologically, or how we are the most underappreciated folks in society. (Personally, I find most interesting the praise that doesn't even pretend to be meant seriously, but still wins applause and laughter.) We should be offended by the underlying assumption that we so thirst for the approval and appreciation of society that this flattery will win us over, but we mostly are not, and mostly it does. Rather than merely tolerating those flattering words, as we should, we recycle them on lists of quotations about librarians that we share with each other in our magazines, websites and listservs. Once you key in on this dynamic of flattery and our consumption of it, you begin to notice it frequently and to notice its effects. That is healthy.

During his campaign and his ALA Presidency, Mitch Freedman (2002-2003) pointed out that we accept this kind of flattery as a substitute for decent pay. That was astute and a very good thing to point out. However, as someone who doesn't think we're so badly paid, and who is also concerned about the future of the profession and the institution of libraries, I think something more fundamental than money is lost in exchange for this flattery, and that is power. When we appreciatively accept flattery from business leaders, politicians or technologists, what happens is that we give ourselves over to them and allow them to lead us; we allow them to win us. We should recognize immediately when we are flattered by people who have an interest in controlling aspects of our institutions or in gaining favorable decisions from us that that is precisely the intention of the flattery. Recognizing this can help us retain the freedom and independence to control the destiny of our profession and the institution of libraries.

By taking note of the flattery that comes our way and our desire to accept it we can also gain a better consciousness of our insecurity as a profession. That insecurity is something that, so far as we recognize it, we usually assign to public perception (so that in order to not be so insecure as a profession what we need to do is convince the public that they should value us more). But the commonness of this flattery of librarians shows that we don't really know how we are perceived by the public—we only know that we are very concerned about what they think, love it when they say they love us, and hate it when they say they don't need us. So, our insecurity, then, is more basic than "public perception;" our estimation of the public's perception of us is largely generated by our insecurity. Rather than trying to convince the public that we are valuable (e.g. with pathetic television ads that try to show our tech-savvy dynamism) we should instead look for the internal sources of our insecurity. Doing that would create more of an impetus to advance the field of Library Science as a whole and to further develop our professional standards, as well as to develop our knowledge and skills as individual professionals. That impetus to improve is removed when we accept the flattery of politicians, technologists and business leaders and adopt a superficial belief, dependent upon continuing to please them, that we are "great."

On Google's Monetization of Libraries

By Rory Litwin
Originally published in *Library Juice* 7:26, December 17, 2004

Google's announcement Monday[1] of plans to digitize millions of books in the collections of the University of Michigan, Harvard, Stanford, NYPL and Oxford and to make them accessible through that ultra-simple search box is causing a new outbreak of Google-fever, for which the cure is to remember some of the principles of librarianship.

Already, Lynn Neary on NPR's "Talk of the Nation" (Dec. 15th) has framed any potential criticism of this development as "sentimental" attachment to brick-and-mortar libraries, but it is not sentimentality that sees the dark side of this development.[2] It is a rational concern for the preservation of a number of the attributes of libraries that give them their inestimable value in a society that aspires to democracy and to the full development of human potential. Google's back-room deal with these universities (which was not worked out in cooperation with the library community though it has implications for libraries as an institution) carries with it a host of problems about which librarians should think carefully before cheering for this corporate giant in its grand plan to assimilate the world's cultural heritage.

Monetization

Google co-founder Larry Page is cited in an article that appeared in Tuesday's *Information World Review* as being a "firm believer in academic libraries being able to 'monetise' the information they hold."[3] Paul Courant, provost at the University of Michigan, is quoted in the *Chronicle of Higher Education* as saying the project is worth "hundreds of millions" of dollars to

---

[1] John Markoff and Edward Wyatt, "Google Is Adding Major Libraries to Its Database," *New York Times*, December 14, 2004, p. A1.
[2] Lynn Neary, "Google's Plan Prompts a Question: What's on the Web?" *Talk of the Nation*, December 15th, 2004.
[3] Mark Chillingworth, "Five top libraries join Google Print revolution," *Information World Review*, December 14, 2004.

his University alone.[4] Google obviously considers that kind of money to be a good investment, which means they expect many hundreds of millions in revenue from these collections, through advertising in the near term and probably other means in the longer term. Already the Google Print™ service, of which this deal is to be a part, provides links to booksellers as well as to libraries. Though they have not announced plans to offer the full text of copyrighted materials on a pay-per-view basis, with fees turned over to copyright owners, it is a technical possibility with the natural force of an economic vacuum in the corporate context. Logically it would seem to be only a matter of time before this mode of access becomes a reality, providing a channel for bypassing both public-interest information policies and the librarian's professional service. The fact that Google is putting libraries "on page A1 above the fold" (in the front page NY Times article), as Barbara Fister put it in an email to COLLIB-L, is not a victory for libraries if the real meaning of this development is simply the transfer of all of this information out of our humanistic institution and into the marketplace. The weighty, loveable, historic notion of "The Library" will doubtless be prominent in Google's marketing of its great reservoir of text, but we would be fooled to think it means that the values indicated by that word (equity of access, collective ownership, privacy, organization, bibliography, and librarianship as a profession) were somehow in play in Google's collection. (Note how Google is already attempting to pander to "sentimental" librarians: "Even before we started Google, we dreamed of making the incredible breadth of information that librarians so lovingly organize searchable online," Larry Page is quoted as saying in Google's Dec. 14 press release. By implication, our "lovingness" only needs their technology to be made useful, and our "loving organization" of those works is ultimately unneeded.)

To spell out the obvious, what this development means is the commercialization of the greatest research libraries in the world with a handshake, suddenly and epochally (and not because of technological inevitability—there are other ways that the digitization of these collections could be handled). The commercialization of libraries has implications both for the institution's democratic character and for the quality of people's research. As Mark Rosenzweig wrote in an email message to multiple lists on Wednesday,

----

[4] Scott Carlson and Jeffrey R. Young, "Google Will Digitize and Search Millions of Books From 5 Leading Research Libraries," *Chronicle of Higher Education*, December 14, 2004.

"There is something mind-boggling about the ability of a single, for-profit company being able to shape the future of a whole sphere of life. Even more so when it enlists the cooperation of the public stewards of that sphere in what amounts to a relinquishment of key elements of responsibility to a unabashedly profit-driven mega-corporation."

I want to examine a more closely the implications of the Googlization of research libraries, with just the beginnings of the needed attention to the loss of privacy, the introduction of commercial bias, questions about democratization and equity of access, the issues of disintermediation, the decontextualization of knowledge, and the closing of the information commons.

Privacy

The privacy of library users in their reading choices has long been held sacred in the library world.[5] In this world, the privacy of individual citizens is understood as a precondition for their autonomous development and their freedom of thought. This is in contrast to the corporate world, where information about individuals as consumers—demographic information, interests, identities, choices—is a commodity that is bought and sold for the purpose of gaining an advantage in the great game of selling you more stuff.[6] Individuals—treated as citizens by libraries and as consumers by the corporate world—have their privacy at stake in Google's conquest of the information commons.[7] As Peter McDonald pointed out in an email to the Progressive Librarians Guild and Social Responsibilities Round Table listservs on Tuesday, Google collects a shocking amount of personal information as it tracks users' searches over time (see Google-watch.org for details[8]). This personal information can be correlated with individual identities with the cooperation of ISP's or with commercial sites that share

---

[5] American Library Association, "Privacy: An Interpretation of the Library Bill of Rights." http://www.ala.org/ala/oif/statementspols/statementsif/interpretations/privacy.htm

[6] Oscar Gandy, "Coming to Terms with the Panoptic Sort," in *Computers, Surveillance & Privacy*, David Lyon and Elia Zureik, eds. (University of Minnesota Press, 1996).

[7] John E. Buschman, *Dismantling the Public Sphere: Situating and Sustaining Librarianship in the Age of the New Public Philosophy* (Libraries Unlimited, 2003).

[8] http://Google-watch.org/

data. At present, this identifying information isn't shared with Google, but the potential and the motive are both there, and the public mood is complacent. Additionally, if Google itself decides to enter the business of selling access to these works, it will have direct access to users' identifying information which it would undoubtedly connect to collected information on search patterns. While libraries and library vendors do a certain amount of usage-tracking for statistical purposes themselves, the strong privacy ethic in libraries militates against the misuse of this information. For example, most public libraries have adopted a policy of destroying personal information once it is no longer absolutely needed, making it unavailable to intelligence agencies whose ability to demand it has been bolstered by the USA PATRIOT Act.[9] If people are using Google to search or access these millions of works, they may naturally expect their privacy as readers and citizens to be respected just as it would be in any library, when in actuality they are being treated as consumers and data sources for the purpose of marketing and with the possibility of political repression. When the ultimate of aim of the disposition of these works shifts from that of enlightenment to that of making money, privacy is one major value that is lost. The value of our privacy is not a matter of mere "sentimentality" but is ultimately a protection of our freedom.

The bias introduced by commercialism

Some say, "What's wrong with advertisements? The business of America is business, and companies have a right to promote their products. How else would we find out about them?" We certainly agree, as a society, that there is a large (apparently ever growing) place for advertisements in our lives. But the field of research, scholarship and education has mostly been off-limits to commercialism, for a simple reason. The aim of research, scholarship and education is truth, and people sense correctly that commercial interests have the potential to distort the discovery and the spread of truth. To a large extent they already do, by funding "friendly" researchers, suppressing research they don't like[10], by directly spreading disinformation via the public relations industry[11], by influencing journalism

---

[9] Laura Flanders, "Librarians Under Siege," *The Nation*, August 5, 2002.

[10] Sheldon Rampton and John Stauber, *Trust Us, We're Experts: How Industry Manipulates Science and Gambles with Your Future* (Tarcher/Penguin, 2002).

[11] John Stauber and Sheldon Rampton, *Toxic Sludge is Good for You: Lies, Damn Lies and the Public Relations Industry.* (Common Courage Press, 1995)

with advertising dollars[12], and by influencing people directly with dishonest advertising. But however compromised it may be, in the world of scholarship and education there is a genuine culture of intellectual honesty that stems from the communal project of seeking and spreading truth for the common good. You do not see advertisements for particular historic works of literature in research libraries, or for particular publishing companies. When a work appears in a bibliography, it is there because of the independent judgment of a scholar or a librarian as to the significance and the relevance of that work; it is not there because somebody is trying to sell it and make money from it. Libraries are full of "pointers" to information, in the form of online catalogs, indexes, large and small bibliographies in books and articles, web-based pathfinders and the personal interactions of librarians and researchers. These "pointers" have the value that they do in part because of the independent judgment behind them and the ability of the professional to match the reader to the right book for them. When a commercial element is added, the "right book" becomes "the book I want to sell." The commercial interest is representing only itself while the unbiased professional is under no pressure to favor any particular vendor or publisher, and is therefore free to attend to the user's personal quest for truth and their efforts to contribute to society's shared store of knowledge. Truth-seekers outside of the context of educational institutions have an equal interest in unbiased information undistorted by commercial interests, but in the wider world they tend to be more vulnerable to that distortion.

Google Print™, even in its introductory phase, plays a major role in introducing advertising into the field of education, scholarship and research, all the more so the more it attempts to enter the higher education "market." At the present time Google claims not to allow commercial interests to distort its search results (though many people, noting the prominence of commercial clutter in their search results, are skeptical of this). But Google's status as a private near-monopoly (in certain respects) means that its reliably "clean" search results cannot be guaranteed by any public policies and could be transformed into pure e-commerce at any time. (If we find this alarming, I should point out, it is not because of "sentimentality" but simply because of our strong values. We should demand that these values be respected.)

---

[12] Robert McChesney, "The Political Economy of Global Communication," in *Capitalism and the Information Age: The Political Economy of the Global Communication Revolution*, Robert McChesney, Ellen Meiksins Wood and John Bellamy Foster, eds. (Monthly Review Press, 1998)

Democratization?

Google is claiming that their digitization project promises to democratize access to these collections of millions of works. I have to admit that research libraries do not really represent paragons of democracy and are not readily accessible to most people, and not only because of geographic barriers. I also have to admit that to the extent that a person will be able to freely download an out-of-copyright work that Google has scanned, access to that particular work has been democratized, and I forgive even librarians' excitement about this development. However, there is a deeper sense in which Google's claim to represent the democratization of information that is presently "locked up" in libraries is a reversal of the truth, and that reversal is dependent upon what is ultimately an odd sense of the meaning of democracy.

When these collections are digitized and made available through that simple search box on the web, something very strange begins to happen. They begin to take on the character of "stuff" in the same way that everything else we download and view in web browsers has the character of "stuff" (similarly to the way that money is "stuff"). There is a bleeding of contexts; with no physical separation and everything on a flat plane, there is little contextual separation between our browsing of personals ads, our online banking, our travel reservations, our eBay, our comics, our news and our Spinoza. All of these activities and contexts become "democratized" in a certain sense, but not the sense we mean when we talk about trying to build a democratic society. Web pages of 7000 words are called "books" and look identical to, or even more impressive than, true online repositories of literature. The information carried by graphic design has increasing importance, and may not bear any relation to truth. The character of everything on the web becomes conditioned by the character of the web itself, and the character of the web is strongly determined by its overall consumer orientation and its relation to the experience of shopping—seeing, choosing, and consuming. As the contents of research libraries becomes "web content," the mode of the use of these materials will be transformed according to the mode of use of the web medium, which sees us skimming, jumping from point to point, impatient, critical by reflex rather than by reflection, superficial and narcissistic. In other words, the web medium tends to "dumb down" the use of what is in it (a phenomenon that may be connected to the relationship to the medium of television). Consumer society has indeed interpreted democracy as something we increase as we dumb down mass media communication and even the educational process in general. So while freer access to out-of-copyright works is undeniably a democratic thing, we should also pay attention to the underpinnings of that mode of access and ask ourselves certain questions: What kind of use of these works is the web medium itself likely to encourage, that is, what does the commercial web do to the nature of research and scholarship? And what does that do to the character of our democracy? And how will these works become connected, via a few short hyperlinks, to the distorting influence of e-commerce?

Here is a less abstract question about how truly democratizing this project will be: How long will it take before the copyright-protected works in these collections are available on a pay-per-download basis, turning the equity-of-access principle of libraries, which is what gives libraries their essential democratic character, into the principle of access for those who can afford it? Contrary to free-marketeers, who see the market as the truest expression of democracy, there is a contradiction inherent between the needs of democracy and the prerogatives of the market. The notion of democracy assumes a rational polity, assumes that the preconditions for an intelligent, thoughtful society exist, while the market tends to nurture what is most stupid in people, preferring to fool them rather than to help build independent minds. Transferring these millions of works from research libraries, even ones at ivory-tower institutions, into a commercial enterprise such as Google, which will make money off of them in any way it can, is superficially democratizing but deeply contrary to democracy's need for information in the public sphere, as useful as it might be to the more fortunate among us who have the ability to make use of it.

Disintermediation and decontextualization

Disintermediation, the substitution of "software solutions" for professional services, has affected most areas of economic activity since the start of the computer revolution, in librarianship no less than in any other field. Information seekers often choose the convenience of the internet over consultation with an information professional, or even the consultation of a bibliography or an index. The stable exception, up to this point, has been in the area of serious research of the kind that requires the use of highly specialized writings, often including those very old works. To access those materials, and to find them in their proper context, a researcher needs to use a library and some of the many research aids that are produced by librarians and scholars. Google's plan will put those works in a giant bucket (so democratizingly) and enable you to pull them out with keywords, kind of like catching fish with a net. So much of this material requires expert knowledge even to comprehend, let alone situate in its proper context, that disintermediated access can in some cases be worse than no access at all.

At this point I should distinguish between disintermediation in general and its specific manifestation in the Google search box. It is possible to build quite a lot of knowledge into a search interface to an information resource. Access to a thesaurus of the controlled vocabulary used by an index can be connected to the search. Reverse-citation information can be built into the display of search results, with linking provided. Multiple search fields can take advantage of extensive cataloging. Even when all of this work is done, the results for the searcher are dependent on her own knowledge level and skill at searching, and many users go away frustrated or go away happy with material that they don't realize is of poor quality or not as relevant as it could be. This is the major problem librarians face with the tools offered over the web by their own institutions.

With the Google interface the problems created by disintermediation reach a new level, because years and years of careful organization of the materials in question will be dissolved in favor of Google's relevance ranking system, which treats every web page and every book in Google Print™ outside of its original context, funneling them all through a single keyword search. (That librarians may have done that organizational work "lovingly," as Larry Page put it, is irrelevant and a trivializing thing to say, if it could even be known. More to the point is that this organizational work was done with the aim of providing access in a meaningful way.)

There is no accommodation, in the Google world, for the myriad scholarly as well as popular jargon and dialects even within single subject areas, which is especially significant when works spanning hundreds of years are in the mix, a situation that leads to a loss of recall as searches based on idiosyncratic keywords miss relevant works that use other terms, and a loss of relevance as works are picked up that use the same keywords in totally different ways. This is part of the reason that subject cataloging and indexing is useful and worth the time of professional catalogers and indexers.

In the Google world, there is no real intelligence determining what documents (or books) are going to be the most helpful to an information seeker, according to their intellectual problem and their knowledge background. Making that determination is not a simple thing; it requires knowledge of intellectual disciplines, an ability to understand people well, and a creative mind. Keyword searches can be useful in certain contexts, but a single keyword search for what is offered as a "whole universe" is no substitute for a reference librarian, no matter how sophisticated the search engine. (To say that librarians are "the most effective search engines yet invented," as John's Hopkins University President William Brody wrote recently[13] is quite demeaning to librarians, for whom search engines are only one brainless tool in a large tool set.) This is one of the reasons libraries employ professional reference librarians to help people with their information needs.

The organization of information in a library, through its catalogs, indexes, and numerous bibliographical sources, is not something to be regarded as having mainly a sentimental value. It is incredibly practical. The "bucket effect" of dumping millions of texts into a database searchable only by keywords, no matter how sophisticated the search engine, represents a major loss if access to those works via Google is compared to access through a library.

I am not forgetting that these research libraries will retain ownership of the original works, and will also own digital copies of the works that they will be able to share in any way that they like, which I concede will be a major benefit of the deal. Realistically, however, as Marc Meola pointed out on COLLIB-L on Wednesday, information seekers will probably just "Google it," trusting an algorithm and thinking they are searching the universe, even more than they do already.

Conclusion

A member of the Livejournal community, "Libraries," posted a link to the *New York Times* article Tuesday, commenting, "We're not being taken over, we're just becoming the greatest information conglomerate of all time."[14] This illustrates the confusion of so many internet librarians who identify with "the Web." "The Web" is not us; it is a medium with its own effects. And Google is not us. Google is not staffed by librarians, and does not operate according to policies that flow out of long traditions of library practice guaranteeing privacy, equity of access, collective ownership of information, information in context, and personal service. This project, as Larry Page has already put it, is about monetizing the holdings of research

---

[13] William Brody, "A Billion-Dollar IPO for Johns Hopkins," *The Johns Hopkins University Gazette*, December 6, 2004.

[14] LittlenoThing, "What I have been dreaming of," Livejournal — Libraries, December 14, 2004.
http://www.livejournal.com/community/libraries/393043.html

libraries. It is about commercializing library collections that it has taken centuries to build. It may be the "greatest information conglomerate of all time," but it is not us. We are nowhere in it; we do not control it or even influence it. We may be invited to imagine that it is "us," that it is "a library" or even that it is "Library," and we may be flattered by the attention, but we should take care to remember what librarianship means in contradistinction to commercialized information, to remember the difference between individuals-as-citizens and individuals-as-consumers and to remember that as librarians we are public stewards of the information commons and have an obligation to preserve and protect it. And, to say it one last time, we must not let anyone write off these concerns as "sentimental." They are not; what they are is simply values-driven.

Now, I suspect that there is no stopping this (though the project is likely to be a great deal more difficult than Google anticipates), and I know that there is no hope of nationalizing Google as a public monopoly, and no hope of raising comparable public funds for a similarly massive public digitization project, at least not the way things are going right now. I also know that in ten years time I will most likely be making good use of some of the material in Google Print™; I don't think I will boycott it. But I hope that by articulating these problems (most of which relate more to general trends than to Google specifically) I can help to advance a critical perspective that will allow us to at least see clearly and to be of use when crucial questions arise where the public interest is at stake.

The Central Problem of Library 2.0: Privacy

By Rory Litwin
Originally published in *Library Juice* (blog), May 22, 2006

Library 2.0 is a powerful idea that finds itself in an awkward predicament. It is an idea that has emerged out of what amounts to a separate discourse within librarianship, that of younger, web-centric librarians who have often have a sense that they are remaking the profession from the ground up for the digital future (and may be correct in having that feeling). The mainstream of librarianship, the older side of the profession, has by now heard of Library 2.0, but understands it poorly or not at all. That older side of the profession may be habituated to modes of practice that in some cases need to die off, but are also the bearers of much important knowledge – of principles and practices – on which the future of librarianship depends. The younger, web-centric generation of librarians is interested in this knowledge in theory, but to the extent that its discourse is separate and web-based it is not communicating with the older generation to the extent that's necessary.

I'm an avid user of Web 2.0 types of sites. I use Livejournal, LibraryThing, Myspace, Last.fm, and other sites with social networking, personalized features and personal information sharing. I am rather addicted to those types of services. I am also at the older end of the user-base of those sites, and communicate more in my professional and private life with librarians of the baby-boom generation than with 20—and even 30-somethings. For that reason I see myself as something of a bridge between the two generational cultures in librarianship.

From the beginning of my involvement with the web, in 1996, I have felt strongly that libraries and the culture of librarianship must be extended into networked communication, with the principles of librarianship as well as the use of the "L" word firmly intact, to preserve the existence of a freely-accessible, non-commercial information and learning space as an alternative to the consumer capitalist information and entertainment space offered by media giants. I have raised questions about what the web medium does to the nature of communication and thought, but these questions have been aimed at directing the shift to the web with intelligence, not at simply avoiding it. I have also pointed it out when library-related efforts on the web have compromised their non-commercial nature without realizing it.

The basic idea of Library 2.0, to transform library services by making them more personalized, more interactive, and more web-based along Web 2.0 lines, has a logic to it that is ineluctable and exciting. I am strongly in favor of the Library 2.0 idea, but want to raise what I think is an important note of caution and consideration as we more forward with experiments with library services that are modeled on Web 2.0 principles. The difficulty that I think we have to grapple with in considering the Library 2.0 idea is that libraries and Web 2.0 services are based on serving two very different essential activities, and those activities have an opposite relationship to privacy.

Web 2.0 websites are, with some exceptions, based primarily on sharing information, but sharing information in a particular way: essentially, they are about seeing and being seen. Libraries are based on sharing information also, but in a different way: they are a place (virtual or physical) to find reading and to read. Reading is so necessarily private and so related to the process of thought as it has evolved over the centuries that its history is congruent with the history of the concept of the private, individual thinking mind in Western culture. In accordance with our conceptualization of the privacy of the act of reading, libraries have traditionally treated the privacy of readers as sacred. Privacy is a central, core value of libraries. This is the reason for librarians' anger over provisions in the USA PATRIOT Act that can force libraries to reveal information about the reading habits of their patrons to the FBI and other government investigators.

Privacy has been an issue for policy specialists in the development of the web from its beginning, as the Electronic Freedom Foundation and others have raised awareness of privacy issues with respect to a host of internet technologies and practices. Many internet users share these concerns about their privacy in theory, but think little of sharing highly personal information on blogs and social networking sites. Most of these sites offer users a degree of control over how their personal information is shared with other users, offering them the ability to limit access to some information to an immediate network of "friends," but these users are often unaware of who all of these "friends" actually are, and often publicly share information for the benefit of one imagined ideal viewer without considering the agendas of potential other, less than ideal viewers. It may sound disrespectful, but I think it's true that users of these sites often lack the maturity that's necessary to make wise decisions about personal information sharing. Additionally, the degree of control that these sites offer to users in sharing their information with other users shifts the focus away from the original reasons for being concerned about privacy, which had to do with the ownership and use of private information by private companies and its accessibility by overzealous and possibly misguided government investigators. A Myspace user may feel confident in her ability to control who can view her profile, but Rupert Murdoch still owns her data.

As serious as privacy concerns may turn out to be, the features of Web 2.0 applications that make them so useful and fun all depend on users sharing private information with the owners of the site, so that it can be processed statistically or shared with others. This presents a problem for librarians who are interested in offering Library 2.0 types of services. If we value reader privacy to the extent that we always have, I think it's clear that our experiments with Library 2.0 services will have uncomfortable limitations. This is probably going to lead many librarians to say that privacy is not as important a consideration as it once was. They will say that the Millennial generation doesn't have the same expectations of libraries in terms of privacy that older generations do, and that we should simply adjust.

I think that we shouldn't accept this idea without examining psychological questions surrounding information sharing and information privacy, and face the fact that a decade from now many of these young people will not have the same attitudes about privacy and information sharing that they exhibit in adolescence and young adulthood. Their decisions concerning privacy on blogs and social networking websites are motivated largely by an interest in being seen, noticed, admired, and potentially in gaining a degree of fame within their milieu. While this is a motivation that's strongly present in any adolescent, an opposite, limiting motivation to protect oneself by keeping personal information private is a motivation that, by contrast, may have to be learned from painful experience. This should tell us that the Millennials may not have reached the time in their lives when they will have learned to place a high value on their privacy. In considering where to compromise reader privacy in offering Library 2.0 services, we should not be too quick to accept the idea that privacy is a concern that technological and cultural change is leaving behind. In many ways our privacy is diminishing, but many people's relative lack of concern for it may have more to do with lack of experience in life than a real change in values. It may also be that in some real way the place of privacy in our culture is changing, but it is a question that is not easily answered and shouldn't be approached too casually. It may take more time before we know the answer.

I would like to see more discussion of privacy in relation to Library 2.0 innovations. I also hope we will be very conscious of the ways in which these ideas sometimes offer to introduce new, social purposes to libraries, beyond just offering new ways of fulfilling already-existing purposes. As we transform librarianship, how aware are we of the full implications of our choice.

Rory Litwin interviews Barbara Tillett

Originally published in *Library Juice* (blog), August 9, 2006

Rory Litwin:

Many *Library Juice* readers who are familiar with Sanford Berman's work on LC subject heading reform have read or heard the name Barbara Tillett. Barbara Tillett has for many years been the chief of the Library of Congress Cataloging Policy and Support Office, and thus has figured into Berman's career-long crusade to reform LC's subject headings with the aim of making them fairer and more accessible. In his inspiring accounts of his crusade to rid *LCSH* of its Eurocentric, sexist, insulting and obscure subject headings, the person of Barbara Tillett often figured in as an obstacle to enlightened progress (never as much as the sheer weight of the great bureaucracy that is LC, but as a heel-dragging bureaucrat and defender of the old guard nonetheless).

My own feeling, in listening to these accounts, is that people like to be inspired by stories that have a hero and a bad guy, but that reality is always more complex. I've often wondered what Barbara Tillett would have to say in answer to some of Berman's more convincing arguments (many if not most of which have indeed, over time, convinced LC), and have felt that the discussion about subject headings and cataloging reform among progressives has been a little poor in the absence of LC's own point of view regarding the various questions that have come up.

Barbara Tillett has agreed to let me interview her about subject heading reform and new developments in cataloging. In the following interview we will discuss some general issues around subject heading reform as well as some specific cases, including the case of the "God" subject heading, which remains as it was when Berman first discussed it in his first book, *Prejudices and Antipathies*.

First of all, Barbara, I want to thank you for agreeing to this interview. I'd like to start by asking you for an explanation of the process of subject heading reform from your point of view, with reference to some of the issues involved and to Sanford Berman's activism. What would you like people to understand about it?

Barbara Tillett:

Thank you for this opportunity! As you know the Library of Congress Subject Headings were originally developed for LC's own collection over 100 years ago. As terminology changes and new topics appear, we update the subject heading terms based both on recommendations from our own catalogers, from about 300 partners in the SACO Program (Subject Cataloging Cooperative Program of the Program for Cooperative Cataloging), and from contributors worldwide. We are very grateful to all the contributors for recommendations. As more users beyond LC began using our system, we provided documentation to describe our principles and policies so others could follow the same practices as our own catalogers, and also to provide consistency among LC's catalogers and those contributing to our cooperative programs. We have a standard process for submitting new proposals for changes and additions to the subject headings that is described in the Subject Cataloging Manual as well as on our Web site: http://www.loc.gov/catdir/cpso/. And the SACO information for submitting proposals can be found at: http://www.loc.gov/catdir/pcc/saco/saco.html.

The general rule for assigning subject headings is to give one or more subject headings that "best summarize the overall contents of the work and provide access to its most important topics." At LC this means we focus on "topics that comprise at least 20% of the work." Other institutions may be able to provide more extensive subject analysis and reach topics in articles and news clippings (as Mr. Berman finds), but we rely on the catalogers discovering terminology in the materials they are cataloging. We also check to see how much we have on a given topic in order to possibly be more specific. Additionally, the use of free-floating subdivisions helps us make headings more specific in a consistent way.

One aspect of "subject heading reform" means keeping the *LCSH* vocabulary updated, and we've been doing that since the beginning of *LCSH*. We constantly maintain the subject headings and try to keep the controlled vocabulary current with today's topics and terminology without changing headings too quickly to terminology that is ephemeral. Sometimes we add the ephemeral term as a cross-reference, for example, we recently added "Culture wars" as a reference under "Culture conflict." We are keenly aware of the impact of any changes on the resources of the Library of Congress catalogers and the resources of our users. At the same time we continuously make changes we feel are important to maintain the currency and viability of *LCSH*.

In the past, it was especially noticeable that changes were not made quickly. For example, the change of "European War, 1914-1918" to "World War, 1914-1918" was made only in 1981. As Mary Kay Pietris noted in a recent email, "For the many years that the list was published infrequently and set in hot lead type, we couldn't respond to change quickly. When we first automated in the 60's, the system was clunky. When the card catalogs were closed in 1981, we were able to make more changes because we didn't have to worry about changing the cards, but the authority work and changing of headings on bib records was still time-consuming and complicated. We didn't get any sort of global update until 2005, ...so we are better equipped to make changes than we were even 25 years ago, but it still isn't easy."

We also are aware that the meaning and connotations of words change over time and vary from culture to culture, so we have made adjustments where terminology once considered appropriate is no longer considered acceptable. We hear from many communities about changing perceptions with terminology and respond as we feel is appropriate to each situation. For example over the years we have changed:

Australian aborigines to Aboriginal Australians (in 2003)

Cripples to Handicapped to People with disabilities (with the latter change in 2002)

Gypsies to Romanies (in 2001)

Negroes to Afro-Americans to African Americans (the latter change in 2000).

We have just changed "Vietnamese Conflict, 1961-1975" to "Vietnam War, 1961-1975."

Our primary users are the US Congress and United States citizens, but we are certainly interested to also address the needs of global users to the degree we are able. The current set of headings reflects the work of hundreds of catalogers and varying philosophies over time, so we are aware that there are inconsistencies, but also cautious about making changes.

Another aspect of "reform" is changing practices. One major step to such reform was the Airlie House meeting on subject subdivision practices held in 1991 after which we changed headings and practices to try to meet the goal of more consistency in terminology and in the order of subdivisions, based on the consensus opinion at the time. The identification of form subdivisions came from the Airlie House meetings and took several years to implement following changes in the MARC format. Another changed practice from 1974 was the introduction of free-floating subdivisions to enable users to construct more specific subject heading strings without having to "establish" each combination. After Airlie House we tried to "tame" the whole free-floating practice to have it be more consistent and rational.

What Mr. Berman may see as his "reform" movement, we see as the normal process of maintaining a controlled vocabulary. Every day we address new and changed headings coming from our catalogers and our SACO Program partners and others worldwide, who use the same procedures as our own Library of Congress staff. No grandstanding is needed, no lobbying of members of Congress or fellow librarians, just the simple act of submitting a formal proposal with evidence that the new or changed heading is needed to catalog library materials. We welcome that assistance.

Litwin:

Would you explain the concept of "literary warrant" as it is involved in establishing a new subject heading? I recall seeing, in some of the materials that Berman distributed to friends, examples of articles where the expression he was advocating as a new subject heading was used.

Tillett:

Literary warrant deals with the need for the use of a subject heading as evidenced in the materials cataloged by the Library of Congress and our partners as well as choosing terminology found in current literature and the language, construction, and style used in *LCSH*. We document the justification for establishing a subject heading in the subject authority records.

Litwin:

In looking at the new ideas for Subject Headings that Berman has advocated, I've noticed that they usually fall into one of two categories of justification: fairness to the people being described, or not wanting to use language that is arguably insulting (e.g. "Romanies" instead of "Gypsies" or "Hansen's Disease" instead of "Leprosy"), and wanting to make works accessible by using ordinary rather than technical or official language (e.g. "light bulbs" instead of "electric lamp, incandescent," which took a while to change).

Tillett:

Can we turn this around to how we see this rather than how Mr. Berman sees it? Most of our correspondence contains helpful and constructive suggestions—what criticism we receive is simply not as he characterizes it. There is no onslaught of letters and emails and faxes from outraged librarians or researchers. For the most part, public criticism comes from Mr. Berman or other individuals he has urged to write to us. We're more inclined to react favorably to constructive suggestions than to coercive techniques such as petitions, hostile articles in the library literature, emotional attacks, or letters of complaint to members of Congress. Methods such as these are almost always counterproductive, whereas more cooperative and positive approaches usually produce good results.

"Fairness" to whom? We want to be informed of headings that some may now consider outdated or offensive, but one group's or one person's viewpoint is not always the general consensus. As noted above we must weigh the impact of change, and test the current literary warrant and appropriateness of terminology in today's society. This involves checking the Web and other current news media to verify terminology that may appear on a new book and checking authoritative sources to assure the suggested new term is acceptable. Often we work in consultation with special interest groups or those who are most knowledgeable about a particular field. For example, in changing "Australian aborigines" to "Aboriginal Australians," we relied on the guidance and expertise of the National Library of Australia. When we were contemplating changing "Handicapped" to "Disabled," it was the forceful advocacy of people and organizations in this field that convinced us that "People with disabilities" is now the appropriate terminology, and that "Disabled" is considered by many to be as offensive as "Handicapped" because it puts the emphasis on the condition rather than on the people. Before we made the change from "Gypsies" to "Romanies," staff members from CPSO attended a seminar on the topic at the Holocaust Museum and consulted closely with a renowned expert and advocate in this field. After we changed the heading to "Romanies," we received complaints from several individuals and a few organizations that opposed our discontinuing usage of the term Gypsies. This is a good example of how there can be differing and conflicting viewpoints that we have to weigh when making subject heading changes, and how difficult it is to please everyone.

"Accessibility" in terms of using ordinary language, for what audience? We have children's headings for that audience, and otherwise *LCSH* is targeting the US public and our Congress. We rely on special thesauri for special audiences, like MeSH for technical medical language to meet the needs of doctors and others in the medical profession, and NASA's thesaurus for aerospace engineers. In demonstrating that a new term is now "ordinary language" or that an old term is now referred to using a new term in "ordinary language," we'd use evidence from the materials we are cataloging. Additionally we do consult newspapers, the Web, and respected authoritative sources–this is back to avoiding ephemeral terminology as main headings–but considering such terms for references.

Litwin:

Sanford Berman has written about one subject heading that he has found controversial that particularly interests me, and I find it a little disturbing that it hasn't been changed. I'm referring to the subject heading for "God," which is still used for the Christian God as well as God without referring to a specific religion, while God in other religions are identified specifically by their religion (e.g. "God, Muslim"). Why isn't the subject heading for the Christian God, "God, Christian?" Having the Christian God referred to by the subject heading "God" without subdivisions in the U.S. government's official classification of all things in effect establishes an official Christian perspective for the United States. An argument based on common usage would be based on the assumption of a Christian population, while the United States is a country of great religious pluralism. Can you tell me if this is an issue that has been discussed at LC, and if it has, what are the considerations at present that have prevented this SH from being updated, or work in favor of its being updated? Can you summarize the discussion within LC?

Tillett:

Because the term "God" refers not only to the Christian God, but also the concept in general, it gets very difficult to clean up 100 years of past practice, but we think we've found a solution using class numbers in combination with reports we think we can get...all this is still to be explored. We now have some global update and other computer assistance capabilities for the massive changes this will entail.

As we now envision it, there would still be the "God" heading alone for the concept in general and comparative terms. We'd follow our practice for other religions to set up "God (Christianity)." For the concept of "God" from the perspective of denominations for any religion, we'd use a subdivision for the denomination under the appropriate "God" heading. This would involve the least disruption to existing headings, and yet still require re-examining hundreds of authority records, as well as many thousands of bibliographic records. We do not take such steps lightly and certainly not without a lot of checking. However, we agree it is long overdue, and I'll keep you posted as we progress in our explorations.

Litwin:

Wow, that is great news. I'd like to talk about one other subject heading that bugs me. When I checked recently, "Zionism" was a broader term for "Jews – Politics and Government." As a Jew who is interested in politics and government but who is not a Zionist, and as someone who is interested in the Reform Jewish opposition to the original Zionist project, this bugs me.

Tillett:

Zionism used to be a BT (broader term) for Jews – Politics and government, but as of 2005 they are now "related terms." (See the *Weekly List* 49, 2005*). In 1986 we converted to the MARC authority format and began distributing subject authority records. At that time we adopted the standard thesaural notation of BT, NT, RT (broader term, narrower term, related term) in place of our see and see also references (x and xx), and converted our existing records using computer algorithms. We continue to adjust where the computer algorithm resulted in a flip that was inappropriate.

*The 27th edition of *LCSH* (2005) has Jews—Politics and government as a NT under Zionism. On *Weekly List* 05-49 for December 7, 2005, the relationship between the two headings was revised. BT Zionism was cancelled from the record for Jews—Politics and government and replaced with an RT Zionism. Jews—Politics and government was added as an RT under Zionism.

Litwin:

Thanks, that's gratifying and interesting. In general, would you say that *LCSH* inevitably reflects politics in some way?

Tillett:

The Library of Congress is the national library for the United States and to some extent we reflect US policy (for example using Burma not Myanmar). We follow Congressional perspectives and those of our State Department to a degree but also apply our own sense of appropriateness and seek to find suitable alternatives to avoid conflicts when we can. An example of that is our establishing the heading Cyprus, Northern to recognize the region without getting into the political status issues of recognizing Northern Cyprus.

Litwin:

Thanks very much for taking the time to explain these issues from LC's perspective.

Dr. Tillett is Chief of the Cataloging Policy and Support Office (CPSO) at the Library of Congress and Acting Chief of the Cataloging Distribution Service. Those divisions of about 45 people are responsible for creating and distributing various authoritative cataloging tools, including *LC Rule Interpretations*, *LC Classification* schedules, *LC Subject Headings*, and other cataloging documentation, such as the *Cataloging Service Bulletin*, *Descriptive Cataloging Manual*, *Subject Cataloging Manual*, etc. She currently serves as the

Library of Congress representative on the Joint Steering Committee for
Revision of the *Anglo-American Cataloguing Rules,* chairs the IFLA
(International Federation of Library Associations and Institutions) Division
IV on Bibliographic Control, and leads the IFLA work towards an
International Cataloguing Code and a Virtual International Authority File.

Dr. Tillett has been active in the American Library Association throughout
her 36 years as a librarian, including founding the Authority Control
Interest Group in 1984 and chairing the ALCTS Cataloging and
Classification Section. She has served on the editorial committees of *ACRL
Publications in Librarianship, Advances in Librarianship,* and continues for
Cataloging & Classification Quarterly, and was a reviewer for *Library Resources &
Technical Services* and *College & Research Libraries.* Her many publications have
focused on cataloging theory and practice, authority control, bibliographic
relationships, conceptual modeling, and library automation. Her
dissertation on bibliographic relationships has been a source for conceptual
designs of computer-based systems for bibliographic control.

Section Three:
Intellectual Freedom and Media
Independence

Four Popular Errors About Free Speech ...An Attack on Complacency and Dissociation

By Rory Litwin
Revised from the original version, published in *Library Juice* 7:10,
May 14, 2004

Our professional ethic of intellectual freedom is something to which we attach a lot of passion, but it involves a number of ideas that we seldom examine. This essay outlines what I consider four "popular errors" about intellectual freedom to make a few points about our relation to freedom of speech as librarians and as people.

Popular error number one: "Ideas aren't dangerous."

Ideas ARE dangerous. Often in discussions of intellectual freedom people assert that ideas are not dangerous, as an argument against censorship. But what this argument really says is "censorship is wrong because ideas aren't worth censoring." But in the end it is because ideas ARE dangerous enough to inspire their censorship that they should be protected. It is the power of ideas to change reality—not their harmlessness—that makes it important for librarians, institutions and governments to support their free expression.

Why is the argument that "ideas aren't dangerous" so typical of librarians? In part, I believe, it is a result of what our profession does with expressions of ideas. We catalog them, organize them, encapsulate them, make them into manageable "things" and manage them. This is of course extraordinarily useful, as we all know. But we should be on guard against allowing this activity to lead us into a denatured and reified conceptualization of ideas and their expression. Too often, when confronted with a challenging idea that is expressed in earnest, we mentally catalog it and file it away as "one perspective," as though in encountering this expression (this person) we are apart from the world, in which being alive means having a perspective of one's own and confronting others'. Because we tend to think of ideas as manageable abstractions, in a separate, otherwordly sphere now called "information," we lose sight of the fact that there are no ideas without the expression of ideas. That expression is a part of life itself. It is the alternately restrained, despondent, flowery, musky, muscular, childlike, coy, agitated, angry and methodical expression of ideas that our profession is dedicated to protecting, not merely the abstract codifications of ideas, from which it is so easy to dissociate.

To be unafraid of ideas, as so many librarians are, is a different thing than to be aware of their power to upset a stable balance, to destroy and create, and still to protect and nurture them. It is the difference between the foolish bravery that is unconscious of danger and the courage that acts through fear. As librarians, we should take ideas seriously enough to be afraid of them, and to protect their full expression nonetheless.

Popular error number two: "The best idea always wins in the marketplace of ideas."

Our arguments in favor of intellectual freedom are sometimes taken to rest on the truism that "the best idea wins in the marketplace of ideas." The implication of this is that the free speech that our society enjoys has created for us the best of all possible worlds, by allowing the citizenry freely to decide from among all of the ideas that society generates and debates. Aside from the question of whether intellectual freedom exists in our society in a deep sense, the assertion that people are engaged enough and rational enough always to chose the best ideas is highly questionable, and to many observers, clearly false. While this questionable assertion may offer a layer of support for opposition to censorship, it has an unfortunate consequence that affects librarians especially, and that is its encouragement of a complacent attitude to discourse. If we believe that "the best idea wins in the marketplace of ideas" by an automatic process, stemming, perhaps, from humanity's fundamental nature as rational and good, then we excuse ourselves from the responsibility to engage with others in a definite way, to apply pressure, to respond from our own perspectives and to make an effort in the world to create a better reality (or at least to protect our world from further deterioration)—as long as we "fight censorship." If "the best idea always wins in the marketplace of ideas" there is no reason for any of us to speak, because we can relax and watch the magic of rational society. But if we don't speak, we lose, because there is no debate, and no real society, without the efforts of people like us. Because the best ideas might NOT win, and very often don't, we must respond. Free speech is not for us to defend only so that other people can exercise it; we must exercise it, too.

Popular error number three: "Being too forceful can stifle debate, and that's censorship."

This popular error is seldom expressed as succinctly and completely as the others discussed here, but it nevertheless commonly affects librarians' thinking about free speech. We frequently see it manifested in professional listserv discussions like this: a strong critic is accused of violating a speaker's right to free speech by "stifling debate." He "stifles debate" by arguing forcefully and confronting the speaker personally and directly. The ironic result is that the critic's speech—and the overall debate—is stifled in the name of intellectual freedom. The frequency with which this pattern is encountered in our profession is an unfortunate sign of a certain narrowness among librarians in the range of expression that, when the rubber meets the road, we actually do protect. Our professional context should provide certain norms, but where these norms restrict expression to an extent that important debates are prevented from moving forward, it is worth noting and correcting.

But what about the original assertion that the critic, in arguing so forcefully and directly against another speaker, really is stifling debate, if that speaker ends up too intimidated to express his ideas fully and effectively? Isn't it true that the critic is stifling speech, and isn't that contrary to intellectual freedom?

I think it is somewhat true and somewhat false. The apparent paradox stems from the fact that as librarians we are both individuals participating in the debates that shape society and professionals fulfilling institutional roles. In debates we sometimes care only to participate in a shared process of thought, but we sometimes have a definite and compelling interest in how things turn out; we care deeply that our side in the argument should ultimately prevail, and are committed to and prepared to make sacrifices for the outcome that we want. That is simply a part of life for a person who is fully and authentically engaged with reality. And it doesn't stop where our professional life begins, as our profession, no less than our national and local politics, is filled with controversial issues, profound questions, and pressing decisions that will shape the future.

Our commitment to intellectual freedom is different from our right and responsibility to participate in public and professional discourse. It is a part of our professional role; that is, it is a part of our commitment as professionals to see to it that the institutions of which we are a part—and society as a whole—support and defend free expression. This is in the interest of everyone who has something to say and wants to hear what others say—including ourselves. Our professional ethic of intellectual freedom supports the freedom of everyone in society—including librarians—to express their ideas. In our professional role, we support this and create and maintain a space for expression; our professional role is infrastructural. But as individuals we use that space to listen and to express ideas ourselves.

This is where we find the greatest significance in the fact that it is the living, breathing, sometimes confrontational expression of ideas that we protect, and not merely the "information" into which those ideas can be denatured and encapsulated. If a critic stifles the speech of his opponent in debate, it is due to both the logic and persuasiveness of his actual expression, and it is the freedom of that expression that we protect, not merely the idea that can be abstracted from it. That is why when people try to help the critic by entreating readers to "ignore the way he says it and just pay attention to the idea he's expressing" (and I used to say this, before I had thought the issue through in these terms) they are actually doing him—and ultimately all of us—a disservice, because they are encouraging readers to make dangerous ideas safe by removing them from the field of confrontation and engagement and encapsulating them in the denatured field of "information."

Popular error number four: "The suppressed idea gains strength."

In the 1950's, when intellectual freedom activists were fighting McCarthyism, anti-communists were urged to join the fight against censorship with the argument that suppressing communist literature would give energy and a strengthened sense of righteousness to the cause of American communism, thus unintentionally helping it. The argument that the suppressed idea gains strength is still a mainstay of popular intellectual freedom philosophy. But is it true? Clearly, injustice can produce resoluteness among the oppressed. But in our own history, did the stifling of socialist opinion in public debate result in a repopularization of the idea of socialism? Not at all. As socialism, the labor movement and related ideas lost their expressions of support, their support died out. It turns out that it is the expression of an idea (given an internal logic), not the suppression of an idea, that gives the idea strength.

The distinction between stifling speech by arguing forcefully within a debate and stifling debate institutionally relates to the idea of justice here. Institutional or governmental censorship or restriction of expression, because they manifest injustice, can create a sense of energy and resolve among the people it affects. Our support for intellectual freedom is, therefore, a matter of justice. But there is no injustice involved in beating your opponent in a passionate debate, if it is free and open debate that accomplishes it. Reason and personality both have a role, and there is no reason why they shouldn't. It is the freedom of life itself that we are protecting in protecting free expression, not merely the freedom to render ideas into a fixed form.

I hope that examining these four "popular errors" at least raises some questions in people's minds about our relation to freedom of speech.

A NOTE ON CIVILITY

In discussing these issues, one of the things I am trying to do is to defend speech that's forceful enough to make people uncomfortable, often in a professional context. The issue of civility comes to many people's minds when they encounter that kind of speech. But the incivility of harsh expression is related to, and often results from, another kind of incivility, which is the incivility of inattention and dissociation. The more we fall into the habit of listening dissociatedly, so that what we hear only registers as "information" crossing a screen and does not engage us as a part of real life, the more a person for whom the real world matters will have to intensify his expression in order to break through and be heard. Civility involves not only speaking to a person as though he is already listening with attention, but listening with attention as well.

The Invisibility of the Alternative Media

By Tami Oliphant
This is a revision of the article originally published in *Library Juice*
5:1, Supplement, January 3, 2002

Introduction

It's 7:30 a.m., and the buzzing alarm wakes Citizen X. Citizen X lingers in bed listening to a news broadcast on the radio. After a brief shower, Citizen X scans the day's headlines for a few minutes before heading off to work. Work involves Internet searching. Citizen X returns home, watches TV for half an hour and then decides to go to a movie. On the way to the theatre, she stops in a bookstore and purchases a magazine, a CD, and a book. After the movie, Citizen X returns home and goes to bed in preparation for another busy day. Imagine that each media item Citizen X used, bought, or read was owned by the same company whose head offices were in another country. Now imagine that you are Citizen X.

In an era of mega-conglomerates, the above scenario is becoming more probable. In 1983, 50 media conglomerates dominated the U.S. mass media (McChesney 21). Presently, approximately 10 companies dominate mass media globally. It is not only the sheer size of these corporations that concerns media watchdogs, but also the trend towards vertical and diagonal integration. Currently, many of these companies not only dominate a selective medium like newspapers, (horizontal integration) but they also control cable TV, movie studios, publishing houses, radio stations, music companies, wireless networks, Internet service providers, and TV production studios. In Canada, media giants like CanWest Global own newspapers, TV stations, radio broadcasting, and interactive media, and Germany's juggernaut Bertelsmann owns TV and radio stations, production studios, publishing houses, magazines, music companies, and newspapers worldwide ("Who Owns What?"). Vertical integration enables companies to control all key elements of the supply chain from production to distribution. For example, a TV cable company might purchase a production firm in order to supply "product" for the company's cable TV outlets. Diagonal integration, moreover, happens when media companies cross sectors—like the gigantic merger of AOL and Time Warner in 2000. This merger combined the Internet with publishing, cinema, and TV.

Compounding the problem of concentrated ownership is what Edward S. Herman and Noam Chomsky describe in their acclaimed work, *Manufacturing Consent*, as a "propaganda model of media control." The authors argue that while mass media serves to inform, entertain, and amuse the populace, it simultaneously instills and propagates the beliefs, values, and norms of the institutional structures that govern society—the ideology of the dominant elites. Thus systematic propaganda is produced by the media through established news "filters." These filters allow private interests, government, and others with access to wealth and power to communicate their messages to the public, thereby determining what news is "fit to print." One of these filters is simply the nature of media ownership. The sheer size, concentrated ownership, immense owner wealth, and quest for profit of the dominant media corporations mean that business priorities can, and do, shape editorial content.

David Cromwell provides evidence of these allegations of editorial interference. "In a 1992 U.S. study of 150 newspaper editors, 90 percent reported that advertisers tried to interfere with newspaper content while 70 percent said advertisers tried to stop new stories altogether" (34). More recently, a survey done by *The Guardian* showed that of 175 editors from around the world who worked on newspapers owned by Rupert Murdoch none challenged the war in Iraq (Greenslade 2). Since 9/11 in particular there have been innumerable examples of editorial interference and bias across all media. However, this is nothing new—writing in 1912, Edward Ross voiced concern about the suppression of the news by capitalist owners as they bought out newspapers formerly run by editor owners; he was concerned about advertisers censoring the news, and he was concerned about reporters' unwillingness to take on "sacred cows" like the railroads (Ross 181-192). Cromwell scathingly describes dominant media as "an integral part of a system of institutionalized greed and violence that is destroying cultures and ecosystems around the planet" (34). While other scholars view the media as more diverse and perhaps less destructive, media certainly do have the power to determine the political agenda, to shape the cultural landscape, and to legitimize certain points of view.

Conversely, the media are also recognized for their key role in promoting international human and cultural rights. In 1948, the United Nations declared in Article 19 of the Universal Declaration of Human Rights that "Everyone has the right to freedom of opinion and expression; this right includes freedom to hold opinions without interference and to seek, receive and impart information and ideas through any media and regardless of frontiers." Birdsall and Rasmussen (32) summarize these ideas as the "right to communicate and be the producer of ideas" so that individuals can partake in cultural life through media. Birdsall suggests that the ability to communicate is what makes us human. So not only is our culture, collective history, ideas, freedom, and ability to communicate with each other affected by media, but possibly our very humanness as well. These human rights outlined by the UN have been under siege through agreements like GATS (General Agreement on Trade and Services) and the neo-liberal policies of the WTO (World Trade Organization) which define media (cultural industries) as being equivalent to any other good or service. These policies effectively make it possible for huge conglomerates to penetrate and dominate foreign markets, thereby further homogenizing media content and reducing an individual's ability to communicate through media.

In our era of convergences and mega-conglomerates there is a pressing need for alternatives to dominant media. Bill Moyers points out that "Free and responsible government by popular consent just can't exist without an informed public ... It's a reality: democracy can't exist without an informed public" (vii). A healthy democratic society needs dissent, debate, and discussion, as well as information about, and advocates for, those who are disenfranchised from the system. The Supreme Court of the United States concurs, stating that "the widest possible dissemination of information from diverse and antagonistic sources is essential to the welfare of the public" (Schwartzman et al. 153). In order to avoid homogenization of media content and instead give equal representation to all viewpoints, and to promote freedom, pluralism, and democracy, citizens need access to alternative media.

So what exactly is alternative media? Some magazines like *The Utne Reader* and the *New Internationalist* are considered "alternative" because of their focus on social issues, but they have national or international distribution and they are definitely not small. Is the libertarian *Wired* still an alternative publication despite being owned by Conde Nast? What makes a Web site or a radio station alternative? Very loose criteria have generally been applied to definitions of alternative media. In the past, alternative media were perceived as having special, specific attributes like being non-commercial, focusing on social responsibility and / or creative expression, or publishers characterized themselves as alternative. All of these criteria are problematic. Because these definitions are so vague, "alternative" can be reduced to mean almost anything. Using these criteria, alternative media becomes indistinguishable from dominant media, and as a result, some have questioned the very existence of alternative media.

Chris Atton provides a much more satisfactory conception of alternative media by focusing on content and the mode of production as the distinguishing features of alternative media.

> I define alternative media as much by their capacity to generate non-standard, often infractory, methods of creation, production and distribution as I do by their content ... Alternative media, I argue, are crucially about offering the means for democratic communication to people who are normally excluded from media production (4).

Echoing Birdsall and Rasmussen's view on the human right to communicate, Michael Traber says:

> The aim is to change towards a more equitable social, cultural, and economic whole in which the individual is not reduced to an object (of the media or the political powers) but is able to find fulfillment as a total human being (qtd. in Atton 16).

Traber suggests that alternative media introduce alternative social actors: the oppressed, the poor, everyday women, labourers, the marginalized, etc. In order to be defined as alternative media, then, content must be innovative and experimental and the processes and modes of production must be democratic and inclusive. Using these two criteria—content and mode of production—the differences between dominant and alternative media become clearer.

Distribution and Wholesale

While vertical integration allows mega-conglomerates to control every stage in the supply chain from media production to distribution, the very nature of alternative media sets them apart from the more traditional supply processes used by dominant media. Alternative publishers do not have the same financial resources as dominant media do, they may refuse advertising or eschew certain advertisers based upon ethical considerations, and they will never attain anywhere near the same circulation figures as their more mainstream counterparts because their potential audience is not as large. Furthermore, many alternative publications have an openly anti-copyright stance or they may be more open to extending fair use laws. For example, many alternative publications allow or encourage open copying of all published material for non-profit use. Because alternative media are different from dominant media, publishers of alternative media face many additional hurdles, particularly in the areas of distribution, indexing, and reviewing media. All of these factors influence the viability and survival of alternative media publications.

Mega mergers are not just an end product media phenomenon: wholesalers, distributors, and retailers are subject to the merger trend also. Currently, four major distributors, Anderson News Company, Chas. Levy (owned by Source Interlink companies), The News Group (a subsidiary of the Canadian owned The Jim Pattison Group), and Hudson News, control the U.S. magazine wholesale and distribution market. Anderson News Company, for example, currently distributes magazines to over 40,000 outlets located in over 45 states. The company also owns Liquid Digital Music, an online music download service used by Wal-Mart and Amazon.com, in addition to owning America's third largest book-store chain, Books-A-Million ("Anderson").

In addition to subscription sales, print magazines rely on sales at the supermarket (42%), discount stores (16.2%), bookstores (12.3%), and other outlets to generate profit ("Challenge" 43). The competition for prime shelf space in retail outlets is intense. As a result, larger, more powerful wholesalers have begun the process of purging themselves of unprofitable titles, imposing handling fees, and setting across-the-board efficiency standards. For example, when Anderson News found that 1,700 of the 4,700 magazines it handles account for more than 90% of the company's retail sales, the remaining 3,000 titles were redirected to a National Production Center where Anderson determined how many copies of each title will be distributed to its retail clients, including ma-and-pa shops and the chain stores (Granatstein 98). Thus Anderson has created a two-tiered system for distribution.

Moreover, Anderson now requires publishers to pay all the handling and distribution costs for their titles. While most of the larger publishing houses are able to absorb the extra costs, the smaller, independent magazines are the most burdened by the new pricing structure (Granatstein 98). Anderson's strategy is to devote more shelf space to better-selling titles, which effectively cuts off small-run magazines. By February 2001, 30,000 retail accounts that sold magazines only a few years ago were not being serviced by the major distributors. These changes in magazine distribution have resulted in the consolidation of wholesalers into just a handful of major players that deliver 90% of the magazines to U.S. newsstands (Buss 42; Owen and Ennis 14).

Lowenstein argues that some titles have remained viable by going through second-tier distributors and wholesalers that encourage greater visibility for their titles in less-congested, smaller shops. This targeted distribution is presumed to work because specialty magazines in specialty stores should attract the customers most interested in the subject, and thus those who are most likely to make a purchase. Another way small magazines are becoming more efficient is by shipping their titles straight to the retailer and bypassing the wholesalers. The retailer cannot return any of the unsold items, but the publisher's discount they receive up-front alleviates costs for the retailer (Lowenstein, "Small" 158).

In a separate article, Lowenstein further explores the possibilities of second-tier distribution. Several smaller companies have picked up titles dropped from the larger wholesalers. Lowenstein cites BigTop Publisher Services, a San Francisco–based distributor, as a success story. Their distribution list includes alternative titles and their number of offerings has increased from 7 to 48 in the past two years (Lowenstein, "Dealing" 155). Big Top's titles average a 70% sell through rate as compared with Andersen's 38–45% rate (Lowenstein, "Dealing" 155). Another example of a successful distributor is Small Press Distribution in Berkeley, California, the only nonprofit wholesaler dedicated exclusively to distributing books from small—and medium-size presses. They teamed up with Poets & Writers to promote small presses in independent bookstores (Rosen 28).

However, these encouraging initiatives do not tell the entire story. Specialty stores that devote space to specialty titles will have a difficult time surviving if they are forced to rely on specialty title sales alone; some media outlets, like independent bookstores, need the revenue generated from mainstream sales in order to offer specialty titles. Not only is alternative media underrepresented in many media outlets, but now a potential purchaser will have to find a specific store that carries the title. Distribution continues to be an obstacle for small-press publications. In this way, specialty stores that are "less congested" and carry specialty titles are being ghettoized. Furthermore, in an era of budget cuts to libraries, a decline in the numbers of independent bookstores, and the bottom line of many monolithic chains, even second-tiered distribution may not provide adequate coverage of titles for the right audience, particularly in areas outside of large urban centres.

Ultimately, what this implies is that any niche publications or magazines with smaller newsstand sales and targeted audiences will suffer from distribution problems. The majority of these publications have a profit margin that renders them irrelevant to large wholesalers with national distribution. Compounding the problem is that many niche publications need to be available nationally or internationally in order to reach their target audience. For example, the magazine *Girlfriends,* a publication aimed at lesbians, must have a large distribution base because the number of lesbians in a given location may not be enough to sustain the publication. In addition, it is just as important, if not more important, for lesbians living in smaller communities to have access to a publication that reflects their interests and their lives, as it is for lesbians living in large urban centres.

The problem with wholesalers and distributors is not restricted to North America, nor to print media. In the U.K., the founder of the program Undercurrents, whose mission is to cover the news stories the news is not covering, cited distribution of their videos as their main obstacle in conveying their footage to the public. Eighty percent of video distribution is controlled by two chains in the U.K., and as a result Undercurrents discovered that interested parties did not know where they could purchase their videos (Cobbing 24).

Distribution is the key for a publication to remain visible, to reach a broad audience, to remain accessible, and ultimately key to the publication's survival. Many alternative publications, however, rely on alternative distribution systems like street-selling, selling in independent book shops, coffeehouses and cafes, and utilizing underground social networks for distribution instead of dominant, commercial distributors and retailers. Not only are many publishers of alternative materials creating a shadow distribution network but they do important work by community building and creating a marginal economy that exists outside of any commercial interests (Sabto 815; Duncombe). However, many of these publications rely on subscriptions, donations, and newsstand sales. If there are fewer and fewer outlets for newsstand, bookstore, and library sales, survival is problematic. As a result, the dominant distribution and wholesale systems render the alternative press invisible.

Indexing

Another way alternative media remains invisible is through indexing or the lack thereof. Large indexing and abstracting companies often overlook alternative publications in their indexes and in their databases. However, some large indexing companies claim there is not a great demand for alternative publications, and they cite this lack of demand as the primary reason why coverage may be lacking in the indexes they produce (Ardito 17).

Stephanie Ardito conducted an informal survey of eleven independently owned magazines mentioned frequently in library literature. Each title was searched in the 1999 edition of Ulrich's *International Periodicals Directory*. Six of the eleven magazines were not indexed in "mainstream" or high subscription database services. However, neither circulation nor readership demand appeared to determine whether or not the title was indexed. For example, *The Source* (370,000 circulation) was not indexed, and *Wired* (400,000 circulation) appears in only two databases. Yet, two publications with a lower subscription base, *The Utne Reader* (260,000 circulation) and *The Village Voice* (248,000 circulation), appear in several sources (16). Neither the age of the publication, nor the subject matter, nor geographical scope, influenced whether or not the magazine was indexed. This informal study raises two questions: when does an "alternative" publication become "mainstream" enough to be included in an index? And, how is a publication deemed worthy of inclusion in an index?

A study done by Lisa Pillow examined the adequacy of indexing for several scholarly African American studies journals. The databases selected for this study were electronic indexing services that are commonly found in large research libraries. The researcher, after analyzing the coverage of African American journals in several different databases, concluded that "the state of indexing for the interdisciplinary field of African American studies is inadequate: no one service provides comprehensive coverage of core scholarly journals ... The 11 services included in the study indexed only 66 percent of the 1997 literature" (5). Similarly, LaFond et. al (7) found that at the University of Albany subscriptions to electronic databases did not substantially increase access to titles covered by the Alternative Press Index.

On an international level, the problem of indexing is particularly acute. A report by W. Wayt Gibbs revealed that many international scientists were excluded from indexes. Commercial indexing services virtually ignore the vast majority of the world's journals. Gibbs reports that "although developing countries encompass 24.1 percent of the world's scientists and 5.3 percent of its research spending, most leading journals publish far smaller proportions of articles ... from those regions" (Gibbs 92).

Furthermore, even if a title is indexed in an online database, the full text of the article may not be available or the print version of the periodical is not easily accessible. The problem is cyclical: if people are not aware of, or cannot access, alternative press publications, no demand will be made for them and ultimately they will continue to be excluded from indexes, where no one will be aware of them and so on.

Reviewing Media

Although many reviewing journals attempt to be as inclusive as possible, reviewing sources use different criteria for evaluating and assessing materials. In some cases, being reviewed in a journal is an endorsement for that title, whereas other journals will review a wide range of titles with a critical eye. Furthermore, it is just as important to remember what materials are not included in reviewing journals as what materials are included, because the vast majority of published materials rarely make it into reviewing media. Some omitted categories of titles include the following: cookbooks, travel guides, reference works, cartoon books, how-to books, inspirational books, self-help books, scholarly books, and genre fiction (Howard 77).

Reviews are often sales tools (Woodward 92) and as a result, larger publishing companies have advantages over smaller publishers; they have signed established authors who generate more coverage in the form of frequent reviews spread over a number of sources, thereby creating access to wider audiences. Although reviewing journals may intend to remain independent, the larger corporations have a greater ability to ensure their titles are included in reviewing journals.

Libraries are often one of the few, and perhaps one of the only, places where marginalized sectors of the public can gain access to alternative publications. However, reliance on mainstream reviewing media for collection development can have dire consequences. Toni Samek succinctly describes the problems that librarians face when attempting to offer a diverse range of materials:

> Self-censorship also plays out on a more unconscious level. Because of the profession's heavy reliance on mainstream review media, publishers and vendors, materials produced by the alternative press and those that reflect alienated social sectors are often under-represented in library collections.
>
> Self-censorship has broad-reaching implications: the reliance on mainstream sources favours not only establishment cultural interests but also economic, social and political interests (41).

The exclusion of the alternative press from mainstream reviewing media—reviewing journals, newspapers, magazines, and television—makes it difficult for alternative publications to become part of current social discourse.

The Alternative Press Online

In 2000, the "Battle of Seattle" marked the first time the Internet was effectively used by activists as a political and organizational tool. This success, to some, provides evidence for the idea of the Internet as the "great equalizer": anyone can launch a Web site for relatively little expense and individuals do not need professional credentials in order to publish. Often individuals act as author, editor, publisher, and distributor. The proliferation of online zines, blogs, wikis, personal sites, and alternative publications appears to support the idea that cyberspace is indeed democratic.

Upon closer examination, it becomes evident that the above assertions are, in fact, erroneous. The Internet has not spawned a competitive media marketplace; as McChesney points out, media giants have too many advantages to be seriously challenged. They have the capital, the programming, the brand names, the advertisers, and the promotional prowess to rule the Internet (20). For example, for the month of March 2006 the Top 10 Nielsen NetRatings Rankings includes at the number one position, Microsoft, number three, Time Warner, number six, News Corp. Online, and at number nine, the Walt Disney Internet Group. These rankings are calculated according to how many hits a Web site receives in a given period of time ("Monthly"). It appears that McChesney's thesis is accurate: the giants have access to far more resources and thus dominate the Internet. In addition, access to the Internet continues to be available only to those who can afford computer equipment and sustained Internet access.

However, ICTs (information and communication technologies) hold much promise for alternative media. Peer to peer file sharing and distribution of material over networks allows publishers to bypass distributors and it also allows easy reproduction and reduced workloads— only a single copy needs to be posted. Time and space are no longer barriers to access. Most importantly, however, the use of ICTs have facilitated the idea of an information commons where the active production and consumption of information, open source software, open copyright, etc., is supported and promoted by organizations and individuals who view access to information as an important component of a democratic society. Because many alternative publishers encourage copying of materials, or are unconcerned about making a profit, the Internet, despite increasing commercial controls, continues to hold promise for alternative media publishers.

Conclusion

The hijacking of media outlets by the mega-conglomerates has resulted in the marginalization of alternative media and has also contributed to the homogenization of the mainstream media. The greatest obstacle for alternative publications regarding access issues is distribution. What is particularly problematic is that alternative publications need to be made widely available in order to reach their typically smaller audience. The lack of wholesalers willing to distribute small-profit alternative publications, the lack of inclusion in indexes, and the reliance on mainstream reviewing journals and vendors to develop library collections, has rendered alternative media, at the very best, marginalized, and at the very worst, invisible.

The invisibility of alternative media in commercial retail outlets highlights the pressing need for alternative media to be made available in libraries. What is communicated in alternative media about our contemporary culture is equally as important as what is documented by dominant media. Ergo, the inclusion of alternative media is necessary for building diverse library collections and for promoting different points of view. In addition, alternative media provide primary source material for scholars as well as material for leisure. One of the stalwart principles of librarianship is providing access to information and upholding this principle must include providing access to alternative sources of information also.

In our era of globalization and mega-conglomeration we are defined as "consumers", not "citizens." Ultimately, concentrated corporate control of the media is harmful to democracy. We need dissenting points of view, we need avenues for personal and cultural expression, and we need the platforms and vehicles to disseminate these alternative points of view. To be able to choose between a hundred things that are all essentially the same thing, is no choice at all. Good morning, Citizen X.

Works Cited

"Anderson News Company: Overview." Hoovers Online. 2006. Hoovers, Inc. 15 April 2006
<http://www.hoovers.com/anderson-news/--ID__54541--/free-co-factsheet.xhtml>.

Ardito, Stephanie C. "The Alternative Press: Newsweeklies and Zines." *Database Magazine*, 44.3 (1999): 14-21.

Atton, Chris. *Alternative Media*. London: Sage Publications, 2002.

Birdsall, William F., and Merrilee Rasmussen. "The Citizen's Right to Communicate." *Citizenship and Participation in the Information Age*. Eds. Manjunuth Pendakur and Roma Harris. Aurora, ON: Garamond Press, 2002.

Buss, Dale. "10 Reasons New Magazines Fail." *Folio: The Magazine for Magazine Management* 30.2 (2001): 41-43.

CanWest Global Communications Corp. 23 March 2001. CanWest Global Communications Corp. 30 March 2001 <http://www.canwestglobal.com/>.

"Challenge at the Checkout." *Folio: The Magazine of Magazine Management* 34.3 (2005): 40-44.

Cobbing, Nick. "Might Not Main." *Whose News?* (Mar. 24, 1995): 24-26.

Cromwell, David. "The Hack and Flack Machine." *New Internationalist* 328 (2000): 34-36.

Duncombe, Stephen. *Notes From Underground: Zines and the Politics of Alternative Culture*. London: Verso, 1997.

Gibbs, W. Wayt. "Lost Science in the Third World." *Scientific American* 273.2 (1995): 92.

Granatstein, Lisa. "Wholesale Changes." *Mediaweek* 9.36 (1999): 98-99.

Greenslade, Roy. "Their Master's Voice." *The Guardian* [London] 17 February 2003: pg. 2.

Howard, Gerhard. "The Cultural Ecology of Book Reviewing." *Publishing Books*. Ed. Everette E. Dennis, Craig L. LaMay, and Edward C. Pease. New Brunswick, NJ: Transaction Publishers, 1997. 75-91.

Lowenstein, Joanna. "Dealing With Distribution Uncertainty." *Folio: The Magazine for Magazine Management* 27.18 (1999): 158-159.

—. "Small Distributors: A Healthy Choice." *Folio: The Magazine for Magazine Management* 27.18 (1999): 155.

McChesney, Robert W. "Oligopoly: The Big Media Game Has Fewer and Fewer Players." *The Progressive* (1999): 20-24.

"Monthly Top Ten Parent Companies." 2006. Nielsen NetRatings. 30 March 2006 <http://www.nielsen-netratings.com/news.jsp?section= dat_to&country=us>

Moyers, Bill. Foreword. *The Future of Media: Resistance and Reform in the 21St Century*. Eds. Robert McChesney, Russell Newman, and Ben Scott. New York: Seven Stories Press, 2005. vii-xxiii.

Owens, Jennifer, and Teresa Ennis. "Latest Wholesaler Merger Shrinks Major Players to Four." *Folio: The Magazine for Magazine Management* 28.2 (1999): 12-14.

Pillow, Lisa. "Scholarly African American Studies Journals: An Evaluation of Electronic Indexing Service Coverage." *Serials Review* 25.4 (1999): 21-29.

Rosen, Judith. "Small is Beautiful." *Publisher's Weekly* 247.49 (2000): 28.

Ross, Edward A. "The Suppression of Important News" *Our Unfree Press: 100 Years of Radical Media Criticism*. Eds. Robert W. McChesney and Ben Scott. New York: The New Press, 2004. 181-192.

Sabto, Michele. "Lo-Fi Tales." *Meanjin* 57.4 (1998): 809-815.

Samek, Toni. "Introducing Intellectual Freedom into the Canadian LIS Curriculum." *Feliciter* 47.1 (2001): 40-43.

Schwartzman, Andrew J., Cheryl Leanza, and Harold Feld. "The Legal Case for Diversity in Broadcast Ownership." *The Future of Media: Resistance and Reform in the 21st Century*. Eds. Robert McChesney, Russell Newman, and Ben Scott. New York: Seven Stories Press, 2005. 149-161.

"Who Owns What?" 18 April 2006. *Columbia Journalism Review*. Ed. Aaron Moore. 5 May 2006. <http://www.cjr.org/tools/owners/>

Woodward, Richard. "Reading in the Dark." *The Village Voice* 44.42 (1999): 92-96.

Some Alternative Press History

(Text of talk for panel on the alternative press at ALA 2003, Toronto)
By Chuck D'Adamo
Co-Editor, Alternative Press Index

This is a revision of the article originally published in *Library Juice* 6:18, August 28, 2003

In 1969, the Alternative Press Center was originally founded as the Radical Research Center at Carleton College in Minnesota. Carleton College never really supported the Center institutionally so the Collective, then including Kathy Martin and Art Jacobs, later joined by Marty Scheel, moved the Center to Rochdale College in Toronto in October 1971. It was renamed the Alternative Press Center. There the collective found inexpensive office space on the 6th floor and living space on the 13th floor. Rochdale College, as some in the room may remember, was an attempt to develop a "free university" space and a collective living experiment. The Canadian government funded the project, something we would rarely see in the United States.

In the summer of 1974, a new collective, Peggy D'Adamo, Michael Burns, and myself, began the move from Baltimore to Toronto to publish the *Alternative Press Index*. We applied for "landed immigrant" status and two of us worked from Rochdale College for a period of time. A serious problem developed which was that Rochdale's residents became involved in a struggle with Toronto's "city fathers" over the space. Rochdale was losing the struggle so the APC collective decided to move to Baltimore.

If you walk by 341 Bloor Street, you can see the 18-story building that was once Rochdale College. Now it is the Senator David A. Croll Apartments, a senior housing project under private-public management, I believe. As I remember, the City considered Rochdale a haven for drug users and US draft-dodgers. However, Rochdale's founders included among its members Dennis Lee, the poet laurette of Ontario who, I imagine, must not have been strung out on drugs in the Rochdale days, but doing some creative writing. His book *Alligator Pie* is one of the top 100 books of Canada.

Now this story is one of many social movement stories connected to the 1960s anti-war, student, and, potentially anti-systemic movements. And there is a link between this piece of social movement history and alternative press history from which I'll try to relate to other examples. The basic idea is that the history of the alternative press is directly related to the history of social movements.

Please note that I am not Paul Buhle, who would have had more learned things to say on this subject.

A democratic society is impossible unless citizens are engaged in active discussion of public policy. Such discussion requires controversy between well-informed citizens.

At least since the French Revolutions of 1789 and 1848, class-based groups, ethnic groups, and social movements of all kinds have had their own newspapers and magazines. Even in the depoliticized United States, there have been times when the numbers of social movement publications were extensive. In 1912, there were 323 socialist newspapers or magazines, many published in foreign languages. And by the end of World War II there were about 200 African-American newspapers (1). Most constituency-based periodicals were partisan and controversial, working for democratic social, political and economic change.

While mainstream newspapers and magazines often publish articles which help citizens to intervene in the political process, it is usually the independent, critical periodicals which generate the innovative reporting important for progressive political intervention. Project Censored and the *Alternative Press Index* are documentary sources here.

Many editors of the alternative press take it as their mission to move readers beyond information to action. Indeed, the independent, "alternative" press has been organically connected to social movements. Publications rise, fall or subsist in circumstances that parallel the movements they represent. Such periodicals serve as forums for debating strategic approaches, for finding common cause among seemingly disparate, often geographically diffuse, constituencies, and, in hard times, for critique (2).

More examples from US history:

- In 1862, writing in the *Douglass Monthly*, Frederick Douglass argued that slavery had become an obstacle to preserving Union, helping to persuade Abraham Lincoln to sign the Emancipation Proclamation.
- Ida Tarbell and other muckraking journalists exposed the nastiness of American capitalism in the pages of *Colliers* and other magazines, helping to facilitate the passage of some of the Progressive era's important regulatory reforms.

- Writing in *The Revolution* in the 19th century, Susan B. Anthony developed a critique of gender discrimination that catalyzed the movement for universal suffrage.
- Second-wave feminists writing in *Feminist Studies, Off Our Backs*, and *Women: a Journal of Liberation* expanded feminist analysis to include violence against women, the poverty of single-mothers, sexual harassment, and, more generally, the politics of the personal.
- From the 1950s through the early 1970s, criticism in the pages of the *IF Stone Bi-Weekly, Monthly Review, The Guardian, Latin American Perspectives, NACLA, The Bulletin of the Atomic Scientists, The Bulletin of Concerned Asian Scholars*, and other periodicals informed the social movements which worked to change US policy on nuclear weapons, Vietnam, and Latin America.

Throughout the twentieth century, oppositional and minority movements, including workers, welfare mothers, people of color, gays and lesbians, and disabled persons have used the alternative press to develop the vision and power their struggles have required. From *The Nation*, founded in 1865, to *The Progressive* (1909), to *Science & Society* (1936), to *Monthly Review* (1949), to *The Black Scholar* (1969), to *In These Times* (1976), to *Z Magazine* (1988), to *Counterpunch* (1993), to the Independent Media Centers of the new century, the independent, critical press reports the news, analyzes the social relations, and nurtures the oppositional movements whose interests are in direct conflict with those of the liberal capitalist oligarchy.

ALTERNATIVE PRESS CENTER

The Radical Research Center, later the Alternative Press Center, was founded in 1969 "to increase awareness of the so-called underground, or critical, press in the United States." Its original—and continuing—project, the *Alternative Press Index*, originally appeared with the subtitle, "An Index to the Publications, which amplify the Cry for Social Change and Social Justice." In 1969, the range of the voices making this "Cry" was becoming increasingly diverse. Consider a few of the 1960s events that the APC began to document through the Index:

- The murder of Fred Hampton and the intense pursuit of other Black Panther leaders by the FBI and other government agencies *The Trial of the Chicago Eight

- The publication of The Bitch Manifesto, The Red Stockings Manifesto and other events catalyzing the increased radicalism of many feminists
- The disintegration of Students for A Democratic Society
- The introduction to US readers of the works of Western Marxists, such as Herbert Marcuse
- The increasing determination of the antiwar movement in the face of the Nixon administration's commitment to pursue and intensify attempts to destroy the National Liberation Front in Vietnam.

Only a handful of stable independent left periodicals, all with limited circulation, including *The Guardian, I.F.Stone's Bi-Weekly, Monthly Review, Liberation, The Nation, New Politics,* and *The Progressive,* were documenting these events and analyzing them from a left perspective during most of the 1960s. But, by 1969, the world of alternative periodicals was expanding. The APC undertook the project of making the range of these reports and critiques accessible to students, scholars, journalists, and other researchers.

In 1969, the *Alternative Press Index* began indexing 72 periodicals. Only 20 of those titles indexed from 1969-71 are still publishing today. However, the Index now covers 300 titles and, since its founding, the API has indexed more than 900 titles. Over the past three decades the APC's collective has tried to follow people active on the left, whether they have settled into academia, community organizing, or single issue advocacy, and to document the publications they are writing and reading. Coverage, thus, has always been wide-ranging, including from the inception of its indexing project titles as diverse as the North American Congress on Latin America's *NACLA Report,* initially a newsletter, the academic *Review of Radical Political Economics,* and Toronto's, *This Magazine,* originally titled *This Magazine is about Schools,* now *This: Because Everything is about Politics.* Theoretical perspectives surveyed include feminism, Marxism, critical theory, structuralism, poststructuralism, critical race theory and queer theory. API titles have documented dozens of political and social movements, including the efforts of women, people of color, rank & file workers, environmentalists, anti-apartheid student groups and Latin American solidarity supporters.

Almost all the radical weeklies and bi-weeklies of the 60s and 70s are gone—Atlanta's *Great Speckled Bird,* the *Ann Arbor Sun,* the *Portland Scribe,* New Orleans's *Nola Express,* the *Berkeley Barb,* New York's *The Guardian* and its negation, the *Liberated Guardian,* the *DC Gazette.* (A few remain such as Vancouver's *Georgia Straights* and Detroit's *Fifth Estate,* though the latter now only publishes quarterly). This partly relates to the waning of the 1960s movements and the lack of development of institution-building skills, but also to the decision of the Underground Press Syndicate to be open to advertising in member newspapers, changing its name at the same time to the Alternative Press Syndicate. *New Times* from Arizona surely benefited from this changed policy as it eventually bought out other alternative weeklies from various cities. Its publisher, Mike Lacey, has justified this by arguing that because of this *New Times* has been able to develop resources for investigative journalism (3). I don't know. Maybe the jury's still out on this.

However, the analytical journals continued to publish and the work of their writers has likely influenced a new generation coming of age in the 1990s and the new century. From the radical caucuses in the academia sprang *Critical Asian Studies* (formerly the *Bulletin of Concerned Asian Scholars*), *Critical Sociology* (formerly *Insurgent Sociologist*), *Feminist Studies, New Political Science, Radical History Review, Radical Philosophy Review, Review of the Fernand Braudel Center, Review of Radical Political Economics*, and others. Of course, the general journals of the New Left continued but with changes—*Arena Journal* from Australia, *Capital & Class* from Britain, *Le Monde Diplomatique* from France, *Monthly Review* from the US, *New Left Review* from Britain, *Socialist Register* from Britain, *Studies in Political Economy* from Canada. While 1960s activists tended to refer their critique to "The System" or "Advanced Industrial Society", relying as they did on maverick scholars who wrote under the pressure of the conservative 1950s, activists in today's alternative globalization movement, many "social anarchists" of varying tendencies, simply say "It's capitalism, stupid."

Two media organizations with which the APC has affinity are Project Censored and the Independent Press Association.

PROJECT CENSORED

Project Censored was founded in 1976 with the purpose to advocate and work to protect First Amendment rights and freedom of information in the United States. It essentially serves as a national "ombudsman by identifying and researching important news stories that are underreported" or censored by the mainstream media (4). The Top 25 Censored Stories and their media guide are key resources for activists. Typically, 80% of the stories that win the awards are from the periodicals that the API covers.

INDEPENDENT PRESS ASSOCIATION

In March 1996, a group of independent, progressive magazine editors, reporters and publishers gathered at the Media and Democracy Congress in San Francisco to discuss the challenges they had in common. Within a few hours of meetings, their shared need for technical assistance, advocacy and fundraising resources moved them to found an organization to work in their interest. The resulting Independent Press Association (IPA) had its inaugural board meeting in August 1996 and, with the help of a few broadminded foundations, hired staff and began operations in September.

Board members have represented a wide range of alternative titles, including *Extra!, Mother Jones, Social Policy, In These Times, City Limits, Third Force* (now *ColorLines*), *Teen Voices*, and *Curve*. Seeking to make the organization both inclusive and responsive to all publications with a social change vision, the IPA board developed a mission statement dedicating the IPA "to promote and support independent periodicals committed to social justice and a free press" by providing "technical assistance to its member publications" and by acting as "a vigorous public advocate of the independent press."

Publications that share IPA's mission can join the organization for an annual membership fee depending on circulation. Direct services include a members-only listserv, free technical assistance manuals, a quarterly newsletter the *Ink Reader*, various discounts, and access to a variety of specialized services. The IPA staff operates a Revolving Loan Fund to help members with direct mail marketing, a bookstore magazine distribution service called Big Top, an ethnic press project in New York City, and offers ad hoc technical assistance in a wide range of areas. In addition, the IPA began in 1999 to display member publications, sometimes in collaboration with the Alternative Press Center, sometimes with *Counterpoise*, at American Library Association conventions.

INDEPENDENT MEDIA CENTERS

The first Independent Media Center was founded to cover the Seattle protests against the World Trade Organization in November and December 1999. This first IMC created an environment for independent media makers of all types (audio, video, print, Internet) to work together covering the protests in a democratic and collaborative manner. It took three months for the Seattle IMC to get organized to provide grassroots coverage of the

Battle of Seattle. It turns out that this was the beginning of a global independent media movement which focuses on reporting on the world-wide struggle against neoliberal capitalism and a range of local issues. There are now over 100 IMCs around the world. I happen to be involved with Baltimore Indymedia. Besides local coverage, we've written on the activities in the streets at national protests in Washington DC and New York City. Baltimore IMC also collaborates with APC staff providing a small, but growing, database of links to articles of the independent, critical press. Most members of our group are activists with social movement experience, and this is true of other IMCs.

In a sense, the current Indymedia movement is like the radical weeklies of the 1960s and 70s. Both are or were urban-based. Both have or had high levels of activist involvement. Both report or reported the advocacy of radical social change. Both express or expressed a commitment to independence and free speech. The IMCs, being Internet-based, are less costly. However, even in the IMC network there's recognition of the crucial value of print periodicals. The New York IMC's *The Indypendent* has recently moved to twice monthly publication and aspires to a weekly publication schedule.

The parallel I am making between the 1960s radical weeklies and the 2000s IMCs is one which notes the social movement-alternative media connection; broad-based left libertarian politics connecting with a similar media movement.

It is also interesting to note how independent media changes over time within a single periodical's history and how this changing connects to changing social movement activity.

There is a thread from *Studies on the Left*, the 1950s origin New Left journal influenced by C.Wright Mills and William Appleman Williams (intellectuals who challenged mainstream sociology and history to the 1960s origin *Socialist Revolution),* where we see the influence of revolutionary Marxists like Hebert Marcuse and Antonio Gramsci. *SR* published the first version of Carl Boggs's studies of *Gramsci's Marxism*, a text well used by cadre of the 1970s New American Movement; the thread continued through the 1980s *Socialist Review* response to the success of right wing Reaganism with a slide back to social democracy and a slippage into the politics of identity in the 1990s to the latest version, *Radical Society,* which attempts to bring strategic thinking and left intellectualism to contemporary global justice concerns. To quote from the journal, "Our inspirations are both old and new—from *The Masses* and Emma Goldman's *Mother Earth* to the Harlem

Renaissance and the Paris Commune, from the end of the cold war to the beginnings of a new global justice movement."

There are at least two other threads from *Studies on the Left* expressive of various trends in the social movements.

One is from *Studies on the Left* to *Socialist Revolution* to *In These Times*. The defining thread here is James Weinstein's project to develop a strategy similiar to the Socialist Party of Eugene Debs, but in a new context. Weinstein's recent book, *The Long Detour: the History and Future of the American Left*, attemps to make his case systematically.

Another is from *Studies on the Left* to *Socialist Revolution* to *Kapitalistate* to *Capitalism Nature Socialism*. The defining thread here is James O'Connor's attempt to develop a neo-Marxist understanding of the capitalist state with strategic intent. The first version of O'Connor's *Fiscal Crisis of the State* appeared in *Socialist Revolution*. He then helped to organize an international group of thinkers around *Kapitalistate* to explore state theory and socialist strategy. Later O'Connor argued that capital's destructive relationship with nature constitutes a "second contradiction of capitalism", the first, of course, that of capital and labor. Thus, *Capitalism Nature Socialism* focuses on case studies of the environmental movement as well as theoretical work providing analysis valuable for an eco-socialist project.

Similar shifting threads of influence can be seen with the independent Left periodicals *Socialisme ou Barbarie* in France, *New Left Review* in Britain, and *Arena* in Australia.

Taking the case of *Socialisme ou Barbarie* we see a development to *Informations et Correspondance Ouvriere* to *Echanges: Bulletin du Reseau Echanges et Mouvement* and the related U.S. periodical *Collective Action Notes*. The thread here is that of the council communism of original *Socialisme ou Barbarie* collective member Henri Simon.

And there is the development from *Socialisme ou Barbarie* to *Libre* and *Textures* (France) to *Thesis Eleven* (Australia) to *Democracy & Nature* (Greece/USA). The thread here is that of Cornelius Castoriadis's critique of Marxism and attempt to develop theoretical basis for a revolutionary libertarian socialist alternative, which he later described as "autonomous society, defined as "self-management of production" and directly democratic "self-government."

I understand that this panel was to address the past, present, and future of alternative materials in libraries. Well, many states in the US are experiencing budget crises. We are losing some subscriptions to the *Alternative Press Index* as a result. And I expect some small circulation alternative magazines are being cut as well. Thinking of the connection between the alternative press and social activism, it seems to me that the role of those librarians who are advocates of the independent, critical press is dual. One role is to fight as a professional worker to maintain and expand library collections of alternative/independent press; the other is to fight with other groups effected by budget cuts as activists to move forward a left libertarian agenda. Thus, librarians must not only be professionals, they must also be activists working in the social movements.

Notes:

1. Weinstein, James. "Celebrating Controversy, Practicing Democracy." Foreword to *Annotations: A Guide to the Independent Critical Press*, 2nd Ed. Alternative Press Center/Independent Press Association, 1999, pp 2-3; see also James Weinstein, *The Decline of Socialism in America, 1912-1925*. Vintage Books, 1969, pp 84-102.

2. Parts of this text draw on "The Independent Critical Press and Democratic Tradition" by Beth Schulman and Charles D'Adamo published as the Introduction to *Annotations: A Guide to the Independent Critical Press*.

3. Response of Mike Lacey to questions on a panel at the Second Media and Democracy Congress in New York City. On the Underground Press Syndicate and related history see Chip Berlet "Muckraking Gadflies Buzz Reality" in *Voices From the Underground: Insider History of the Vietnam Era Underground Press*. Edited by Ken Wachsberger. MICA Press: 1993, pp 63-80.

4. Peter Phillips & Project Censored. *Censored 1998: The News that Didn't make the News—the Year's Top 25 Censored Stories*. Seven Stories Press: 1998. p 352.

Selected Bibliography:

Alternative Press Index, 1969-present. Alternative Press Center.

Buhle, Mari Jo, Paul Buhle, Dan Georgakas (editors). *Encyclopedia of the American Left*. University of Illinois Press, 1990.

Echanges et Mouvement. "What is Echanges et Mouvement as a Group?" *Collective Action Notes,* No. 14-15: 31-32.

Jones, Marie F. (general editor). *Annotations: A Guide to the Independent Critical Press.* Alternative Press Center and Independent Press Association, 1999.

Lewis, Roger. *Outlaws of America, the Underground Press and Its Context.* Pelican, 1972.

Peck, Abe. *Uncovering the Sixties: the Life & Times of the Underground Press.* Pantheon, 1985.

Phillips, Peter & Project Censored. *Censored: The Top 25 Censored Stories.* Seven Stories Press, annually.

Samek, Toni. *Intellectual Freedom & Social Responsibility in American Librarianship, 1967-1974.* McFarland, 2001.

Swados, Harvey. *Years of Conscience: The Muckrakers.* New York: World Publishing Company. 1962.

Weinstein, James. *The Decline of Socialism in America, 1912-1925.* New York: Vintage Books, 1969.

Selected Entries from the *Encyclopedia of the American Left*:
"Appeal to Reason," pp 51-52
"Black Panther Party," pp 96-98
"Daily Worker," pp 178-82
"Dissent," p 195
"Freedomways," pp 244-45
"In These Times," pp 350-51
"International Socialist Review," pp 374-75
"Liberation News Service," pp 422-24
"The Masses," pp 452-54
"Month Review," pp 483-85
"Mother Earth," p 492
"National Guardian and Guardian," pp 502-04
"New International/New Politics," p 516
"New Left," pp 516-23
"New Masses," pp 526-27

"North American Congress on Latin America," p 538
"Partisan Review," pp 556-58
"Peoples World," pp 573-74
"Progressiv,e" pp 596-99
"Radical Economics," pp 621-23
"Radical Professional & Academic Journals," pp 636-38
"Ramparts Magazine," pp 639-40
"Science & Society," pp 679-80
"Socialism and Feminism," pp 707-11
"Southern Exposure," p 737
"Student Nonviolent Coordinating Committee," pp 755-57
"Students for a Democratic Society," pp 757-58
"Stone, I.F. (1907-1989)," p 751
"Studies on the Left," pp 758-59
"Underground Press," pp 791-93
"Women: a Journal of Liberation," pp 831-32
"Women's Studies," pp 842-44

Selected Web Sites:
http://www.altpress.org/
http://www.indymedia.org/
http://www.indypress.org/
http://www.projectcensored.org/

Information-Seeking During Wartime: Reconsidering the Role of the Library in Increasing User Self-Sufficiency

By Doug Horne

This article was originally published in *Library Juice* 7:22, October 22, 2004

As a life-long news addict and career information professional, information seeking habits are always of interest to me. I am either trying to figure out how to get people what they need when they need it, or I have a personal interest in getting the good information first. Information seeking reaches a new level of intensity when a "breaking news story", a crisis, or some other event of global interest becomes a focus of attention. The Internet has made it all the more possible to remain up-to-date, consult many sources and viewpoints, and get the information as it becomes available. In recent cases, each subsequent international news story has produced new strategies for obtaining information, as developing Internet technologies put the tools for gathering and disseminating information into the hands of an increasingly large group of people. When an event like the 2003 invasion of Iraq took place, the huge range of possibilities for online sources of information lead to a lengthy and involved search for the "best" information and unique insight into the events. This type of information gathering can be a great challenge and the world of information has become all the more rich and daunting as the possibilities for sources of information have grown exponentially with the advent of networked information and instantaneous global communication.

In 1991 as the war in Iraq broke out, we were introduced to a new type of reporting of information. While Viet Nam had been the war fought on the evening news, Iraq was the war in which we watched live footage of the bombing of Baghdad in grainy night-vision images of tracers in the sky. Occasionally, we would see reporters in a Baghdad hotel giving live accounts of life in a city under attack. On the first night of this war the public library I was working in at the time completely emptied as people watched prime-time broadcasting of the bombing of a city. At the time this was a new phenomenon and both television and radio provided constant coverage. During lulls in the action we were shown videotaped footage of bombs being dropped, and the impact of precision weapons on targets. All of this was carefully delivered in press briefings that were the sole access the press had to the military. In this conflict, we were offered the strange combination of tremendous new technology for delivering coverage of war, coupled with a very controlled release of the available information. We were frequently watching live broadcasts but the authorities, very aware of the power of the media at the time, made great efforts to try to ensure that the message getting out was under their control. In 1991, it was still possible to control the relatively small number of media outlets, and journalists were not allowed to roam freely in Iraq but were fed information through press briefings.

Teaching university students how to research this type of event a couple of years later, I would relate the first piece of advice imparted in my undergraduate international relations classes: read the newspaper. Better yet, read more than one newspaper. For the new crop of now Internet savvy students who thought they didn't need such a primitive method of retrieving information, I related the following experience. During Desert Storm in 1991, one of the most dramatic events was the Iraqi retreat from Kuwait City along what was called the Basra Highway. The US media related in press releases how Air Force F-15s and A6s intercepted and destroyed the retreating Iraqi military as they raced North in a huge victory for the coalition. The *Times* reported "roads leading north from Kuwait City were clogged with Iraqi military vehicles." (Apple, 1991) Later, browsing our library's copy of the *Times of London*, which at that time was received in paper and thus was always behind, I read a very different account of this event. In this version, a panicked Iraqi military had escaped Kuwait City in any civilian vehicles they could find and were racing North in what was described as "anything that had wheels" and "brand new Mercedes, Range Rovers, and luxury American limousines." (Airs, 1991) This unfortunate convoy was cut off at a bottleneck in the highway and destroyed like fish in a barrel by the American air power, the vehicles gradually piling up behind each other and fanning out into the desert as each tried to get around the carnage. My example simply pointed out the importance of reading multiple sources and gaining multiple viewpoints, then assessing the accumulated information. One source is rarely enough to provide a well-rounded account of events and most sources have a political stance or agenda, even when the intention is to remain objective. In 1991, most people still only had access to a small number of media outlets, using television, radio, and print media. The voices most heard were North American, and to find alternate viewpoints required a good deal of effort.

From the start the 2003 version of the war in Iraq was different. "Embedded" journalists rode into battle with the troops with everything broadcast live via satellite. The promise of embedding journalists was that this war would be transparent, and we would witness the reality of the events as they unfolded on the front line. With a thoroughly promoted and anticipated "starting time" for the war, people sat down to watch it begin and saw many correspondents head north into the Iraqi frontier. Unfortunately, war in real time turned out to be extremely boring. Hours of footage shot through the window of a military vehicle rolling across endless desert did not impart a great deal of information, and did not hold the attention for long. Network broadcasts provided little more satisfaction as we were provided with a very narrowly focused account of the events, often from nothing more than a stationary camera focused on a Baghdad intersection. Putting the camera in the hands of individuals in the field gave us a very personal and detailed view of the events that we received immediately, but these views were still those filtered through the major television networks, and thus limited in scope. Despite significant advances in technology, receiving messages from the mainstream media left one only as informed as when reading a single newspaper in 1991, and many of us were also suspicious of the "good news" message we were uniformly receiving from these outlets. In fact, the views of combat journalists in Viet Nam were far more informative and provided more in-depth coverage, even though they took time to compose and had to be shipped out of the country to be published.

For those of us who had been paying attention to the buildup to the Iraq conflict, we knew that there were better sources of information than the mainstream media. For some time, I had been debating all things political on an Internet bulletin board. The participants were mostly young, well-read, opinionated people who were very good at keeping up-to-date and using the Internet to back up their claims. Whenever I had discussed such forums in the Library setting, they had always been dismissed as places for subjective ranting, lacking the academic rigor that we required in our information sources. What was clear to me from my very early visits to this forum, however, was that this community did not tolerate poor arguments and unreliable sources. In fact, one learned quite quickly to thoroughly research one's arguments, as the other members of the forum were quite merciless in their attacks on flawed reasoning and sources. Those who became known for sloppy reasoning might not be banished, but they were most certainly labeled and known to the community. It's true that the discussions often didn't meet the standards of academia, but that does not diminish the fact that informed and well-read people were expressing themselves, relating information from many international viewpoints (one was a young person in Lebanon, another a member of the US military), and often comparing favourably with major news outlets in terms of how quickly they communicated the latest news. The advantage of this type of forum was that the participants expressed a wide range of viewpoints, which was a refreshing change from the homogeneity of the media's message. I was quite impressed by the ability of these people to very quickly find interesting and obscure sources of information and to use the Internet to its fullest potential. Activity on these boards generally fluctuated with the activity on the ground in Iraq and in the media, so that when the war began in earnest information was passed at a high rate of speed.

At a certain point in the conflict as information was flooding in from many sources I felt the need to ask these people to list their favourite information sources. The results were varied and fascinating, and I made a large bookmark file to keep track of it all. These people certainly didn't need my advice about reading a wide range of newspapers, as they read any and all that could be found. The most significant fact to emerge was that the availability of newspapers on the Internet leads these people to read not just major North American papers, but to branch out to interesting sources around the world. While The *NY Times*, *The Times of London*, and *The Guardian* were popular choices, quality sources were visited wherever they might be found. These included the *Sydney Morning Herald*, *The Ha'aretz Daily*, *The Lebanon Daily Star*, and *The Sacramento Bee*. The papers were often chosen exclusively for the quality of coverage and local writers. While any source can provide wire service coverage, intelligent analysis of the issues was highly valued during these confusing times. While I had access to quite a number of newspapers in my student days, I had no way to search as far and wide as these people could on a regular basis from the comfort of their homes. There was a strong desire expressed to seek out a wide range of viewpoints, and to find more than the wire services had to offer.

Many of the participants also consulted Al-Jazeera on a regular basis. This was an interesting new addition for those in search of information. In the 1991 war, there was no information flowing from Arab side of the war, and I don't recall ever hearing an Iraqi opinion on the situation. This new source of information sprang up somewhere between 1991 and 2003 and made its way rapidly into our consciousness with the new Gulf War. Perhaps the most significant inroads made by Al-Jazeera occurred as CNN reporters were asked to leave Iraq temporarily at the beginning of the US attack on Baghdad, and all of the live feeds of the bombings (watched by millions), were provided by Al-Jazeera with their logo only partially covered at the bottom of our television screens. (Goodman, 2003) I suspect that many people never noticed the Al-Jazeera logo on their screens, but the impact of their coverage was clear and significant. This was also the same news network that broadcast footage of captured US soldiers early in the conflict, leading to a great deal of ethical debate about the treatment of prisoners. (El Deeb, 2003) While its introduction to our world of information was controversial, it was clear from the beginning that this news source was credible and tended to be present when news was being made in the Arab world. In fact, once one got used to the idea, Al-Jazeera seemed very similar in nature to CNN. For those of us suspicious of the major media outlets, a dissenting voice was welcome, particularly one that obviously possessed significant resources. Some clearly felt that this dissenting and loud voice was a threat, as the Al-Jazeera web site was repeatedly hacked and made unavailable during periods early in the conflict. This lead to the interesting phenomenon of people posting instructions on how to watch Al-Jazeera television broadcasts live on one's computer, and others providing summaries of this news source on their own sites. As with everything on the web, it turned out to be impossible to silence an information source if it wishes to be heard.

One of the most remarkable sources of information available from the Internet during the Iraq conflict was a website called simply called "War in Iraq," (http://www.iraqwar.ru) a half English half Russian site with details regularly posted on troop movements and major military engagements. While we were watching embedded reporters in the western media, this site seemed to be monitoring military communication inside Iraq and reporting detailed troop movements and combat operations. These stories were very different from the others we were hearing, and the reports seemed more authentic, relating the difficulties and ugliness of war. This source was unlike anything I had seen before, describing in great detail the progress of battles that were mentioned only in passing by the major media outlets. While it seemed reasonable to assume at the time that these were authentic accounts, many of them have been verified since. As the US troops approached Baghdad this web-site temporarily packed up and, suggesting that they were leaving the country with the Russian embassy, disappeared for a few days. The site began updating again in the same interesting manner shortly thereafter and recently went offline. (remnants of this site can be viewed by searching at http://www.webarchive.org) The site claimed to be gathering information by monitoring military radio and there seemed to be no reason to doubt this as the reports were detailed and mirrored the reports coming through other outlets. Such a point of view had been completely unavailable in previous conflicts, and the discussion forums on this site were particularly unique, pitting Russian visitors against those from the US.

The possibility of receiving first person reports from the front line was fascinating for those in search of the most detailed information. While this type of reporting had been possible previously, instantaneous reporting from the front lines was new. For those on the move, initial television reports delivered by satellite telephone were disappointingly grainy and out of synch. The obvious tool to provide continually updated information was the blog. This source of information has been routinely devalued in the past as "vanity publishing" by researchers and information professionals. Indeed, many thousands of blogs are nothing more than a diary for people with little to say, but in the hands of the right people they can be a unique insight into the minds of otherwise inaccessible viewpoints. Now a standard form of communication, the situation of war brought the blog to the centre of public attention. These websites featuring frequent posts can be easily and quickly updated, and being largely text-based are not overly demanding of bandwidth or processing power. Perhaps the most famous of the blogs came straight out of Baghdad beginning well before the war, featuring a young Iraqi named Salam Pax. Called "Where's Raed?", this blog quickly became known as a unique viewpoint from inside the society and city being dominated by Saddam Hussein. What may have been most surprising about this depiction of life in Iraq was simply how normal it all seemed. While it is easy to think of the "other side" as an alien environment, it was clear that Salam was just a young person in large city. Salam was able to tell us from the site of the action when a missile landed or a bomber flew overhead. While CNN could relate the story with the detachment of a foreigner in a strange land filtered by the US military, Pax was telling of the experience while sitting in a residential living room. As the inevitable invasion approached the depictions of Baghdad became darker and more uncertain. One image that stuck in my mind was of Ba'ath party members digging in on the streets and stacking weapons on the corners for the citizens to keep in their houses. The intention and consequence of this distribution of weapons is now very clear in an Iraq in which everyone seems to be armed.

Where's Raed? (http://dearraed.blogspot.com/) was just one of many blogs being published from inside Iraq during this conflict. While there were blogs produced by mainstream media and American soldiers in Iraq, the

more interesting ones were those from otherwise unheard voices.
Warblogs.cc (http://www.warblogs.cc) provided an aggregating service of
headlines from around the world combined with the personal observances
of its creator as he crossed the border from Turkey and explored Northern
Iraq. Blogs such as "Back to Iraq" (http://www.back-to-iraq.com) and
"Baghdad Burning" (http://riverbend.blogspot.com) are just two sources of
information coming from Iraq that are not aligned with any particular
authority but supply reports of day to day life in the country. There are also
a number of blogs maintained by those fighting against the occupation.
Such a thing would have been inconceivable in the last war in Iraq, but the
level of organization and sophistication of the opposition is significantly
different this time. The opposition is also clearly aware of the power of
information and they realize that providing an alternative voice makes a
huge difference in the message getting out to the world. Perhaps the most
remarkable of these websites is 'The Iraqi Resistance"
(http://www.albasrah.net/moqawama/english/iraqi_resistance.htm),
devoted to day to day reporting of activities in Iraq. While many would
consider this to be anti-American propaganda, it is a fairly straightforward
(although obviously biased) accounting. It provides weekly activity reports
that often reflect what can be heard elsewhere, although told from a
viewpoint not often heard in the Western media. I was also very interested
in the photo gallery on this site, as it displays a series of images very different
from those seen elsewhere. As one might expect, the images are clearly
depicting the negative aspects of the war, but they are eerily reminiscent of
images from Viet Nam. American soldiers suffering the horrors of war are
the standard here, but the site wisely stops short of the grisly to simply focus
on the fact that war is ugly and sad. The fact that an increasing number of
people are media-savvy is obvious here, as the maintainers of this site seem
to realize what will draw in the sympathetic visitor, but don't go so far as to
turn off most people with the sensational. In fact, rather than showing the
expected images of triumphant opposition forces, the selection is clearly
carefully selected to increase support for their side of the issues. The
viewpoint they communicate is important, as it is clearly reflective of a
reality, whether or not it is one many people in the West want to view.

The pace at which information was being made available during the
war made sites with frequent updates and information from a wide variety
of sources very valuable. While the larger news sites that are frequently
considered the most reliable still offered a great deal of information, there
were many other options. *The New York Times*, The BBC, CNN, and other
major new outlets are now able to update at a moments notice (a practice

perfected after the experience of the Internet being a primary source of information on September 11 and at times being incapable of keeping up with demand). (LeFebvre, 2002) News aggregators, however, have probably never been as popular and as useful as they were early in the Iraq war. These sites bring together news from a variety of sites to produce a complete up-to-date picture of the news, albeit generally with an identifiable political slant. Perhaps the most well known of these sites is *The Drudge Report* (http://www.drudge.com), providing quite a large number of politics-related headlines from many sources. Although Drudge is controversial and shunned by many as transparently ideological, what he does is very useful. These digests of the news make for convenient "one-stop" picture of the state of things and allow one to see articles that might otherwise require a great deal of searching. It is important to be careful, however, to balance one's input by visiting a number of sites and gathering different viewpoints.

During the most information intensive moments of the recent Gulf war, it was helpful to visit several aggregators a day (and at times several times per day). One that I visited regularly was the *Agonist* (http://scoop.agonist.org), a site that combined the blog of a reporter in Iraq with links to breaking news from a variety of sources. Others included the Independent Media Center (http://www.indymedia.org), and the rather obvious but often overlooked Google news (http://news.google.com). A great source that really came into it's own during this conflict was the *World Press Review* online (http://www.worldpress.org) which is a truly international collection of world news, collecting material from virtually everywhere. I also noticed that people were turning to sites with more sophisticated analysis of events as well as examination of the media itself, like that found in *The Economist* (http://www.economist.com), MEMRI (the Middle East Media Research Institute, (http://www.memri.org), Mediastudy.com (http://www.mediastudy.com), or sources like the Cato Institute (http://www.cato.org/index.html). With all of these sources available, the mainstream media seemed like the least likely source for information when things were happening quickly. The major networks in the west have been criticized for taking on an overly positive tone on stories related to the war, and seemed a bit to keen to run stories that were clearly being looked at with a more skeptical eye by other outlets. (Regan, 2004) For those of us interested in getting as close as possible to what's "really happening" viewing the commonly seen pictures of Saddam's statue being pulled down was not sufficient, when the alternative new sources had the wider angle shots showing it to be a carefully controlled media event. (Watson, 2003) By this point in the war, those of us who had been following it through the Internet identified this event immediately as one requiring further investigation, and multiple sources provided alternative views.

The rapid development of the information environment in response to the increased demand for information at the beginning of the recent Iraq conflict was a fascinating thing to watch for the information professional. While people in the West (and likely those in the Middle East as well) initially tuned into the usual media outlets to view the promised embedded journalists ride across the border into Iraq, the curious very quickly began to search out other outlets. While the official outlets provided coverage, homegrown sources of information quickly became a very important alternative. People quite simply referred to the source that provided the most up-to-date and credible information. In this war, the availability of many different viewpoints caused the curious to seek out as many versions of the stories as were available, and this lead to perhaps the most startling of revelations relating to people and their information seeking habits. Many of the knowledgeable and well-read people I spoke to were doing their own searching and determining the value of information on their own. None of these people were turning to the Library for the information, and while many recognized the value of libraries and their materials, the fact that information was restricted to registered users in the case of universities, or was limited in scope in the case of public libraries, meant that these people simply went elsewhere, and got results. They occasionally envied my access to historical newspapers, or expensive journals, but this didn't cause them to seek them out. On reflection, I realized that I also was not turning to the very library that I worked in every day. I also realized that all of the sources that I was finding and being referred to were not the sources that my Library was offering to users on a regular basis. While the available information had exploded in volume and variety, those asking at the Library were still being pointed to the traditional sources, meeting our criteria of academic quality. An entire world of information and alternative viewpoints was virtually invisible to the Library, and a large number of people were bypassing the Library without a second thought.

In curiosity one evening I decided to visit my own library's website, and realized (to my dismay), that the site seemed quite lifeless compared to all of the dynamic sites I had been visiting to find up-to-date information. While many websites, and many people, reflected a world in constant change and turmoil, our site seemed completely oblivious to the events in the world around it. We were hardly alone. As reported in *Library Journal*: "While antiwar rallies have occurred in front of several campus libraries nationwide, many academic facilities haven't altered their homepages in response to the war. The main library pages for Columbia, Cornell, Princeton, Yale, Harvard, and Brown universities, plus the University of Pennsylvania and Dartmouth College—the Ivy League—offered no immediate links. Several large state university library web sites—including Florida, Michigan, Wisconsin, North Caroline, and Texas—were similarly unchanged." (Rogers, 2003) A number of times when I have raised this issue, the response to this concern has been that it is not the role of the library to provide this type of information, and I have found this troubling. While libraries do have a very important job to do in preserving and maintaining the information of academia, they clearly also have a mission to provide access to current information from all sources that might be useful to the academic enterprise. The idea that libraries should be identifying and disseminating quality information is as true now as it ever has been, but it seemed that we are now missing a great deal of the available information. In my days in university, the library collected a wide range of newspapers from around the world, journals on all topics, and such things as access to the Reuters newswire. Aside from what could be found on radio or television, the library was the place to turn for information of any type. It was disturbing to me that one of the most read-about and documented events of our time was not being reflected by the major point of interface with libraries. People were watching the events intensely; they were the subject of headlines and hours of television coverage, and surely people had questions or were curious to find out what was going on beyond the major news outlets.

User needs and expectations have clearly changed since the Gulf War of 1991 and information seeking habits experienced anecdotally during the recent conflict suggest how much things have changed. In many respects librarians have ceased to have exclusive claim to being the authorities on searching for information. In the case of searching out information on current events such as occurred during the war, the anecdotal evidence would seem to suggest that users are also not counting on libraries to collect or disseminate this type of information. If we adjust our perceptions of our place in the academic process libraries still have a valuable role to play, particularly in light of the increasingly large universe of information available to our users. As in the past, we must stress the availability of information and the value of seeking out multiple sources of information (well beyond the major newspapers suggested in 1992). With the huge variety of available sources it is more important than ever to focus on some traditional roles of the librarian. These most certainly include information literacy, helping the user to understand what information is, and the many forms that it takes. The user must not only be able to find the information, but also be able to critically assess its value wherever it may be found. More than ever in this era of Internet resources, this aspect of information literacy is absolutely crucial to teaching users to successfully carry out research, and to independently accomplish this in an environment in which we no longer control all aspects of collections and access to them.

While it seems that the fact that library users may not feel a need to visit the library to fulfill their information needs is simply bad news, it seems quite reasonable to suggest that librarians should see this as the proverbial "wake up call." In fact, I would suggest that we should not accept a new limited role in which we are no longer the experts in finding and distributing the information to users. As our users' opportunities for information gathering grow at an increasing rate, we need more than ever to survey and understand their needs. As far back as 1996 the need to reassess how we provide added value to the academic process was being expressed in a Follett Lecture by Carla J. Stoffle:

> "Academic Libraries have always seen themselves as adding value in the scholarly communication and information delivery processes by organizing knowledge that is created and packaged (usually in book or journal form) outside the library. We have done this primarily by providing access through cataloguing and classification systems, and by creating in-house indexes and bibliographies. Now libraries have the potential to participate in the creation of new knowledge packages and access tools. We can increase the availabilities of information that heretofore have not been accessible, by using electronic publishing and new information access and telecommunications advances including the internet, web browsers, multimedia programming and mark-up languages, scanning and imaging hardware and software." (Stoffle, 1996)

While many of the technologies mentioned in Stoffle's talk are now taken for granted, the idea expressed is very significant, and perhaps even more relevant today. We are even more involved today in the process of dealing with information packaged outside the library, and our challenge is to add value by making it accessible and providing the tools to identify the valuable resources. Even more important is the concept of creating "new knowledge packages" which may now extend far beyond the creation of indices and bibliographies. In fact, we may create tools that deliver customized information based on user preferences, behaviour, or characteristics such as academic programs or curriculum. These types of services, along with information literacy and critical thinking skills that the library can add to the learning process, create the "added value" that the library can bring to the academic process.

At this point, libraries are beginning to respond to the challenge of re-assessing user needs and library roles in the face of increasing access to online information. There are certainly more useful pathfinders appearing on library websites to point users to resources online and the variety of material included is growing to include some of the new types of information available. While a positive step, this does not address the fact that many of the users do not turn to the library as the source of this information in the first place. The difficult step to take is to admit that many users are bypassing the library for this part of the information seeking process, because they can search independently and quite often are able to access all of the information that they need to complete their work. Having come to understand this position in the process of research, it is then the job of those in libraries to determine how the professional skills of librarians may continue to bring added value to this process. While anecdotal evidence (and reference statistics) suggests that fewer people are coming to the library to take advantage of our traditional services (Kyrilladou, 2000), we are the people with knowledge of the world of information and a history of teaching information literacy. Our users are still seeking information and it is more abundantly available than ever before. The fact that the finding aids and classification systems are now scattered, imprecise, and possess as many variations as there are sources, means that our information literacy skills are now more needed than ever before. It is essential, however, that we also utilize our skills and experience with user needs assessment to monitor this constantly changing world and keep up to date with new sources and means of distribution of information. If we do not do this, the Iraq war of 2003 will just be one of the early examples of our users bypassing the library in their search for information.

References

Airs, Gordon and Wills, Colin. (1991, March 2). Landscape of Carnage on the Basra Road. *The Times*, p.1.

Apple, R.W. (1991, February 26) U.S. Cites 'Tremendous Success' in Kuwait Action. *New York Times*, p. A1.

El Deeb, Sarah. (2003) Al Jazeera Says it has Duty to Show World Casualties From Both Sides. *SFGate.com* (March 27, 2003). Retrieved June 27, 2004 from the World Wide Web: http://www.sfgate.com/cgi-

bin/article.cgi?f=/news/archive/2003/03/27/international1151EST0621.
DTL.

Goodman, Tim. (2003, March 22) Baghdad Booted CNN before 'awe'
struck U.S. Broadcasters Shift to Arab TV Cameras to Show Bombing, *San
Francisco Chronicle*, p.w-2.

Kyrilladou, Martha. (2000) Research Library Trends: ARL Statistics.
Journal of Academic Librarianship 26(6), 427-436.

Lefebvre, William. (2002). Computer Systems Laboratory Colloquium:
CNN.com—Facing a World Crisis. Retrieved July 12, 2004 from the
World Wide Web:
http://www.stanford.edu/class/ee/380/Abtsracts/020213.html.

Regan, Tom. (2004) Media Knocked for Iraq War Coverage: Experts
Say US too Soft, Foreign Media Often Too Hard. Retrieved July 12,
2004 from the World Wide Web:
http://www.csmonitor.com/2004/0211/dailyUpdate.html?s=entt.

Rogers, Michael. (2003) For Libraries, It's Mostly Quiet on the Middle East
Info Front. *Library Journal* 128(8), p.16.

Stoffle, Carla J. (1996). The Emergence of Education and Knowledge
Management as Major Functions of the Digital Library. Follett Lecture
Series. Retrieved January 6, 2004 from the World Wide Web:
http://www.ukoln.ac.uk/services/papers/follett/stoffle/paper.html.

Sunderland, Alan. (2003) Eye Witness Report: The Toppling of the Statue
of Saddam was a Staged Media Event: Interview with Neville Watson.
Retrieved   June   17,   2004   from   the   World   Wide   Web:
http://www.globalresearch.ca/articles/WAT304A.html.

Section Four:
Librarians: Culture and Identity

A Librarian's Confession

By Rory Litwin
Originally published in *Library Juice* 7:18, August 27, 2004

The *New Breed Librarian (NBL)* online magazine of 2001 and 2002 was all about how the younger generation of librarians is busting the old stereotypes that say we are introverted, stuffy, conservative, shy, perhaps officious, humorless, pedantic, dowdy, drab, and probably live alone with a beloved cat. "Not so!" it argued, "Librarians are hip, radical, wild, have indy street cred, talk in slang, go to the hippest rock shows, are anarchistic, and want to make the world safe for skateboarders and free-form muralists!" (It didn't say that literally, but that was part of the idea, along with more lofty ideas about our devotion to the democratic ethos of the modern library, as well as ideas about younger librarians' affinity for computers.)

I was interviewed in the first issue of the *NBL* as a prime example of a librarian who is not what a librarian is thought of as being—this because of my commitment to the radical potential of libraries as a model institution in society, my interest in making libraries better, and in general my youthful passion for libraries and librarianship as something that I see in an exciting light (as well as for being a webmaster and having an electronic newsletter). I fit the profile of a stereotype-busting librarian in a number of other ways as well—I've been arrested in political protests, I've been to plenty of hip rock shows, I've used a variety of illegal drugs, I've contracted a few STDs (dim memories now), I have a couple of tattoos, I'm a gen-Xer from the socially liberal environment of the San Francisco Bay Area, and I've shown a tendency to iconoclasm. Surely I represent the New Breed of librarians, right? Defying that awful stereotype? Right?

Well, not exactly. I've come to realize, as I've eased into the latter half of my fourth decade of life, that to see and represent myself in that way would not be entirely just to myself as a person, nor to the profession of librarianship.

Let me explain why.

I had many reasons for becoming a librarian; together they added up to the profession "fitting" me. The profession fits me because it serves the ideals of democracy and is a public institution—that is to say, it fits me ideologically; but the nature of the work suits my temperament as well. I am and have always been a true nerd; this nerdiness is connected to my selfless attitude at the reference desk and my passionate love of reference materials. It really couldn't be any other way. Despite the resume of hipness that I am capable of producing, I fit the librarian stereotype more than I defy it. I am and have always been a shy, introverted guy, intellectually inclined, with mediocre social skills and a sexuality that is frequently called into question. The Myers-Briggs personality test says I am an ISTJ, which, if it is not the personality type of the majority of librarians, is certainly the stereotype's type. Despite my political progressivism, I have a definite conservative tendency, in terms of my everyday behavior, dress, judgmental ethical sensibilities and a somewhat buttoned-down, hesitant and unadventurous nature. I also live alone with my beloved cat.

Generally speaking, these are facts about myself of which I've never been completely comfortable, and have at times wanted to deny. But I have come to realize that they are related to positive traits that serve me well as a librarian (and no less so as a person). That is what we should realize about the librarian stereotype. Every human trait has a valuable and a less-functional face to it. We tend to talk about the librarian stereotype strictly in terms of its undesirable aspects. But it is related to our strengths as librarians also—to our thoughtfulness, our focus, our desire to help. I've quoted Will Manley on our stereotype before. In *American Libraries*, May 1996, he wrote:

> "The world generally sees us as steady, serious, and studious. Unfortunately, steady, serious, and studious are often mistaken for strict, staid, and stuffy. That stereotype seems unfair and unkind until we compare it with other, more unpleasant occupational stereotypes: Lawyers are liars, politicians are crooks, doctors are greedy, athletes are stupid, journalists are egomaniacs. In comparison, our stuffiness doesn't look so bad."

In a sense, I am saying that we should embrace our stereotype in order to emphasize its positive aspects (without allowing ourselves to be reduced to that stereotype, as that would rob us of our individuality and diversity). The stereotype fits only a few of us perfectly, but anger over not being represented fairly by it shouldn't lead us to deny the ways in which we do fit the traditional understanding of what a librarian is like, because there is much that is true and positive in that idea. We should be proud of being librarians according to what the word "librarian" is commonly understood to mean, and should assert our value on that basis—not on the basis that the public has misconceptions about us and doesn't realize, for example, that we are computer experts (which most of us are not) or that we have pierced tongues (which most of us do not). We should not underestimate the degree to which we are already valued by society for the qualities we are understood to have and the use to which we put those qualities.

I am writing this because I am finding that as I "own myself" to a greater degree as a person, I also own myself to a greater degree as a librarian. Our profession as a whole could stand to do something similar.

A Critique of Anarchist Librarianship

By Rory Litwin
This is a revision of an article originally published in *Library Juice* 7:25, December 3, 2004

First, I'd like to provide a little background for my treatment of this subject. On the Progressive Librarians Guild discussion list recently, John Buschman attacked the "anarchist librarian" identity that rose to noticeability in the late nineties, thanks primarily to Chuck Munson's website and email discussion list. John's reasons for attacking it at the time he did were left obscure in his messages, but it is clear enough from his writings that it is something he has thought about for some time and associates, tenuously, with postmodern emphases on identity generally. His attack asserted that "anarchist librarians" are poseurs, committed only to an identification with a well-understandable ideal but without actual political commitments; that anarchism is an adolescent political identification that rather irresponsibly rejects involvement with existing institutions and real politics, preferring childish "DIY" projects whose dependence on the infrastructure and culture of those institutions it does not acknowledge; that "anarchist librarians" are not truly a part of the political left but are merely hipsters. Their anarchism should not be taken seriously, he asserts; when criticized about the incongruity of "anarchist librarianship" they reply that the questioner should study and learn about the seriousness of anarchism as a political philosophy, but they, at the same time, are not seen to follow any serious anarchist practice or to engage in serious discussions of problems of anarchist librarianship, instead simply capitalizing on the incongruity of the "anarchist librarian" label by being "difficult to understand" and therefore hipper than the naive questioners.

I will admit at the outset that I partially agree with this assessment; I think there is a degree of uncomfortable truth in it. At the same time, my association with individual anarchist librarians, whom I originally met in at ALA conferences while I was still in library school and have met with personally at intervals for years afterwards at library conferences and Anarchist Book Fairs, teaches me that they at least deserve to be taken seriously, and that anarchism, as a political philosophy, is often misunderstood, and that because of this an examination of some of the implications of "anarchist librarianship" is warranted. Among the anarchist librarians who originally got me thinking about these issues are Chuck Munson, whom I just mentioned and whom I appreciate because he is sincere in the true Godwinian sense; Howard Besser, the former LIS professor who now leads the Moving Image Archiving and Preservation program at NYU (though he has always liked to say he has to decline the great honor of being called a librarian because he is a mere professor); Julie Herrada, who curates the Labadie collection of historic anarchist material at the University of Michigan; Jessamyn West of Librarian.net fame, who, though she no longer calls herself an anarchist, still holds the same values; Laura Quilter, who is now studying law at one of the top law schools in the country and mixes anarchist ideals with a practical, admirable, real-world effort to make the world a better place; and though he has never quite identified himself as part of this group, Chuck D'Adamo of the Alternative Press Center, who is very sophisticated theoretically and is unquestionably politically committed and active. I respect all of these individuals and know them well enough to know that, for them, their anarchism has been more than a mere pose but, in different ways, represents the outcome of a long and passionate thought process and a genuine political orientation to life.

My own conclusion is, however, different. Regarding anarchism, I certainly sympathize with the idea of a society in which people are rational and sensitive enough that law and government are not needed (except perhaps for things like the provision of infrastructural regulation), but I cannot imagine that it is law and government that prevents this society from coming into being, and I also cannot imagine that any society in which people organize themselves to achieve communal ends can be free of hierarchy and relations of authority, whether acknowledged or not. Regarding anarchist librarianship, I think that there are real contradictions inherent in the idea, and that it is immature for anarchist librarians simply to gloss over those contradictions, which they often do.

I'm not going to provide an exposition of anarchist theory, but I will say that if you think anarchism is primarily about Freedom, I can join in with the anarchist librarians who say that you could probably use a little education in its theory. Godwin, Proudhon, Bakunin, and Kropotkin, who were the founders of anarchism as a political movement, each had a vision in which freedom was important primarily as a means of bringing about a rational, responsible community of individuals, but in each case it would be a community that would be self-governing via informal censure—not necessarily all that libertarian (unless you are a follower of Max Stirner, who founded a separate tradition during that time period).

I am also not going to attempt a critique of the contemporary anarchist movement, except to mention that while as a political identity it is no different from any other radical political identity in its affordance of a whole range of inauthentic as well as authentic ways of claiming it, I think it does tend to attract a greater number of privileged white people who want to be "Left" in a way that doesn't force any tough choices or sacrifices, because its absolutist nature allows its believers to wash their hands of realities that don't measure up to its ideal of human society (such as electoral politics).

What I am going to do is show why I believe that the "anarchist librarian" identity does involve a real contradiction, while being as fair as I can to librarians who are anarchists.

It was Jessamyn West who provided the prototype for the defense of anarchist librarianship, saying,

> I've said it once, and I'm sure I'll say it a zillion more times: anarchists are NOT against organization, or pro-disorder; they are against centralized forms of governance and hierarchical power structures in general. So, while hierarchy in the workplace is a problem, hierarchy in the card catalog is not.

Unfortunately for those of us who remain unedified, she has pretty much left it at that (though she did attempt to address my line of questions in an interview I did with her in *Library Juice* in 2002).

My argument is that hierarchy in the card catalog is in fact linked to hierarchy in the workplace, and it has to do with the fundamental basis of modern librarianship in a collection of standards for the organization of information. Modern librarianship has its beginnings in the very un-anarchistic nineteenth century phenomenon of multiplying efficiency and productivity through the standardization of processes and tools. In a broader sense, this standardization is at the heart of the Industrial Revolution and the process of rationalization that went along with it, to which the anarchist movement was part of a large reaction. Melvil Dewey, among others, contributed immensely to the standardization project that makes up the bulk of library science. Standardized cataloging and classification are the primary examples, but there are many others, including such things as the physical dimensions of a catalog card and the "Library Hand," both dead standards now but functioning in their day. Standardization of all of the methods of librarianship brought major benefits: it enabled cooperation between libraries and it unified the profession so that when one had learned the standard methods and tools one could function as a librarian in any library. The twentieth century only saw the standards of the profession extended into new technological areas. Libraries have also made use of standards that exist in the broader infrastructural context at a variety of levels, ranging from the barcode standard to the age-old standard of the sequence of letters in the alphabet. But it is the standards that are specific to librarianship that give libraries the skeleton of a unified institution.

Technical standards, as Chuck Munson has pointed out to me, are generally created in a collegial, cooperative setting (in a process that he likes to say is anarchistic). He likes to cite the development of the standards underlying internet protocol and the open source software that drives so much of the internet as examples of anarchistically-produced standards and tools. There is certainly a cooperative spirit operating in these areas of technology development, but once the technology and the standards are developed it requires the authority of hierarchical, usually large organizations (corporations, scientific and professional societies, universities and governments) to bring them into common adoption. Furthermore, all of that collegial, cooperative, scientific work is only possible in the context of an infrastructure that is institutionally supported by these hierarchical, authority-bearing organizations. Even open-source software development is tied to such institutions, albeit often indirectly. (A perfect historical example of what I am talking about is the introduction of the Carolingian miniscule standard for the Roman alphabetic script. This standard was created and used by the intelligentsia of the Carolingian renaissance, but depended on the regime of King Charlemagne for its promulgation and control.)

In the library world, the MARC format, MARCXML, MODS, METS, Z39.50 and a host of other technical standards are maintained by the Library of Congress, as are the Library of Congress Classification System and the Library of Congress Subject Headings. These standards and others like them form the basis of the practice of librarianship as a unified profession. (A shared ideology and a body of intellectual doctrine are extremely important as well, and are historically tied to the development of early standards, but the standardized methods play a skeletal role in the body of the institution.) There is always collegial criticism of these standards, and LC and other standards developing organizations respond to that criticism, but there is nearly universal acknowledgement that even a flawed standard is better than no standard. In fact, it is the recognition of the importance of standards that is the reason for the continued pressure on LC to reform its Subject Heading list. There is cooperative, collegial work involved in the setting of various standards, to be sure, but what the Library of Congress has to do with them is more than just "the office work," (the phrase that anarchists like to use to dismiss administrative functions). The Library of Congress, in the case of the standards it maintains, organizes that activity and provides the authority so that what results in each case is a standard that whole organizations can adopt in order to be able to cooperate with other organizations. Similarly, the American Library Association is the publisher of, and provides the authority for, the Anglo American Cataloging Rules.

Hierarchical structures of authority, I should point out, are not automatically "undemocratic," though anarchists would tend to have it that they are. Organizations institute bureaucratic structures partially in order to prevent individuals from having too much power and acting arbitrarily. Societies institute formal voting procedures in order to make authority accountable to the people. These systems never function perfectly, and often do not even function well, but the belief that life without them is more democratic, or that hierarchy and relations of authority and coercion do not exist where they are not formalized or acknowledged, is false. (An important statement along these was radical feminist Jo Freeman's 1970 essay, "On the tyranny of structurelessness," which is available on the web, at http://www.jofreeman.com/joreen/tyranny.htm. Jo Freeman sympathized with the values that motivate anarchists, and was highly concerned with democratic process.)

In response to this line of thinking, one member of the Anarchist Librarians discussion list asserted the relevance of the difference between "authority of" and "authority over"—standards, she would have it, being created and adopted purely by the "authority of" type of relation. Evidence supporting this argument would be in the fact that standards are generally produced by non-governmental organizations and are promulgated and accepted without the force of law (NIST notwithstanding). They are more like regulations than laws, only there is no penalty for not following them other than being less able to participate in larger systems.

Unless, of course, you are a worker.

If you are a cataloger in a large library and you decide you would like to use the Hennepin County List for subject headings, instead of the standard LC subject headings used by your institution, or if you would like to give all of your web pages unix-standard "html" filenames instead of the Microsoft-standard "htm" that your library uses (hypothetically), you will learn quickly that the promulgation of standards is an "authority-over" game where the rubber meets the road. Standards are spread not by free individuals but by organizations with a hierarchical structure. Their use demands that individuals subordinate themselves, at least minimally, to the larger organizations in which they participate. This is true even in the most democratic organizations that exist or can be imagined, because it is the basic principle of organized activity.

But I have assumed that anarchists agree with the value of large-scale organization and the efficiencies that it brings. Some anarchists argue that people can be highly organized without hierarchical relationships of authority (though in the end it is article of faith not unlike belief in the Kingdom of Heaven). Most anarchists, however, in my experience, eschew organized structures altogether and emphasize localism and individualism. It may be that Jessamyn West is actually an exception to the rule (so to speak), and most anarchist librarians ultimately prioritize localism over the value of a unified profession, and would be quite happy to see librarianship consisting of small, democratic, autonomous libraries doing everything for themselves, each in different ways, without shared systems that facilitate cooperation and without a unified sense of what a library professional is and knows. That is possible. It is, however, so far away from both the professional's and the common public's understanding of what librarianship is that the sense of contradiction in the idea of an "anarchist librarian" would be validated. Anarchist librarians could argue that this is what makes their vision radical; I would only point out that it is incompatible with 20th and 21st century library practice as we have known it and would necessitate a severe loss of functionality; it would be a pre-modern librarianship.

To take this position, I should point out, is not to reject the value of localism altogether; compromises can be made between the interests of organizing on a large scale and maintaining local autonomy to meet local needs, as the Hennepin County Library did during Sanford Berman's years as head cataloger and other libraries do in other ways. Such compromise positions should not be confused with anarchist positions, however, because they recognize the importance of some degree of membership in larger organizational structures and standards regimes, and that is precisely what anarchism, based as it is on an absolute principle, doesn't allow.

Anarchists value their history and generally see great value in the preservation of the cultural record and in its accessibility, and have natural affinities with librarianship's role as a cultural and informational commons where civil liberties are held sacred. The contradiction lies in the fact that librarianship, as an institution and a project of society at large, demands larger structures of organization than are possible to achieve without formalized hierarchical relationships and formally specialized roles. Anarchist librarians take for granted, and simply do not see, what this society-wide organization of the institution does for the practice of librarianship, or do not see that it involves, at many levels, hierarchical structures and a kind of large-scale organized activity that is precluded by their beliefs.

Despite my view of the importance of standardization in the development of modern librarianship, I am not blind to the ways in which the overall process of rationalization and the subsequent rise of the information society have given rise to oppressive social arrangements and have been used to maintain inequality. My position as a socialist is that we can balance freedom and organization in a society that maintains dynamic, organized, highly functional, democratically controlled institutions for the sake of humanity as a whole (rather than for controlling classes). (Librarianship and socialism, as I feel is obvious, are deeply compatible. They are more compatible, as we are seeing increasingly with the erosion of the public sector by privatization and anti-tax policies, than libraries and capitalism.)

For further reading:

Agger, Ben. "Work and Authority in Marcuse and Habermas." *Human Studies* 2 (1979). pp. 191-208.

Freeman, Jo. "The Tyranny of Structurelessness." *Berkeley Journal of Sociology*, 17 (1971-1972). pp. 151-165.

Litwin, Rory and West, Jessamyn. "Interview with Jessamyn West." *Library Juice Concentrate*. Library Juice Press, 2006. pp. 147-152.

Mattli, Walter and Büthe, Tim. "Setting international standards: Technological rationality or primacy of power?" *World Politics* 56 (October, 2003). pp. 1-42.

Olshan, Marc A. "Standards-making organizations and the rationalization of American life." *The Sociological Quarterly*. 34, No. 2 (1993). p. 319-335.

Ritter, Alan. *Anarchism: a theoretical analysis*. Cambridge University Press, 1980.

Interview with Jessamyn West

By Rory Litwin and Jessamyn West
Originally published in *Library Juice* 5:35, November 28, 2002

RL: Jessamyn, you recently told me that you were thinking of stopping using the "anarchist librarian" label to describe yourself. Is that because your social-political theory is changing, or because you don't want to define yourself by those two attributes alone, or because of something else?

JW: It's a bit of both. I find the label less than useful. I know what I mean by it, but I feel like people think "oh, bomb-lobbing starbucks breaking angry girl who can't get a date." Since I'm trying to be clear, I may move to something like decentralist or anti-corporate which does sum up more of what my issues are. Basically, the label is shorthand for a long-winded explanation of purposes. Prior to WTO, it aligned more closely with my identity as I saw it, and now, even though my identity hasn't changed much, the label means something different. Also, for the purposes of librarianship, it's easy enough to say "radical librarian"—especially to non-librarians— and have them know what you mean, more or less. I still identify in every way with the anarchist librarians, I just don't find the monniker very useful when I am trying to explain what I am about.

RL: I can appreciate that. When you have a chance to have a conversation with someone who is curious, and you do reveal that you are an anarchist, do they often say, "Isn't an anarchist librarian a contradiction in terms?" How do you respond to that? Do you say "Well, I might not exactly be an anarchist in the sense that you're thinking." If so, maybe you could explain a little bit more in depth for *Library Juice* readers what your political philosophy is. Personally, neither "anti-corporate" nor "decentralist" means precisely the same thing as anarchist, as I understand the word, though "decentralist" might be closer. (I'm an anti-corporate socialist who believes in a moderate degree of centralism—with accountability—in organizations, myself.)

JW: Well, I always say that anyone who asks me whether the anarchist libraran thing is an oxymoron is just begging for a lecture on anarchism. I say that we're not against organzation and in many ways we're not really against structure, we're just against externally created rules and systems—governance from without, if you will—and basically think that decision making happens better in non-hierarchical, non-power dominated organizations. In fact, in most anarchistic collectives I know, there is actually a great deal of structure to stand in for all the little assumptions people make about how people ought to behave that are not necessarily the normative ideals in anarchistic relationships.

So, in summary, I think the things that drew me to anarchism as a philosophy [note that I am specifically not saying as a governance structure here] are the lack of hierarchies in the personal and work-type relationships, as well as the general mistrust of power and governance. The finer points are, mistrust of corporate capitalism specifically as I see it being played out in the US lately [the notion that all progress and all expansion is necessarily a good thing and everything "primitive" and/or old fashioned is necessarily a bad thing] as well as seeing everything suddenly have a price tag. Things without price tags [social good, health, literacy, the value of knowing your neighbors] wind up getting de-emphasized because no one can figure out how to make a buck off of them, or you see some really pathetic examples of people trying.

And, on a more positive note, I have always been drawn to, and practice, the very anarchistic idea of mutual aid. That is, you help people and they help you, not because of any external coercion, but because it is the right thing to do, end of story. This sort of good faith can get abused in a work environment where every five minutes you work that someone isn't paying you for suddenly gets tabulated as "surplus value" being extracted from your good graces. That's not the sort of world I want to live in. Not that anarchists have a stranglehold of the mutual aid idea, but that they along with the Catholic Workers & Quakers and many others make community service a very central part of their faiths, above even the quest for the almighty dollar or the idea of private property, etc.

In my ideal world, then, people would organize in small, self-governed communities and decide for themseles what the structure of relationships, jobs and financial structures would be. And yes, this might mean going without power plants and automobiles and plastic shoes and whatever. I don't care, I truly don't. I'd eat potatoes for a lifetime if I could just live in a world where singing and dancing are as valued as governing and Power

Point. Obviously there are no easy steps from now to then, but as far as a dream goes, I like it and I'm sticking to it. In the meantime, I try to be a good citizen, a good friend, a good person and a good worker.

RL: I think that's a description of what anarchism means to you that will be informative to a lot of readers. But it leaves me wondering, a bit, where certain structures and practices in the profession fit in. For example, disregarding for the moment whether the MARC format has a long future, it's an instance of a standard, or a rule, in a sense, that serves a group of users which is far too large for each member to have input into that standard and how it is developed and promulgated. Nobody is going to be clubbed for not using the MARC standard correctly, but isn't it an example of a rule or structure that is imposed from without (that is, from outside local communities of professionals), and controlled by a more-or-less remote, central authority (the Library of Congress Network Development and MARC Standards Office)? How do things like the MARC standard and other standards (technical and professional) fit into your vision of a de-centralized, "governance from within" librarianship?

JW: that's a good question. I think there are good examples in the open source movement where you can still have standards, they are just created by the groups that will be using them, have a standard format, standard methods for updating, and standard processes to go through to amend them. Then, if people think they are some sort of super-genius, they are welcome to go all nutso and make their own variant of the standard, see who comes to their tea party, etc. The oss4lib project is the most hopeful-seeming one of these, as far as projects by people I know personally.

Anarchist structures don't mean that everyone does everything, just that the choices of who does what are decided in some format by the group at large, and are also malleable by the group at large if something seems to be going in the wrong direction. Most of the Internet protocols were developed loosely in this way. They benefitted from the fact that most people were trying to use the technology to do fairly limited and specific things, but as a design-by-committee project, much of it succeeded. I fall asleep at night sometimes thinking of how the LC subject headings would turn out if they were all in a huge database accessible and alterable by everyone. It would be chaotic and likely mostly awful, of course, but at least there would be an entry for "Jessamyn—Super-genius." And, I know you are familiar with only-sort-of-hierarchical Dmoz.org which is a blessing for some people and a total nightmare for others. My experience there has been positive, but the negative interactions other people experience are also very real.

The whole set of issues surrounding interdependent systems and the anarchistic model is something I find fascinating. That is often people's first repsonse to anarchistic ideas: "Oh yeah, who runs the trains??" And I think the answer has something to do with co-operation but also something to do with the necessity of trains and a re-engineering of a society that isn't necssarily based on people who go to jobs and come home from jobs and aggressively seek leisure activities. This is sort of a hippy-dippy response, I am aware, but while there is certainly a good use for MARC records—and they were a real milestone in terms of interchangeable data well before most people had heard of the Internet—the average user would be happy just being able to use a keyword search to look up author or title or, heck, book size and color. The anarchistic political/philosophical model does not neatly map on to every workplace environment, and I don't think I mean that I am searching for an "anarchist LIBRARY" necessarily, just that I'd like to bring my political ideas and my workplace ideas more in line with each other. I am not concerned, for example, with the tyranny that may be present in alphabetical order.

RL: Interesting. So, thinking about the various libraries where you've worked, how would you like to see libraries changed, organizationally and in terms of services, so that they are more in line with your vision of, let's say, a liberated world?

JW: well I'm not sure. I can easily visualize my perfect library environment in my mind, but the linear path from here to there is what is much less clear. I think my perfect library would mimic the older private library style with some changes. There would be a great deal of inter-communication between smaller libraries that shared catalogs but had specialized collections of books. They would probably be located in people's homes and would be much more reading-room oriented than checkout oriented. They would be somewhat detatched from the more academic and archival libraries which would almost necessarily have to be big and more comprenhesive.

I think about the small libraries of Vermont—where each one reflects their own small communities and each one is in a lovely building that is a resource to the community and I think "What if this space were open 16 hours a day?" "What if people could leave their own books and zines as well as what the librarian selects?" "What if everyone in the town got to take a stint on the reference desk and field questions about their own particular subject specialty?" "What if there was a co-op model with a few paid staff and many volunteers who took work shifts to attain membership status to the library?" There are upsides and downsides to this approach, certainly, but I think a lot of the downsides [what if people moved into the library, what if the religious right filled the library with religous tracts?] would just help the public ascertain problems they were having in their own communities that needed addressing. Homeless people camping out in the library is not, at its core, a library problem, it's a social problem—Why do we have people in our society who don't have places to go?

So, my shorter answer for present-day libraries goes something like this:

- smaller libraries, smaller staff, less employee hierarchy
- rotating job assignments, more patron participation
- community ownership of libaries in a real way, co-op model
- library as a place to store patron's books as well as reference materials, computers, music etc.
- comfortable spaces, more human, less industrial
- open system of rules and policies, malleable and flexible and transparent
- libraries open when people want to use them, not necessarily the 9-5
- shifts anticipated by librarians.
- reference by email or phone or however patrons need them
- house calls

Granted, this system works much better in an idealized small community. I'm not much of a real futurist when it comes to libraries, but I have gone to serveral infoshops and reading rooms and generally find their atmospheres—with real-people furniture and staff sitting right there where you sit—to be very pleasing. My dream, of course, is to be able to live in a library, so this is a selfish personal vision as well as my own liberation theology.

RL: Well, you certainly have an inspiring vision, one that I think presents a lot of juicy practical problems for future librarians to solve. Is there anything else you'd like to say to *Library Juice* readers?

JW: Not much, just that I think it's important that since jobs are where many of us spend upwards of 30-40% of our lives, we should work hard towards making that time not only positive and useful for ourselves, but also use that time to basically support, legitimize and strengthen the lives of those whom we come in contact with. I really believe—sap that I am—in trying to live the ideal world you envision for yourself as much as possible, as difficult or as scary as that might be. Thanks for giving me this opportunity to mumble on about this.

Jessamyn West can be found at http://librarian.net and
http://Jessamyn.com

Section Five:
Cuba

Rhonda L. Neugebauer Reports on her March, 2000 Trip to Cuba

By Rhonda Neugebauer
Originally published in *Library Juice* 3:34, Supplement, September 6, 2000

In March of this year, seventeen U.S. librarians, scholars and educators participated in an 11-day educational tour of libraries, archives, universities, and cultural and historical sites in Cuba. Organized by Rhonda Neugebauer, the delegation traveled to five cities and held discussions with Cuban librarians and informational professionals about their work, philosophy, values, their perceptions of their role in society and their obligation to provide access and delivery of information to their patrons.

Issues of mutual interest to both groups were explored and various aspects of U.S. and Cuban librarianship were examined. We were impressed by the dedication and plain hard work of our Cuban counterparts, their ability to provide a high level of service with limited resources, and their commitment to the continued development of services and collections throughout the country. Above all, we were impressed by the Cubans' willingness to share their experiences and their desire to establish relationships and strengthen exchange programs with United States libraries.

This article reports on the highlights of our tour, conveys some of our impressions of this island nation and describes what we learned of Cuban libraries and librarianship. It explains in some detail the Jose Marti National Library, the National Technical Library School and the Cuban Library Association (ASCUBI).

The similarities between Cuban and U.S. libraries are striking. Cuban librarians carry out many of the same activities as do their North American counterparts. They strive to build broad in-depth collections that reflect their cultural and national identity and provide information and reference services to researchers, other professionals and the public. They organize and preserve materials in diverse formats, create tools that aid patrons in the use of their collections and increasingly employ electronic technologies to format, communicate and deliver information. They also organize and participate in continuing education and degree programs, conferences, instructional workshops and professional associations. They lobby for increased funding and create national programs to facilitate library services and distance education.

Cuban librarians are concerned about the effective use of their limited resources and the development of appropriate technology and Internet tools. Their ethics and values are reflected in their work to professionalize training programs for librarians and to organize Cuban libraries in a manner that provides for the equitable distribution of materials and services to all parts of the country, especially to the historically underserved rural areas.

However, Cuban librarians face formidable challenges. Cuba is a poor country of about 11 million people, and it is small, about the size of the state of Pennsylvania. The economy is heavily dependent upon agriculture and tourism for the foreign exchange that is required to purchase commodities from abroad, including such items as food, fuel, clothing and books that are needed to supplement national production. For the past forty years, the U.S. has imposed an economic embargo that prohibits trade with Cuba. As a consequence, Cuba has existed in a kind of economic limbo vis-a-vis the rest of the world. In the early 1990s, the economy was thrown into disarray with the collapse of the socialist bloc and since then, Cuba has had to find new trading partners and financing.

This dire economic environment has had a severe impact upon the nation. Consequently, inadequate library budgets inhibit the development of collections, services and preservation programs, severely restricting the purchase of such basics as books and journal subscriptions. In the 1990s, the economic problems were severe enough to reduce drastically most publishing efforts throughout the country. Even today, while publishing has partially recovered, press runs are still greatly reduced and fewer new titles and journal issues are published.

Cuban libraries also face a chronic shortage of resources. The office supplies that we take for granted—paper, ballpoint pens, paper clips and computers—are hard to come by. The country faces regular problems with the telephone system and international telecommunications that impede library development. Despite these rather formidable obstacles, Cuban librarians are determined to find solutions to these problems and they have made progress toward their goals of collection building and improving services. They continue to add materials to their collections through exchange and donation and the development of new programs.

One innovative program has been the establishment of subscriber groups wherein patrons contribute books or pay a small sum (10 pesos per year*) to borrow new books. These groups, called Minerva Clubs, invite patron support for and donations to public library popular fiction collections and are an example of the way in which Cuban libraries have responded to increased need for books in face of the decline in publishing. The Minerva Clubs, started with donations of materials from Spain, serve large numbers of people and help libraries buy multiple copies of high-demand titles. Also, many libraries have developed a variety of children's programs with story times, games days, theater presentations and art and music appreciation days.

The Jose Marti National Library (Biblioteca Nacional "Jose Marti"):

At the Jose Marti National Library, our delegation met with Director Dr. Eliades Acosta Matos and about two dozen staff members who described the library, its collections and services. The National Library, founded in 1901, holds approximately three million items, including books, photographs, rare books, maps, music and materials in Braille. The librarians oversee several active publishing projects, including the *Bibliografia Cubana* and the *Revista de la Biblioteca Nacional*. In addition to serving as the main repository for Cuban intellectual patrimony, the National Library also provides services to the public including circulation, reference and children's services and serves as the principal organizer of a network of some 387 public libraries throughout the country. Librarians at the National Library provide training, cataloging and reference tools, program planning support, continuing education programs and technological support to public libraries as well as to about 500 school libraries, 500 health center libraries and 1000 information centers in the Havana area.

After introductions and descriptions of the library's services and collections, Dr. Acosta brought up the issue of censorship and intellectual freedom in Cuban libraries. He said, "The materials we have in our libraries offer a variety of perspectives on the revolution. In our collections, we want diversity. We want to add materials of all types and perspectives. We have books by U.S. authors and books by Cubans that live abroad. We would like more materials that are published abroad, but we just do not have the funds to purchase them. That is why our exchange programs with libraries around the world are so important. Through exchange (canje), we add materials that we could not possibly purchase because of the cost. Many titles from abroad are in our libraries because of the exchange relations we have had with U.S. and other foreign libraries for decades. In addition to attempting to preserve the national patrimony, our collection development policies reflect the needs and desires of our people to be exposed to all kinds of ideas and perspectives."

The National Library's plans for development include automation of their main and departmental catalogs, a union catalog for the country's public libraries, website development (photos taken of our meeting and an accompanying story were mounted on the news section of the website within an hour of our visit), Internet connections for public libraries, the publication of bibliographies, exhibitions of cultural artifacts and books, authors' presentations and the expansion of the new recreational reading Minerva Clubs to all of the localities that request them.

The National Technical Library School (Escuela Nacional de Tecnicos de Bibliotecas):

Talks with library school administrators and teachers were an important component of our trip. The enthusiasm of both the teachers and the students was infectious, but the outdated teaching materials alarmed us and spurred several of us to ask what we could do to help find more suitable equipment and add more current library science titles. Although education in Cuba is free, support for equipment, materials and teaching materials is seriously deficient (a situation found almost everywhere in the country). Several U.S. participants in the program decided, on the spot, to find ways to help the library school by sending library science texts and other professional materials. The school's head of reference, Cátedra Haya, mentioned that the school would appreciate receiving any discarded copies of *American Libraries, Library Journal, School Library Journal, Dewey Decimal Classification and Relative Index* (they currently work with the 17th edition), encyclopedias, thesauri, or software manuals. Even English language editions of reference works are useful because English is taught at the school.

The National Technical Library School was founded in 1962 in the wake of the Literacy Campaign. The mission of the school is to provide technical and reference training for students who will work in public or regional libraries as "técnicos medios" (library technicians/ paraprofessionals). Students come to attend the school from all regions of the country. They receive free housing, meals and a stipend as well as free tuition. The school currently offers a two and one-half year study program for nearly 300 students who work towards a library technician degree after finishing their high school studies.

Fifty-five teachers are affiliated with the school (some teach part time about their specialties). The school offers a curriculum that includes courses on general library topics (reference, cataloging, collection development, history of the book, the book trade and publishing, bookbinding, etc.), yearly practicums in nearby libraries, visits to all types of libraries, and, during the third year, a semester-long assignment in an institution near the student's home town. Reports, exams, and a "trabajo de titulación" (a work similar to a thesis) are also required.

On our tour of the school, we saw classrooms, workrooms where the students compile projects and reports (some are similar to poster sessions), the computer room (with four 386 machines, only one of which has a hard drive), the typing room (typing is taught because most of the libraries in which graduates will work do not have computers yet), the school's archives and the library. Their future development plans are to obtain newer equipment and teaching materials, to add Internet access, to automate the school archives and library holdings and to establish more exchanges with libraries abroad. (The director of the school was in Mexico at the time of our visit, working to set up an exchange with Mexico to allow students to study abroad.)

The Cuban Library Association (Asociación Cubana de Bibliotecarios, ASCUBI):

Our delegation met with ASCUBI representatives in the National Technical Library School where they had just set up new offices. Marta Terry, President of ASCUBI, and nine members of the national Executive Board welcomed us to Cuba and described the work of the association. ASCUBI has been active in international organizations including IFLA and it was the lead organizer of the 1994 IFLA conference held in Cuba. The national association has about 1200 members and represents all library workers, including both librarians and library technicians. There are chapters in nine of the 14 provinces. Because of the low membership fees ASCUBI maintains, there is little or no money to send librarians to international conferences. Cuban library workers pay a membership fee of about one peso per month for dues to ASCUBI (about US$.60 a year). ASCUBI representatives expressed considerable interest in U.S. librarianship and ways in which they might participate in ALA initiatives.

American Library Association's Sister Libraries Initiative:

At most of the libraries, we presented the Spanish language brochure prepared by ALA that details the new Sister Libraries Initiative. The Initiative encourages U.S. and foreign libraries to form relationships that promote the sharing of information and problem-solving techniques while participants learn about other cultures and the global issues facing all libraries.

The host libraries were presented with mementos (bags, pens, and pins) from the Libraries Build Communities campaign organized by ALA President Sarah Long. The Cuban librarians were impressed with the program's goal of matching libraries for mutual support and education. Several of them promised to investigate the possibility of joining the ALA effort. The ALA International Relations Office deserves special recognition for sending the information and gifts to distribute to our Cuban hosts.

Note about "Independent Libraries":

Several members of our delegation visited two of the so-called "independent libraries." These "libraries" operate out of private homes. One family had a bookshelf of materials that seemed ordinary by Cuban standards; the other family had no books. The families told us that they receive books and other materials by mail and by hand delivery. The second family we visited stated that materials (books, reprints of magazine articles and print copies of website pages) were delivered to them regularly by persons from the U.S. Interests Section; others were published and donated by the Cuban American National Foundation (an anti-Castro organization in Miami). We were told that the families received monthly deliveries of these materials and some monies from contacts in Miami and Mexico. Both families told us of their long histories of opposition to the Cuban government and the usefulness of the materials delivered by the U.S. Interests Section personnel in their efforts to encourage opposition to the Cuban government.

Based on this experience, it is my opinion that the information circulated on innumerable library listservs, including several ALA listservs, about these "independent" libraries, the "confiscation" of library materials and the persecution of their owners is either totally false or greatly exaggerated. The individuals that operate these "libraries" are not independent and they are not librarians. They are uncredentialed and they depend for materials upon donations from sources that oppose the Cuban government.

Based upon personal observation and interviews with the individuals in charge of these "libraries," I have concluded that these individuals are dissidents who distribute anti-government propaganda from their homes. Some of these materials are provided by the U.S. government and by individuals in Miami who pay for the materials and postage. The individuals involved in these activities cannot be considered independent of interests outside of Cuba.

*The official exchange rate in Cuban banks is 1 peso to the dollar. The exchange rate outside of banks but still official is 20 pesos to the dollar. So, the 10 pesos per year charge could be considered the equivalent of $10 or $ .50, depending on where one might exchange the pesos.

Cuban libraries and institutions on the Internet:

1. José Martí National Library: http://www.lib.cult.cu
To see the photos of our visit, go to
http://www.lib.cult.cu/noticias/Marzo/IIencuentro.htm

2. Instituto de Información Científica y Tecnólogica
(Institute of Scientific and Technological Information): http://www.idict.cu

3. Academia de Ciencias (Academy of Sciences):
http://www3.cuba.cu/ciencia/acc/

4. Association of Cuban Librarianship (ASCUBI): President, Marta Terry
martaterry@hotmail.com

5. Escuela Nacional de Técnicos de Biblioteca (National Technical
Library School, Vice Director Moraima D. Lorigados Hernandez), Calle
34, no. 513 entre Quinta y Septima Avenidas, Municipio Playa, Ciudad de
la Habana, Cuba. Telephone: 22-4502 or 29-4461

6. University of Havana Library:
http://www.uh.cu/biblioteca/Web_page_BC.htm

7. Biblioteca Provincial Ruben Martinez Villena (Public Library): Obispo
59, entre Oficio y Baratillo, Habana, Cuba; bpvillena@binanet.lib.cult.cu

8. Casa de las Americas: http://www.cult.cu/casa/
Director, Ernesto Sierra. beacasa@cult.cu

9. Cuba Museum Guide: http://www.cubaweb.cu/museos/

10. Instituto Cubano del Libro (Cuban Book Institute):
http://www.cubarte.cult.cu/libro/icl/

11. List of public libraries (partial list): http://binanet.lib.cult.cu/red.htm

12. Sociedad Cubana de Ciencias de la Informacion (Cuban Society of
Information Science): http://www.idict.cu/socict/socict.htm

13. Instituto Cubano de Amistad con los Pueblos (Cuban Institute of
Friendship with People): http://www2.ceniai.inf.cu//ICAP/ ;
icap@ceniai.inf.cu

Ann Sparanese's Paper on Cuba for the IRC Latin America and Caribbean Subcommittee

By Ann Sparanese
Originally published in *Library Juice* 4:9 Supplement, March 14, 2001

January 8, 2001

To: Pat Wand, Chairperson, ALA IRC Latin American & Caribbean Subcommittee
From: Ann C. Sparanese, SRRT Action Councilor
Subject: Hearing on Charges by "Friends of Cuban Libraries"

Thank you for inviting me to speak before your Subcommittee. These notes have been prepared for your consideration. I am the head of Adult & Young Adult Services at the Englewood Public Library in New Jersey. I have been an active member of ALA for ten years. As well as serving on SRRT Action Council and its International Responsibilities Task Force, I have been a member of YALSA's Best Books for Young Adults Committee, the AFL-CIO/ALA Joint Committee on Library Service to Labor Groups, and I am the current Chairperson of RUSA's John Sessions Memorial Award Committee. I also have a long history of interest in, and travel to, Cuba. I attended the 1994 IFLA Conference in Havana and my most recent visit was this past November, when I visited Cuban libraries and met with Havana members of ASCUBI, the Cuban Library Association. I have followed with interest, and argued against, the allegations of Mr. Kent since he began his campaign in 1999. The Social Responsibilities Round Table passed a resolution regarding the FCL at midwinter conference one year ago. Mr. Kent would like to present his proposal as a no-brainer, a simple question, a single pure concept: intellectual freedom. But it is not. This paper is respectfully submitted with the hope that the subcommittee may approach Mr. Kent's requests with a fuller appreciation of history, the facts and the issues.

1. Who Are the "Friends of Cuban Libraries?"

This is how Robert Kent and Jorge Sanguinetty described themselves at the outset of their campaign for Cuban "independent libraries."[1]

"Before going to the debate, however, the Friends of Cuban Libraries would like to answer some inquiries from the public regarding the goals and origin of our organization. The Friends of Cuban Libraries, founded on June 1, 1999, is an independent, nonpartisan, nonprofit organization which supports Cuba's independent libraries. We oppose censorship and all other violations of intellectual freedom, as defined by the Universal Declaration of Human Rights, regardless of the ideology or leadership of whatever Cuban government is in office. The founders of the organization are Jorge Sanguinetty and Robert Kent. Jorge Sanguinetty resides in Miami. He was the head of Cuba's Department of National Investment Planning before he left the country in 1967. He was later associated with the Brookings Institution and the UN Development Programme. He is the founder and president of Devtech, Inc. He is also a newspaper columnist and a commentator on Radio Marti. Robert Kent is a librarian who lives in New York City. He has visited Cuba many times and has Cuban friends whose viewpoints cover the political spectrum. During his visits to Cuba Robert Kent has assisted Cuban, American, and internationally-based human rights organizations with deliveries of medicines, small sums of money, and other forms of humanitarian aid. On four occasions he has taken books and pamphlets to Cuba for Freedom House and the Center for a Free Cuba, human rights organizations which have received publication grants from the U.S. Agency for International Development; on three occasions his travel expenses were paid wholly or in part by Freedom House or the Center for a Free Cuba. On his last trip to Cuba in February, 1999, Robert Kent was arrested and deported from the country."

Many references to Mr. Sanguinetty appear on the WWW. He speaks widely on the subject of returning free market enterprise to Cuba. As a commentator on Radio Marti, Mr. Sanguinetty is or was an employee of the United States government. Cubans on the island have always listened to Miami radio and even some TV stations. But Radio Marti is a propaganda

---

[1]   See http://internet.ggu.edu/university_library/if/cuba.html. Most of the activities carried out by the FCL take place on the listserves, of which this site has an "anthology."

station directly controlled by the most right-wing elements of the Cuban-American exile community, the Cuban American National Foundation (CANF). It is not a neutral voice or a bastion of "free expression." It has never aired the voices of liberal elements of the Cuban-American community who favor the normalization of relations with Cuba. Mr. Sanguinetty is simply a professional propagandist. In October 1995, President Clinton presented a $500,000 government grant to Freedom House for publishing and distributing pamphlets and books in Cuba.[2] The funds were also devoted to paying for individuals to travel to Cuba as tourists in order to make contact with dissident groups, organize them and fund them.[3] Robert Kent is evidently one of these couriers—another propagandist on an illegal, paid-for mission on behalf of Freedom House. He is not the only American to be sent on such a mission[4] and be deported. Kent evidently believes that by acknowledging his sponsor, this somehow legitimizes his activities. But it only demonstrates the nature of his campaign as part and parcel of stated US foreign policy intended to destabilize Cuba.

2. What Are the "Independent Libraries"?

The "independent libraries" are private book collections in peoples' homes. Mr. Kent and the right-wing Cuban-American propaganda outlets, call them "independent libraries" and even "public libraries." These "independent libraries" are one of a number of "projects" initiated and supported by a virtual entity calling itself "Cubanet" (www.cubanet.org) and an expatriate anti-Castro political entity calling itself the Directorio Revolucionario Democratico Cubano. The Cubanet website describes what the "independent libraries" are, how they got started and who funds and solicits for them. The index page says that the organization exists to "assist [Cuba's] independent sector develop [sic] a civil society..." This is the wording used in both the Torricelli and the Helms Burton Acts, both of which require that the US government finance efforts to subvert the Cuban society in the name of strengthening "civil society." You will see on the "Who We Are" page that Cubanet, located in Hialeah, Florida, is financially supported by the National Endowment for Democracy, the

---

[2] Franklin, Jane. *Cuba and The United States: A Chronological History*. Melbourne, Ocean Press, 1997. p375.
[3] Calvo, Hernando and Katlijn Declercq. *The Cuban Exile Movement: Dissidents or Mercenaries?* New York, Ocean Press, 2000. p.130.
[4] Ibid.

United States Agency for International Development (USAID) and
"private" "anonymous" donors. The "exterior" representative of the
"independent libraries" is the Directorio Revoucionario Democratico
Cubano, also located in Hialeah.[5]

3. Who are the Independent Librarians?

You will read on the pages of Cubanet about the individual "libraries"
and their personnel. Not one of the people listed is actually a librarian. Not
one has ever been a librarian. Most, however, are leaders or officers of
various dissident political parties, such as the Partido Cubano de
Renovacion Ortodoxa and the Partido Solidaridad Democratica. This is
documented on Cubanet, although Mr. Kent never mentions these party
affiliations in his FCL press releases. We know absolutely nothing about the
principles, programs or activities of these parties, or why they have been
allegedly targeted. We don't know whether their activities are lawful or
unlawful under Cuban law. Kent maintains that their activities are solely
related to their books—but in reality we have no idea whether this is true
and in fact, one of these "librarians" told one of our ALA colleagues that
this was not true! By using the terms "beleaguered," "librarians" and the
buzzwords "freedom of expression" and "colleagues" Mr. Kent hopes to get
the a priori support of librarians who might not look beneath this veneer.
After all, isn't this the reason that the subcommittee will be considering their
case in the first place? But I wonder if ALA is willing to establish the
precedent that all politicians with private book collections who decide to call
themselves "librarians," are therefore our "colleagues"?

4. Who funds Cubanet, the Directorio, and the "independent libraries"—
and why is this important?

A recent book entitled *Psy War Against Cuba* by Jon Elliston (Ocean
Press, 1999), reveals, using declassified US government documents, the
history of a small piece of the 40-year-old propaganda war waged by our
country against the government of Cuba. The US has spent hundreds of
millions of taxpayers' dollars over these years to subvert and overthrow the
current Cuban government—US activities have included complete

---

[5] Another of its stated purposes is "informs the world about Cuba's reality", but
their news pages simply report only anti-government events or incidents.

economic embargo, assassinations and assassination attempts, sabotage, bombings, invasions, and "psyops." When even the fall of the Soviet Union and the devastation of the Cuban economy in the early 1990's did not produce the desired effect, the US embarked on additional, subtler, campaigns to overthrow the Cuban government from within. One element of this approach is the funneling of monetary support to dissident groups wherever they can be found, or created. This includes bringing cash into the country through couriers such as Mr. Kent, and increasing support to expatriate groups operating inside the US, such as the Directorio, Cubanet and especially, the Cuban American National Foundation (CANF). The website Afrocubaweb (www.afrocubaweb.org) has gathered information from the Miami Herald and other sources to document the recipients of this US funding. USAID, a US government Agency, supported the Directorio Revolucionario Democratico Cubano to the amount of $554,835 during 1999. This is the group that supports the "independent librarians" in Cuba and is listed as their "foreign representative." The money that they send to Cuba, as well as the "small amounts" of cash that Mr. Kent carried illegally to Cuba violates Cuban law, which does not allow foreign funding of their political process. Neither does the United States allow foreign funding of its own political process—the furor around alleged Chinese "contributions" to the Democratic Party is a case in point. The "independent libraries" may be independent of their own government, but they are not independent of the US government. The US government is not the only anti-Castro entity that has adjusted its policy to changing times—the most right-wing forces in the Cuban expatriate community have also stepped up their support of dissident elements inside Cuba over the last few years. The *Miami Herald* reported in September 2000 that "the leading institution of this city's exile community plans to quadruple the amount of money it sends to dissident leaders on the island..." This leading institution is the Cuban American National Foundation (CANF), and the article reports that part of the group's $10,000,000 budget will begin "flowing to the island through sympathetic dissidents by the end of the year." More specifically, CANF will, among other declared activities, "increase funds to buy books for its [Cuba's] independent libraries."[6]

---

[6] "In Miami, Cuban Exile Group Shifts Focus" by Scott Wilson. *The Washington Post Foreign Service*. Thursday, September 14, 2000; Page A03. As quoted at http://afrocubaweb.org/dissidents.htm.

5. What is CANF? What is its record on free expression, intellectual freedom, and democratic rights here in the USA?

The Cuban American National Foundation (CANF) was founded by Jorge Mas Canosa, a veteran of the Bay of Pigs invasion and CIA operative, at the behest of the Reagan administration in 1982. It has become the most wealthy and powerful voice of the right-wing Cuban community in South Florida and has wielded extraordinary political power for the last twenty years. It has been connected to violence and terrorism both in Cuba and in Miami. Its newest tactic, as described above, is to "support" dissidents in Cuba, including buying books for "independent" libraries, presumably to support "freedom of expression" in Cuba. Mr. Kent and Mr. Sanguinetty claim to be proponents of human rights and frequently refer to the "landmark" IFLA "report." But they seem to have no problem with their libraries' CANF connection, even though CANF was the subject of a truly "landmark" report issued by Americas Watch, a division of Human Rights Watch, in 1992. The Americas Watch report on CANF is the first that organization ever issued against a human rights violator in a city of the United States. It states that "a 'repressive climate for freedom of expression' had been created by anti-Castro Cuban-American leaders in which violence and intimidation had been used to quiet exiles who favor a softening of policies toward Cuba."[7] The executive director of Americas Watch at that time, said "We do not know of any other community in the United States with this level of intimidation and lack of freedom to dissent."[8] The report documents "how Miami Cubans who are opposed to the Cuban government harass political opponents with bombings, vandalism, beatings and death threats."[9] A campaign spearheaded by CANF against the *Miami Herald* in the early nineties resulted in bombings of *Herald* newpaper boxes and death threats to staff.[10] Pressure from CANF closed the Cuban Museum of Arts and Culture because it showed work by artists who had not "broken" with Cuba.[11] Anyone who followed the Elian Gonzalez case this past year noted that tolerance for dissenting views by Cuban Americans was

---

[7] "Miami Leaders are Condemned by Rights Unit" by Larry Rohter. *New York Times*, August 19, 1992 Section A, Page 8, retrieved from Lexis-Nexis.
[8] Ibid.
[9] Franklin, p.300.
[10] 10 Op.cit.
[11] Franklin, p 241, 242, 252,277.

completely lacking in Florida and a hostile atmosphere was maintained by CANF during the duration of the affair. Can you imagine what the life expectancy of a pro-Castro "independent library" in the middle of Little Havana would be, given this history? CANF does not respect freedom of expression or democratic rights in the USA, yet it is a direct financial supporter of Mr. Kent's independent libraries. Neither Mr.Kent nor Mr. Sanguinetty have disowned this support—in fact they haven't even mentioned it! They have not chosen to examine or criticize the lack of free expression among the very people that give them succor and publicity here at home, yet they claim to be its great champions in Cuba!

6. What about free expression and democratic rights in Cuba?

There is no doubt that political dissidence has its consequences in Cuba. Those who want to overthrow the current socialist government are considered political problems. Because of the declared and well-funded US policy of seeking to destabilize Cuba by creating and/or instigating social unrest, the Cuban people consider these people to be agents of US policy and enemies of the nation. This view is shared by the former head of the US Interests Section in Cuba, former Ambassador Wayne Smith who says: "Since 1985, we have stated publicly that we will encourage and openly finance dissident and human rights groups in Cuba; this too is in our interest. The United States isn't financing all those groups—only the ones that are best know internationally. Those dissidents and human rights groups in Cuba—that are nothing but a few people—are only important to the extent that they serve us in a single cause: that of destabilizing Fidel Castro's regime."[12] This is the reality of a small country that has been in a virtual state of siege by the most powerful country in the world for more than 40 years. The US has engaged in invasion, sabotage, assassination attempts against its leader and even the maintenance of a military base against the will of the Cuban people, as well as well-documented psyop and propaganda campaigns. With the economic blockade, the US has sought to bring the Cuban people to their knees by depriving them of sources of foodstuffs and denying medicine to their children.[13] Ambassador Smith: "Through these two policies, economic pressure and human rights—we

---

[12] Calvo & Declercq, pp 156, (interview with Ambassador Smith.)

[13] "Denial of Food and Medicine: The Impact of the U.S. Embargo on Health and Nutrition in Cuba," A Report from the American Association for World Health, March 1997.

want to force the overthrow of Fidel Castro and then install a transitional government that we like—to reinstate the people we want and thus, control Cuba again."[14] It is a fact of life that democratic rights suffer in any nation under siege or engaged in war. A view of our own history will illuminate this point: simply look at the what happened to the American people's freedom of expression, constitutional rights and human rights during the Civil War, WWI, WWII, the Cold War McCarthy period and even during our most recent wars. Can we realistically expect and demand that Cuba be the model of democratic rights in the face of the unrelenting US economic and political aggression? Cuba does not have a perfect human rights record. But are we simply to condemn Cuba for this situation? Don't we, as US citizens, whose tax dollar has been used for so many years to create this situation, have a special responsibility to look at the full picture? Shouldn't our first concern be to change the policy that has directly contributed to the limitation of democratic rights in Cuba? Even the UN special rapporteur for human rights, while critical of Cuba, credited the US policy for making the situation worse than it might otherwise be.[15] Mssrs. Kent and Sanguinetty are asking this committee and the ALA for a sweeping condemnation of Cuba on the basis of human rights. But are not food, education, medical care, income, freedom from violence, and literacy "human rights"? The Cuban people enjoy free medical care—despite the US denial of Cuba's right to purchase basic medical products—and have one of the highest per capita rate of doctors in the world. All Cuban children attend school and enjoy free education through university. The Cuban people are an extraordinarily literate people with many more libraries and books than people in most of the undeveloped world, despite Mr. Kent's attempts to ridicule their library collections with absurd claims that have been refuted by Cuban librarians. Cuban workers have the right to an income even if they have been laid off from work; they have a society free from violence and no Cuban child has ever been killed by a gun in his/her school. Racism, as we know it in the US, is not present there and vestiges of racism are actively combated at all levels of society. If these are taken as measures of human rights, Cuba comes out looking very good indeed. This is not to say that intellectual freedom and complete freedom of expression are not important. But Cuba's exceptional success in fulfilling these basic human needs explains why the majority of the Cuban people are not anxious to trade their current situation for the "free market", "wealthy exiles get their

---

[14] Calvo & Declercq, p160.
[15] Franklin, p 330.

property back" plans of Kent/Sanguinetty's sponsors in Miami and the US government. Before the ALA passes judgment on Cuba, even in the area of free expression, we need to look at the whole picture and we need to have some first-hand experience. We cannot simply act on what one ill-informed librarian and a professional expatriate propagandist—both with US government backing—tell us.

7. How does US policy towards Cuba affect free expression and intellectual freedom for US citizens?

For close to forty years, in various permutations, the US has maintained a travel ban, which specifically denies the right of US citizens to visit Cuba outside a small set of "legal" and "licensed" exceptions. This means that if any US citizen (any US librarian, for instance) wants to travel to Cuba, simply to see for her/himself what is going on there (not for any specifically academic or professional purpose), this is against US law and punishable by fines and/or imprisonment. If members of this subcommittee want to visit Cuban libraries, simply to chat with your counterparts and even seek out the "independent librarians"—it is not the Cuban government that is preventing you, it is the US government! This is clearly an issue of intellectual freedom[16]—but not to Mssrs. Kent and Sanguinetty. They are purists. They are only concerned about freedom of expression and intellectual freedom in Cuba—not in the US—and only for Cubans in Cuba, not in Miami! This is utter hypocrisy. Because of this forty-year war against Cuba by the United States, it is not just Cuban citizens who have seen their democratic rights limited, it is US citizens as well. To deliberately ignore this reality reveals the claims and motives of Mr. Kent and Mr. Sanguinetty as deeply suspect.

8. What About the IFLA Report?

Why has the FCL been able to go forward with their accusations? The answer is a report by the recently formed IFLA—FAIFE (Free Access to

---

[16] In "The Right to Travel: The Effect of Travel Restrictions on Scientific Collaboration Between American and Cuban Scientists," the American Association for the Advancement of Science is every bit as critical of the United States in limiting travel as it is of Cuba! The report notes that the US government does not recognize the right to travel as an internationally recognized fundamental right. http://shr.aaas.org/rtt/report/one.htm.

Information and Freedom of Expression) Committee. The sole basis for this action—the first such action taken by committee—was the Friends of Cuban Libraries allegations, and several phone conversations with the alleged librarians involved. No member of FAIFE ever visited these "libraries" or attempted to. No "investigation" whatsoever was undertaken beyond these phone contacts. Parts of the report were taken verbatim from the papers of Mr. Kent and Mr. Sanguinetty. Even the FAIFE report acknowledges the role of financing by "foreign interests," but it does not seem to find this point very important. It does not address the issue of who these "librarians" really are, but accepts FCL's allegations that they are librarians. The IFLA investigation meets no standards. Nevertheless, it has bestowed on Mr. Kent's cause a certain legitimacy and has allowed Kent to go the Canadian Library Association, and other groups, which also reacted to the IFLA report and did no independent investigation. In an especially crass but clever move, Kent even managed to get a recently imprisoned Chinese American librarian to make statements about a situation about which he has no knowledge. Perhaps IFLA can be forgiven for not understanding the nature of US hostility toward Cuba, and the lengths to which the US and the right-wing Cuban expatriate elements will go to further their aims of overthrowing the Cuban government. But the American Library Association will have no such excuse. Our own members and colleagues have visited Cuban libraries and the "independents" (without prior notification) and have testified as to their inauthenticity. They must be listened to. This is already more than IFLA cared to do. The IFLA report, and all that followed because of it, cannot be allowed to grant any further imprimatur to the Kent/Sanguinetty campaign.

9. What about our real colleagues—the librarians of Cuba?

The charges that have been spread by Kent and his FCL have deeply offended our real colleagues, the librarians of Cuba, and our sister library association, ASCUBI. Our real colleagues are beleaguered by shortages of things as simple as paper, professional literature, computers and printers—and much of this has to do with their inability, because of the US blockade, to purchase any items from US companies (or foreign companies doing business with the US). Computers cannot be brought to Cuba from the US legally, even as a donation by licensed travelers. True "friends of Cuban libraries" would be concerned about these matters. It is time that we begin to know our real counterparts/colleagues in Cuba. It is time that we begin to have the kinds of conversations and exchanges on all subjects—including intellectual freedom and censorship. It is US policy, not Cuban policy, which prevents us from doing so. As the representative of US librarians, the ALA has an obligation first to address our own country's limitation of freedom of expression and the freedom to travel, then to criticize others. The American Library Association cannot allow itself to be the willing instrument of a US government/CANF-sponsored disinformation campaign. If the ALA takes any action at all on Cuba, it should be to call for an end to the embargo and the hostile US policy towards Cuba which harms the democratic rights, including freedom of expression, of both the Cuban and US people. ALA should begin in the spirit of the resolution passed by the US librarians who attended the IFLA conference in Havana in August 1994.

Ann C. Sparanese, MLS
Head of Adult & Young Adult Services
Englewood Public Library
Englewood, NJ 07631

The Status of Gays in Cuba: Myth and Reality

By Larry R. Oberg
Published in an earlier version in *Library Juice* 4:9, Supplement,
March 14, 2001

Based upon a memoir by the late self-exiled Cuban writer Reynaldo
Arenas, the film *Before Night Falls*, released in 2000, chronicles the author's
coming of age and repression as a homosexual and artist by Cuban
authorities in the early days of the Cuban revolution. Arenas wrote his
memoir in New York shortly before his death from AIDS in 1990, some ten
years after leaving Cuba in the Mariel exodus. Apart from any artistic
considerations, questions have arisen concerning the accuracy of Arenas's
descriptions of the past persecution of Cuban gays and the usefulness of the
memoir and film as guides to the current status of gays and lesbians on the
island.

Between March 2000 and April 2002, I spent more than four months in
Cuba on four separate occasions, working as a librarian on a range of
research projects with my Cuban colleagues. Most of that time was spent in
Havana, but also in numerous other cities, including Matanzas, Trinidad,
and Santiago de Cuba. As a gay man, I was motivated to find out as much
as I could about the status of Cuba's gay and lesbian population. What I
experienced, read, and was told made me suspect that Arenas's portrayal of
his personal life as a gay man in the early years of Cuba's revolution may
have been exaggerated. For example, his fantastic claim, arrived at by
"complicated mathematical calculations," to have bedded some 5,000 men
by the age of 25 is hardly plausible and, if we are to believe him, every
young stud on the island was constantly on the alert to jump his bones.
Well, perhaps not.

Interestingly, Arenas' apparently insatiable sexual appetite does not
come through in Julian Schnabel's sanitized film version of the memoirs, in
which he is depicted as little more than an inveterate flirt. I cannot claim to
know whether Arenas' description of the repression that he and other gays
suffered during that particular moment in Cuban history is accurate. But,
whatever the truth of the matter, I can attest to the fact that the condition
and status of gay men and lesbians on the island today can only be
described as much improved.

To prepare for my visits, I read Canadian Ian Lumsden's 1996 introduction to Cuban gay life, *Machos, Maricones, and Gays: Cuba and Homosexuality*. Lumsden, a lukewarm supporter of the Cuban revolution, provides us with a useful history of the treatment of gays during the early days of the revolution and surveys their status in contemporary Cuban society. I also watched Sonja de Vries's 1995 documentary, *Gay Cuba*, which consists of a series of interviews with gay men and lesbians who speak frankly of their lives and relationships with friends, family, and coworkers. (One of the producers of the film, an interviewee himself, now works as a tour guide and gave me useful background information on the film.) *Gay Cuba* was shown at the annual International Festival of New Latin American Cinema in Havana to public and critical acclaim. Nonetheless, some of the Cuban gays with whom I spoke expressed reservations about the film, suggesting that, while it is generally accurate, it nonetheless presents an incomplete portrait of gay life on the island nation.

Gay Cuba is not, however, the only filmed account of gay life in Cuba. Several other documentaries are available. A particularly interesting one, released in 1996, is *Mariposas en el andamio* (*Butterflies on the Scaffold*). Mariposa, a metaphor for drag queen, is used here to refer to someone who transforms himself into something beautiful to be admired by all. The film documents the daily life and performances of drag artists in a Havana neighborhood called La Guinera. At my request, I was invited to La Guinera for a private show. Extremely poor before the revolution, La Guinera today is recognized by the United Nations for exemplary community development, but remains what might be called working class. Many of these drag shows are sponsored by the local CDRs (Committees for the Defense of the Revolution), and all play to large and enthusiastic audiences.

What I found during my time in Cuba was a gay community with many parallels to those of Europe and North America, as well as a number of differences. For one thing, all laws that discriminate against Cuban gays have been removed from the books. Earlier efforts to legislate behavior in Cuba gave rise to the Public Ostentation Law. Enacted in the 1930s, it was used effectively for decades to harass gay people who refused to remain closeted. Aimed at those who "flaunted" their homosexuality, the law defined public and even private homosexual acts that might be witnessed involuntarily by others as offenses punishable by fine and detention. The Public Ostentation Law was repealed by the revolutionary government in 1988. The legal situation of gays in Cuba today is usefully contrasted with, for example, that of the United States where many states retain outdated anti-sodomy laws and repressive legislation aimed at gays increasingly is enacted at the state level and proposed at the national level.

While in Cuba, I spoke with scores of gays, mostly men, and encountered none who said that their government was persecuting them, although many older gays did talk about the "bad old days." Most, however, reported incidents of private discrimination by individuals, and all resented the residual machista attitudes that remain stubbornly embedded in some levels of Cuban society. Nourished for centuries by Spanish colonialism, the Catholic Church, and a quasi-reverential attitude towards the traditional heterosexual family, these attitudes not only perpetuate prejudice against gays but also result in more highly polarized sex roles than generally exist in North American and European societies. No one with whom I spoke, however, reported active or systematic repression by the state.

One question that I asked many of my informants was, "Would you feel comfortable holdings hands with your boyfriend on the street?" Several responded with a qualified yes and a few stated that they do just that. Indeed, two men or two women holdings hands is not an altogether uncommon sight, at least not in Havana. But some also stated that they would stop holding hands at the approach of a police officer. Urban Cuban police forces recruit a high percentage of young macho males from the provinces, many with a chip on their shoulder against gays.

It is important to put Cuba's past record of mistreatment of gays into perspective. While context rarely excuses negative behavior, it is worth remembering that Cuba was scarcely alone in its anti-gay attitudes and actions. For example, in the Boise, Idaho, of the 1950s, scores of gay men were persecuted, driven from their homes, pursued when they fled to other states, and imprisoned in what came to be known as the Boys of Boise scandal, one of the most infamous anti-gay actions in United States history. Florida, home to so many Cuban expatriates, has a dreadful record of gay rights abuses, and in 1990, in Adrian, Michigan, the police staked out a public park for months on end before arresting nearly twenty men on charges of public indecency. Almost all were married and self-identified as heterosexuals. Many were arrested in their homes in front of wives, children, and in a couple of instances, grandchildren.

Cuba's past record on gay rights may be no better than that of most Western societies, but it can be argued that gay people in Cuba are better off today than those in any other Latin American society and even in parts of North America and Europe. It wasn't too long ago, for example, that death squads in Rio de Janeiro were sent out to cleanse the city of its "queers." In the United States, the problem is more likely to be private violence underpinned by a pervasive hatred of gay people, as in the murders of Matthew Shepard, Brandon Teena, Billy Jack Gaither, and countless others.

Like North American and European societies, Cuba is undergoing a profound review and reconceptualization of its attitudes towards gays and lesbians. The 1994 film Fresa y chocolate (Strawberry and Chocolate) is the first Cuban film to deal openly and directly with homosexuality. Directed by Tomas Guitérrez Alea, the film has been widely praised. What is less well known is that it was also wildly popular across the island, playing simultaneously at ten or twelve Havana theaters to lines several blocks long. Its popularity was, no doubt, a response to a repressed desire on the part of Cubans to talk more openly about this issue.

Another seminal incident along the road to acceptance for Cuban gays occurred in 1996. Pablo Milanes, a Cuban nova trova singer who has achieved quasi-sainthood among the island's population, wrote a song about love between two men entitled "El pecado original" ("Original Sin"). Pablito, as he is affectionately known, dedicated the song to all Cuban homosexuals. Introduced at his annual holiday concert held in the vast Carlos Marx Theater in the Miramar neighborhood of Havana, "El pecado" original took the audience and the country by storm and did much to advance the cause of gay acceptance. It is of interest to note that, in the 1960's, Milanes was briefly confined to one of the UMAP (Military Units for Aid to Production) work camps set up to rehabilitate prostitutes, gays, and others considered to be delinquents. Although short-lived, the UMAP camps represent the low point in revolutionary Cuba's treatment of its gay and lesbian citizens.

One of the most striking things about Cuba is the vitality of its cultural and intellectual life throughout the island, particularly in Havana. Gay themes are prevalent in the theatre, in lectures, and in concerts. In December, 2000, I attended a play entitled *Muerte en el bosque* (*A Death in the Woods*), produced by the Teatro Sotano in Havana's Vedado neighborhood. Based upon the acclaimed novel Mascaras (Masks), by Leonardo Padura Fuentes, the play follows a police investigation into the murder of a Havana drag queen, a plot device that allows for an examination of Cuban attitudes and prejudices towards gays at every level of society.

On a lighter note, a group called La Danza Voluminosa, which features large dancers, produced an alternately amusing and touching ballet version of Racine's *Phèdre*. The director opted for gender-blind casting and, indeed, a man danced the title role. A one-man—yes, one man—stage version of *Strawberry and Chocolate* played to considerable success a few years ago. And, at the 22nd International Festival of New Latin American Cinema held in Havana in December 2000, perhaps half of the films shown had gay themes or subtexts. In 2001, Emilio Bejel published *Gay Cuban Nation*. The book is a fascinating scholarly study of the impact of homosexuality on Cuban politics, society, and culture, as seen through the writings of its gay artists, both past and present.

A striking contradiction in Cuban society today is the contrast between the rich cultural and intellectual life that is widely available and easily affordable, and salaries that make the purchase of a pair of shoes an event for which one must plan. Cubans purchase theatre tickets in pesos nacional (MN, i.e., moneda nacional; valued at approximately five U. S. cents). Tickets for the National Ballet cost Cubans five pesos nacional; theatrical plays, eight; musical extravaganzas and ballet festival performances, ten. Admission to first-run films costs two pesos nacional. Foreign tourists pay in pesos convertibles (CUC or tourist dollar; valued at approximately 1.8 U. S. dollars). Admission to the National Ballet costs tourists 20 pesos convertibles. For most other theatrical events tourists pay the same number of pesos as Cubans, but in pesos convertibles, not pesos nacional. Tourists are allowed, however, to pay at the cinemas in pesos nacional.

In Havana, gay-run and gay-clientele restaurants are not hard to find. Try, for example, the elegant French cuisine at Le Chansonnier or La Guarida, the latter located in the apartment in which Strawberry and Chocolate was filmed. Until its recent closing, the famous, indeed somewhat infamous, Fiat bar on the Malecon attracted hundreds of gay twenty-somethings who, on weekend nights, spilled across this emblematic Havana thoroughfare to line the sidewalk along the sea wall. Midnight mass on Christmas Eve at the Havana cathedral and any performance by the National Ballet at the Gran Teatro de la Habana attract scores of Cuban gays.

Gay culture in Cuba without doubt was repressed, sometimes severely, during the period described by Arenas in *Before Night Falls*. But where was it not in that pre-Stonewall era? This, however, is not the reality that I found in today's Cuba. Indeed, it is unlikely that the slick and trendy Out magazine would feature Havana as "The new gay hot spot ... hot boys, drag-heavy bars, and a whole lot more" in its February 2001 issue, if Cuba were as repressive as its critics would have us believe.

It is ultimately unproductive to hold Cuba to an abstract standard that no other country in the world, certainly not my own, can claim to have reached. It is more useful to view this small island nation within the context of current reality. How well is Cuba doing compared to the rest of Latin

America? How well is it doing relative to our own countries? How much progress has been made over the past forty years on a variety of fronts—literacy, education, health care, housing, the status of women, and of course gay rights? When we respond honestly to these questions, we see a vision of Cuba that is sharply different from that propounded by Cuba's detractors.

This is a revised version of an article that first appeared in the November-December 2001 issue (v.8, no.6) of The Gay & Lesbian Review Worldwide.

Québec, Qc 2006
Le 20 mars 2006

Section Six:
Various and Sundry Readings

Library Limericks

By Carol Reid
(Not previously published)

On my way to looking up another word, in the book that has all the words...
poetaster: a writer of mediocre verse; rhymester; would-be poet

There once was a poor poetaster
Whose boss acted more like his master;
He said, "You're too slow,
If you don't want to go,
You will have to write worser and faster."

And with that poetastic first attempt, it was off to the libraries!

A gentleman named Ranganathan
Had five things he put all his faith in:
To each book its reader...
We made him our leader;
He wrote *Colon Classification*.

There once was an icon named Dewey,
Who at dubious letters went "phooey!"
Some thought he was biased...
Was he chauvinist or shyest?
Or was he in fact a real roué?

There once was a catter called Cutter
Who numbers and letters would mutter,
While matching each word
(Some folks found him absurd),
Through his 2-figure tables he'd putter.

For three legendary libraries, in literature and in life

There was a librarian named Borges
Who into the world made great forays;

He welcomed the rabble
To the Tower of Babel:
A book store of infinite mores.

In 1911 a fire
Destroyed much to which we aspire,
But allies worldwide
Rallied right to our side,
And restored the State Library (Empire).

The library at Alexandria,
A lexicological dandy, a
Sine qua non,
It had great élan,
One like it, there'd never again be a.

For the Hawaiian librarians and their successful battle against Baker & Taylor in 1997

They say be not borrower nor lender,
Though such services we love to render;
We never grow weary
Of any a query,
So long as you're no venal vendor.

A couple in honor of cataloger extraordinaire Sanford Berman

There once was a Berman named Sandy
Who with LC honchos would bandy
The best subject heading
Searchers should be getting,
No matter how risqué or randy.

Tristram Shandy was a hypothetical immortal historian who would take one year to transcribe the events of a single day. Although he would fall further and further behind as time went on, paradoxically he would still eventually write a history for all time!
~Bertrand Russell

There once was a maverick called Sandy
Who with needed headings was handy;
He wasn't a bad guy,

A bit of a gadfly,
A true latter-day Tristram Shandy.

Dedicated to all dedicated librarians who love something else on the side

There once was a bored cataloger
Who doggedly worked as a blogger;
He wanted to write
And stay up half the night,
Not grind in machines like a cog (grrr...)

Librarians love acronyms,
At times they seem almost like whims,
We mark tags with MARC,
And we spark things in SPARC,
And we go out on lingo-like limbs.

For Nicholson Baker

Novelist Nicholson Baker,
To some of us he took the cake for
Critiquing our actions
And creating factions:
A library mover and shaker.

For Nancy Pearl

A lusty librarian named Pearl
Decided her faves to unfurl,
She took bun and all,
And she posed for a doll,
Offending the occasional churl.

For Miss Ruth Brown

Bette Davis in the movie *Storm Center*
Played librarian and little boy's mentor:
There's a book she won't retire,
He irately sets a fire,
Then, ironically, all feel contenter.

Some people are fond of book banning,
Not satisfied merely with panning
The works they dislike;
Instead, they would strike
Such titles the wide world from spanning.

Like flowers, collections need weeding,
Since shelf space we're constantly needing;
We can sell them in sales,
Give to schools or to jails,
Yet our book-loving hearts are still bleeding.

Please bring all your books back on time,
If you don't, though, it isn't a crime,
You can pay a small fee
(It has happened to me!)
But be quick or your debt it will climb.

For Richard Wright whose story is told in the children's book Richard Wright and the Library Card, *based on his autobiography* Black Boy

Richard Wright wrote of the day
Into literacy he found a way:
With a White card he'd borrow
Books to ease his sorrow…
In the wide world of words he would stay.

For Charlie Parker

A rare bird named Charles used the atlas
To find a feline for the catless,
A cat who can swing
And can look at a king
And can bring jazz and ska to the scatless.

There was once a librarian lover
Who did not judge a bed by its cover;
He was named Casanova,
Blamed it on the bossa nova,

Around Ladies' Lingerie he would hover.

There once was an old preservationist,
Who of all in the lab was the patientest;
He said, "What, me worry?"
Adding, "What is the hurry?
It's not like I am a Creationist!"

So what rhymes with librarian??

There once was a Bolshevik librarian,
A pro-samizdat proletarian;
He classed for the cause,
But what gave him some pause
Were authorities authoritarian.

There once was a very old librarian,
An actual octogenarian;
She was wizened and wise,
Wore an all-knowing guise,
And a comfy smock she looked quite airy in.

There once was a puerile librarian
Who stockpiled *Conan the Barbarian*;
He'd eschew a film classic
For movie parks Jurassic,
And those with Mo, Curly, and Larry in.

For Stephen King, one of the most frequently "challenged" authors of the 1990s

There once was a ghoulish librarian,
Ate lunches of book paste and carrion;
He'd happily hush you,
But just as soon crush you,
That horrific inhumanitarian.

Some of my bets friends...

A patron approached the librarian,
A dyslexic request he was carryin'—

A nice enough feller,
Though very bad speller,
He asked her was the dictionary in.

Merriam-Webster *defines* walleyed *as "having walleyes or affected with walleye" or "marked by a wild irrational staring of the eyes." A librarian once wrote that "the problem of 'starers' had become a hot topic among public librarians in North Carolina." Around the same time she asked her homeless relative what he thought of the library and he told her that the main branch had "too many people working in there. They don't have anything to do but sit at their desks and stare at you all day long." "I like to remind myself of this story,"* she says, *"every time I start thinking that I have the one true perspective on something."*

There once was a walleyed librarian
Who stared at each Tom, Dick, and Harry in
Their cubicles and carrels;
From Internet perils,
They were saved from tarnation and tarryin'.

To my man Dan, the longest word lover I know

There once was a British librarian,
Antidisestablishmentarian,
Declined to eat liver,
Reclined on a river:
That riparian vegetarian contrarian!

Some men they regard the librarian
As an unsexy mere secretary in
Flats and a bun,
The kind not called "Hon,"
But they're not the kind we'll be marryin'!

For my friend Nate

Atlas Shrugged, shrugged the librarian,
Is out, but we've more libertarian
Books by Ayn Rand,
And some that are banned,
And others that really are nary in!

There once was a New Age librarian,
Ate health food and was an Aquarian;
He always recycled
And to work bicycled,
And practiced a lifestyle agrarian.

There once was a lanky librarian,
Blonde, lofty, and quite frankly Aryan,
But her friends were all Jews,
Very liberal her views,
And her call to help all it was clarion.

For the followers of Voltaire, master of Enlightenment, whose personal library now resides in the Russian National Library at St. Petersburg

There once was a philosophe-librarian,
A wine-and-fromagey Voltairean;
His ideés were fixes,
And his friends were French geeks,
Sporting wear they looked fairly mohairy in.

There once was a careful librarian,
Who studied whatever looked scary in
The workplace and stacks;
Her warnings were facts,
Like the mine that they found the canary in.

Batgirl, by day a librarian,
Shelved both books and crooks with a flair,
Reinvented the type
And never yelled *CRIPE!*
An adorable disciplinarian.

And for all kidlit devotees ... past, present, and future...

There once was an unborn librarian,
Bookworm in the womb—she was wary in
Her cramped and close quarters;
She'd put in her orders

For all tales that there is a fairy in!

Postscript: For my own biblio-niblings * *Willa, Woody, Mary, Julian, and Alex:*

There was a librarian named Willa
Who filed in folders manila;
She liked things in order,
A bit of a hoarder,
Kept chaos down to a scintilla.

How much book could a Woody read?
Since that Woody could speed read...
He could read a rack,
Plus another stack,
And be back for more, indeed!

There was a librarian named Mary
Who worked, of course, at the library;
She liked to tuck books
Into crannies and nooks,
Leaving room for some new ones to spare, see?

If you do a search that is Boolean,
There you will always see Julian;
With *and* not *or*,
His less is more,
And his library haul is Herculean.

Alex hails from Ethiopia,
A once cultural cornucopia...
We all do love her dearly,
But can't always read her clearly,
With our transcontinental presbyopia.

* *Niblings* is a neologism reported in the *Atlantic Monthly* to denote nieces and
nephews, the offspring of one's siblings.

Some Meditations on Those "Amusing Searches"

By Rory Litwin
Originally published in *Library Juice* 6:24, November 13, 2003

Each month in *Library Juice* I publish a list of a dozen or two searches that led to pages on libr.org in the previous month—amusing, or at least head-scratching, stuff. (They are compiled on the *Library Juice* website at http://libr.org/Juice/amusing.html.) It has occurred to me that many of these searches are trying to tell us something about information seeking behavior, and that we can actually learn from them when we are done giggling. I've made a stab at a typology of the "amusing search," with lessons and questions arising from each.

The Embarrassing Information Need

Here are a few choice searches of the "embarrassing," type, which range from the fetishistic to the bizarre to the simply sensitive. (I am removing the obvious searches for specific types of porn, though some would say these also represent legitimate information-seeking behavior.)

- beach 2001 bare breasts sociology
- characteristics of men prefered by gays
- questioning if masturbation effects your intelligence
- origins of 4 20
- how to cultivate a submissive woman
- how much are back issues of Hustler magazine worth
- human milk embarrassed
- instructions making gas mask b o n g s
- BUNION FETISH
- los angeles what to say in voir dire to avoid being on a jury
- searching to see if i have a warant on me
- electronic penis stretcher
- people who hate the oak lawn library
- I NEED WEAPONS

(The all-caps were in the original searches.)

These represent legitimate questions that an information seeker would likely be very embarrassed to pose to a real live librarian, whether because of fear of disapproval or as a matter of sheer privacy. We can draw a couple of different conclusions from this. One is simply that given the relative privacy that users (rightly or wrongly) assume that they have on the net, disintermediation in information services has an aspect that can sometimes be a positive thing; it provides a new freedom to explore. Some might argue, on the other hand, that the real life encounter has an important moral dimension that can confront a person with his own sense of shame, and that this can be a good thing. For example, the guy needing weapons might have second thoughts about his plans to waste his family when he finds himself in a conversation with a librarian who, despite her commitment to intellectual freedom, can't entirely control her subtle, or not so subtle, expression of alarm (in other cases it might be disgust or amusement) in response to the question, and the information seeker will be influenced to return to a better side of his nature. If our commitment to intellectual freedom is thorough, however, we should support the right of an information seeker to access whatever information they might be looking for without interference based on our own values, and we should acknowledge that privacy in information seeking is a positive aspect of disintermediation. (Personally, I think that it's a mixed bag and a phenomenon which should prompt questions of ourselves about the idea of absolute intellectual freedom.)

All Over the Map

Some of the amusing searches I've collected illustrate that web searchers use search engines for a wider range of information needs than librarians generally claim to or are expected to address. Some of the searches in the previous list illustrate this; here are some more:

- hippy yearbook quotes
- pictures of anger managements classes
- frankenberry jew
- idi amin's location
- what is the procedure for being strip searched at an airport
- "mary minow" (husband OR married)
- i hate jcrew models
- weird pictures of Jesus Christ

- find top secret information thta your not supposed to know about
- pics of stupid lazy people
- kellogs Once you pop, you can't stop
- fold dollar to find info on Sept.11
- scary background music for powerpoint
- wav library "ta da"

I should definitely point out that the world of information needs that librarians are capable of addressing is larger than the world of information needs that we are generally expected to address. So, there are frequently web searches on subjects that a librarian could handle quite well, but that a person wouldn't consider asking a librarian about because he or she doesn't think of these subjects as the kinds of things that there are likely to have been books written about. Leaving aside the fact that there is no subject too off-the-wall to have a book written about it, and the fact that librarians provide more than just books, there are information needs that an information-seeker might be justified in satisfying for himself via the web for reasons other than privacy or convenience. For example, information about individuals who are not public figures is not really in the province of libraries to collect, but it is possible to find such information on the web. Another example is the case where a person needs some type of a computer file (such as background music for a powerpoint presentation, desktop wallpaper or sounds for his or her system); the web is the logical place to go, because the file needs to end up on his or her own computer anyway. (This is an example, however, that begs us to explore our definition of information. As librarians we function with a definition of information that has to do with imparting knowledge and informing decisions, but we also tend to accept the "information age" definition of information, which refers to anything that can be transmitted by electrical signals, whether software, music, movies, pictures, or information in the older sense. On reflection, we might decide that a need for a digital file that the user ends up owning is more of a collecting or gathering (or shopping) need than an information need. This is a question worth exploring.)

In terms of information needs that public librarians would love to help with but which are too unconventional or "unserious" to bring the library to mind for most users, there is the question of how to promote the library and the librarian as an approachable helper. This is where the discussion of the image and stereotype of librarians, which sometimes seems self-involved, has actual relevance. We want users to feel comfortable coming to us with questions about "whatever." We want them to feel that we are comfortable speaking in their vernacular, and many of us want to tell the rest of the profession that it is and should be our vernacular too. But it is a difficult thing to communicate the importance of thoroughness, accuracy and information literacy without reproducing the impression that we are, if not sexless, not exactly cool. I believe that the problem may be inextricable from the nature of what we do at one level, but that at the same time it can be very helpful in many cases to use an informal manner, even to the point of not communicating so called "professionalism," when communicating with information seekers.

Children and the Otherwise Naive and Uneducated

Many web searches reveal searchers who are "not clear on the concept." They either don't know how web searches work, or they are ignorant of essential aspects of the subjects they are trying to investigate. Here are some examples:

- I need a job in San Jose that pays very well with no experience
- am i gay
- how many mins to Pinar del rio
- www. hippies clothes.com
- what might happen to france
- roman numberals
- summary of supermodels in a report format
- who owns words?
- bun laden
- What is the purpose of a Tree [why do we need them]
- using words for a proffesional request letter
- how to make manipulative female neighbor stay away
- what kind of conditions do potatoes need and provide
- When did the Information Age take place?
- how do I become seriously rich
- WHAT PART OF THE CONSTITUTION WOULD YOU DELETE ESSAY(Caps in original)

These people obviously need professional help, and we are just the professionals to provide it. But first, how can we help them find us? "Ask a Librarian" services are part of the answer, but it makes me wonder: why doesn't ALA take some of the $1 million it's devoted to that "@ Your

Library™" campaign and pay for banner ads on the web that lead to "Ask a Librarian" services? And to the extent to which we might consider it important to get people off their asses and into the library, some effective marketing on the part of local libraries seems in order. Press releases are an effective tool to reach the public which are underutilized by most libraries due to the perception that a good Public Relations program requires a PR professional. It isn't necessarily the case, as librarians would find if they chose to read some of the books on PR that sit on their own shelves. Of course, most libraries don't have a big surplus of staff time to devote to more than immediate problems, and this is part of the reason our professional associations are important. In any case, "marketing" of library services, for lack of a better word, is needed if we wish to extend these services into new territory.

People Enjoy Surfing Around

I get tons of searches like these, which seem to be aimed at nothing in particular:

- wabbits
- scary shit
- Women
- words with frog
- nobody
- juice – wheatgrass - barley
- surreal OR mentioned OR cemetery OR exempt OR scantiest
- pure unadulterated bullshit
- "largest"

These are people whose primary information need seems to be to surf around, but presumably they prefer to do it while looking at a TV-type screen in the privacy of their own home than to browse the catalog and shelves of their local library (at least at that moment). There are a lot of reasons for this. One interesting one is the instant availability of the sense of surprise that search engines offer. Who knows what will turn up—that I can access immediately—if I type in "scary shit?" It's fun and it doesn't require an attention span. Library use, on the other hand, does require an attention span. The thing about attention span that constructivist educators, who advocate lots of audio-visual accomodation to young learners' lack of it, don't acknowledge is that our attention spans are what they are because we have practiced and cultivated the art of attention, and we have done so because it has been expected of us by our parents, our teachers, and our society. If we are in a McCluhan-esque post-literate society, conditioned by technological revolutions which have superseded the printing press, the question of the role of libraries in that society arises with a new insecurity. Are we primarily the preservers and representatives of a possibly obsolete print culture, or should we gradually transform ourselves into facilitators of access primarily to sensory culture? This question can be found at the heart of problems facing librarianship in the 21st Century, but we don't know quite how to deal with it head-on.

Selected Quotes for the Week

From *Library Juice*, 1998-2005

"The more we try to get a grip on information, the more it slips through our fingers like a ghost. Information, in fact, is the ghost of meaning, and our society's worship of the ghost signals a continuing loss of meaning."
  -Stephen L. Talbott

"The fragmentation of rational knowledge in the postmodern world has produced a focus on information that is unaware of its history."
  -Marcus Breen, "Information does not equal knowledge: theorizing the political economy of virtuality." *Journal of Computer Mediated Communication* 3(3)

"The eternal conflict of good and the best with bad and the worst is on. The librarian must be the librarian militant before he can be the librarian triumphant. At the end of another century, when a conference like this is held, our descendants will look back with wonder to find that we have so long been satisfied to leave the control of the all-pervading, all-influencing newspaper in the hands of people who have behind them no motive better than 'the almighty dollar.'"
  -Melvil Dewey, in "The Relation of The State to the Public Library," originally reprinted from the *Transactions and Proceedings of the Second International Library Conference,* 1889, and published in *American Library Philosophy: An Anthology,* selected by Barbara McCrimmon, Hamden, CT: The Shoe String Press, 1975.

"I consider it important, indeed urgently necessary, for intellectual workers to get together, both to protect their own economic status and, also, generally speaking, to secure their influence in the political field."
  -Albert Einstein, 1938, in a comment explaining why he joined the American Federation of Teachers local number 552 as a charter member.

"When I was in prison, I was wrapped up in all those deep books. That Tolstoy crap—people shouldn't read that stuff."
 -Mike Tyson, in *The San Francisco Chronicle*, 12/31/96

"Never regard your study as a duty, but as the enviable opportunity to learn to know the liberating influence of beauty in the realm of spirit for your own personal joy and to the profit of the community to which your later work belongs."
 -Albert Einstein

"Of all the professions, librarianship is probably the most derivative and synthetic, is the most dependent upon the more formal disciplines for its own theoretical structure and its corpus of practice. In the past librarians have been disposed to view this characteristic as a fundamental weakness, and it has therefore generated a considerable feeling of professional inferiority. Yet this very quality has given librarianship a uniquely strategic position of leadership in the integration of human knowledge, and it could make of librarianship a great unifying force, not only in the world of scholarship, but also throughout all human life."
 -Jesse Shera, *The Foundations for Education in Librarianship*, pp. 202-3

"When you take 'Personnel Issues in Information Management,' you learn how to supervise library employees, not how to be one. When you take 'Library Administration,' you would do well to remember that you are the one who is being administered, at least in the beginning and probably for a long time. ...[T]he program of instruction leads you to believe (in a twist on the old Huey Long boast, 'Every Man a King'): 'Every Librarian a Supervisor.' Now, common sense indicates that this will not be the case. Libraries are hierarchical. To suggest that each new group of graduates will soon be Supervisors is not based in reality... So prepare yourself, learn about unions, 'the folks that brought you the weekend'..."
 -James Danky, "Libraries: They Would Have Been a Good Idea," a talk given April 17, 1997 at the University of Illinois, Urbana-Champaign, and published in Sanford Berman and James Danky, eds., *Alternative Library Literature 1996-97*, Jefferson, NC: McFarland, 1998

"I don't think we should be automating information professionals out of business. Quite the contrary, I think we should be giving them a bigger job: reaching out to support the collective cognition of particular communities. This might include systems to support the creation, circulation, and transformation of particular genres of materials. It might include setting up and configuring mailing lists or other, more sophisticated tools for shared thinking. It might include both face-to-face and remote assistance. Distributed alliances of librarians might support specific distributed communities, while comparing notes with one another and sharing tools."
  -Phil Agre, "The End of Information and the Future of Libraries,"
  Progressive Librarian 12/13, Spring/Summer 1997

"Librarians would do well to remember *Moses* or *Pieta* and think somewhat less frequently of Shannon and Weaver."
  -Jesse Shera, "Librarianship and Information Science," in Fritz Machlup and Una Mansfield, *The Study of Information: Interdisciplinary Messages* (NY: John Wiley and Sons, 1983)

"The librarian's mission should be, not like up to now, a mere handling of the book as an object, but rather a know how (mise au point) of the book as a vital function."
  - Jose Ortega y Gasset, *Mission del Bibliotecario*

"All of the books in the world contain no more information than is broadcast as video in a single large American city in a single year. Not all bits have equal value."
  -Carl Sagan

"There is no escaping from ourselves. The human dilemma is as it has always been, and we solve nothing fundamental by cloaking ourselves in technological glory."
  -Neil Postman, "Informing Ourselves to Death" (German Informatics Society, October 11, 1990)

"It is especially the narrowing of the range of public discourse in a market-dominated information industry that requires vigilant librarians who recognize that libraries in a corporate sense symbolize the totality of human knowledge in all modes of knowing. As consumers of information products, library systems could, for example, use their collective purchasing power to remain critical of the ethical consequences of convergence and concentration industry trends for their collection and interpretive functions."
-Archie L. Dick, "Epistemological Positions in Library and Information Science," *Library Quarterly*, Vol. 69, no. 3, July 1999, pp. 305-323

"We librarians ostensibly subscribe to the "balanced collection" professional ethic. Intellectual freedom, our raison d'etre, needs a garden of diversity in which to flourish. So we can certainly demand equal time for women's material after 5,000 years of male worldview! I define "women's material" as material useful to women, which works directly in our interest like a fine tool, which does not ignore, trivialize, or lie to us."
-Celeste West, "The library as motherlode: a feminist view," In James P. Danky and Elliot Shore, eds., *Alternative Materials in Libraries*. (Scarecrow, 1982)

"A man should hear a little music, read a little poetry, and see a fine picture every day of his life, in order that worldly cares may not obliterate the sense of the beautiful which God has implanted in the human soul."
-Johann Wolfgang von Goethe

"An oligarchy of private capital...cannot be effectively checked even by a democratically organized political society [because] under existing conditions, private capitalists inevitably control, directly or indirectly, the main sources of information."
-Albert Einstein, quoted in a *Nation* piece about how *Time* magazine neglected to mention, in its bio on their "Person of the Century," that Einstein was a socialist. *The Nation*, vol. 270, no. 3, January 24, 2000.

"Any dictator would admire the uniformity and obedience of the [U.S.] media."
-Noam Chomsky

"What seemed to me to be at stake at this time was a kind of censorship by effect, at the very source, where decisions are made as to what is identified as news, what information is chosen for dissemination, what ideas and views are considered acceptable, or desireable, to publish and disseminate. And the source was shrinking. Open censorship can be fought openly, and often successfully. But, how can librarians assure the broadest representation of information, opinions, and creative expression in the face of the growing concentration of ownership of communication channels?"
-Zoia Horn, *Zoia! Memoirs of Zoia Horn, Battler for the People's Right to Know,* McFarland, 1995

"To ensure a comprehensive and non-sectarian collection of material on all subjects requires a social project of great complexity. Yet as people charged with providing public access to knowledge easily equal to that of the academic, the doctor or the politician. They have the task of providing a democratic society with the information to preserve, even to improve that democracy. They are required to be unbiased and to serve everyone equally. Censorship promotes elitism, the enemy of democracy. Selection should act as a leveller. It should not ignore marginal interests. If they are to work effectively as agents for social and cultural education librarians need to engage in an activism that is largely lacking in the profession."
-Chris Atton, *Alternative Literature: A Practical Guide for Librarians,* Gower, 1996

"Creating an un-McDonaldized culture in the library is much easier when the library has un-McDonaldized librarians. These individuals can be actively recruited by going beyond the stadard requirement of an ALA-accredited MLS, an affinity for technology, knowledge of a foreign language, or other conventional criteria. Asking a candidate for evidence of creativity, whether in terms of unusual projects undertaken or a bold vision of the future, could be one way to guage a person's potential."
-Brian Quinn, "The McDonaldization of Academic Libraries?" *College and Research Libraries* May, 2000, vol. 61 no. 3

"Question managerial prerogatives"
-Sanford Berman

"Librarians persist in sublimating librarianship to the lure of the machine."
-Jesse Shera, "Librarianship and Information Science," in Fritz Machlupu and Una Mansfield (eds.), *The Study of Information: Interdisciplinary Messages*, New York: Wiley, 1983

"Business equates information with profit. Librarians must equate information with understanding. The role of the librarian is to distinguish between data and information, between facts and knowledge, and to be concerned not only with the "what" and the "how" but also with the "why.""
-Patricia Glass Schuman, in Leslie M. Campbell, "Keeping Watch on the Waterfront: Social Responsibility in Legal and Library Professional Organizations," *Law Library Journal*, Summer, 2000, vol. 92, no. 3, pp.263-286

"Many librarians hold the reassuring belief that all information in neutral and therefore the library's collection development decisions do not involve judgments about whether some information is good or bad. But for many librarians and community activists this is not the case. The belief that some information is morally wrong and that the use of these resources can lead to moral decay reflects the same concern of early library leaders."
-Mark Alfino and Linda Pierce, *Information Ethics for Librarians*, p.99 (McFarland, 1997)

"We must not confuse the thrill of acquiring or distributing information quickly with the more daunting task of converting it into knowledge and wisdom."
-Principles of Technorealism—Principle 4

"It is of great importance that the general public be given the opportunity to experience, consciously and intelligently, the efforts and results of scientific research. It is not sufficient that each result be taken up, elaborated, and applied by few specialists in the field. Restricting the body of knowledge to a small group deadens the philosophical spirit of a people and leads to spiritual poverty."
-Albert Einstein

"Perhaps this is an obvious point, but the democratic postulate is that the media are independent and committed to discovering and reporting the truth, and that they do not merely reflect the world as powerful groups wish it to be perceived. Leaders of the media claim that their news choices rest on unbiased professional and objective criteria, and they have support for this contention in the intellectual community. If, however, the powerful are able to fix the premises of discourse, to decide what the general populace is allowed to see, hear, and think about, and to "manage" public opinion by regular propaganda campaigns, the standard view of how the system works is at serious odds with reality."
 -Noam Chomsky, *Manufacturing Consent*, preface, pg xi

"Silence is the language of complicity."
 -Unknown

"It's no exaggeration to say that in the information age, texts aren't read, they're searched. But, as Heraclitus said, "If you do not expect the unexpected, you will not find it." To search a text instead of reading it is to renounce its capacity to surprise us, to make of the text more than ever before a tool, and to restrict its range of implication and suggestion to the ends we assign it."
 -Chris Fujiwara, in "Disintermediated!" *Hermenaut* #14

"It is arguable that the success of business propaganda in persuading us, for so long, that we are free from propaganda is one of the most significant propaganda acheivments of the twentieth century."
 -Alex Carey, "Managing Public Opinion: The Corporate Offensive," 1978, in *Taking the Risk Out Of Democracy*.

"If you don't read much, you really don't know much. You're dangerous."
 -Jim Trelease, quoted in "The No-Book Report: Skim It and Weep," *The Washington Post*, Monday, May 14, 2001; Page C01

"One distinguishing feature of contemporary culture in America is that information is consumed for diversion rather than for consequential purposes. Paradoxically, in other words, information of all kinds is processed as low-level cognitive distraction, a form of mass entertainment. The collapsing of news, data, broadcast, and leisure media has resulted in an entertainment culture where the act of consuming information is as diversionary as watching a variety show or a situation comedy... The simple term 'information' may no longer be adequate to describe the spectrum of input available to human beings in their capacities as data processors."
-Joseph Urgo, *In the Age of Distraction,* University of Mississippi Press, 2000

"It would be a serious intellectual mistake to confuse information that functions as entertainment with actual, or knowledge-based, information. It would be a mistake as well to simply ignore the cognitive implications of information processing as entertainment. Real information, such as who controls wealth and property in the United States, why prison building outdistances school construction, or comparative rates of upward and downward mobility, is as difficult to locate as it ever was and must be culled from the kinds of books and journals not featured and sometimes not even carried by the megabookstore at the strip mall or reported on by television features."
-Joseph Urgo, *In the Age of Distraction,* University of Mississippi Press, 2000

"Private capitalists inevitably control, directly or indirectly, the main sources of information. It is thus extremely difficult, and indeed in most cases quite impossible, for the individual citizen to come to objective conclusions and to make intelligent use of his political rights."
-Albert Einstein

"Education for freedom must begin by stating facts and enunciating values, and must go on to develop appropriate techniques for realizing the values and for combating those who, for whatever reason, choose to ignore the facts or deny the values."
-Aldous Huxley, *Brave New World Revisited,* (New York: Harper & Row, 1965), p96

"If I allowed my honest opinions to appear in one issue of my paper, before 24 hours my occupation would be gone. The business of a journalist is to destroy the truth; to lie outright; to pervert; to vilify; to fawn at the feet of mammon, and to sell his country and his race for his daily bread. You know it and I know it and what folly is this toasting an independent press ... Our talents, our possibilities and our lives are all the property of other men. We are intellectual prostitutes."
  -John Swinton of the *New York Times* toasting his profession before the New York Press Club in 1953.

"I'm a voracious reader. You have to read to survive. People who read for pleasure are wasting their time. Reading isn't fun; it's indispensable."
  -Woody Allen

"Whenever you find yourself on the side of the majority, it's time to pause and reflect."
  -Mark Twain

"This is the most information intensive war you can imagine.... We're going to lie about things."
  -Military officer involved in planning the response to the World Trade Center attack. (*Washington Post*, 9/24/01)

"We have an obligation to communicate. Here, we take the time to talk with one another... and to listen. We believe that information is meant to move and that information moves people. "
  -Enron's last published annual report

"The corporate grip on opinion in the United States is one of the wonders of the Western world. No First World country has ever managed to eliminate so entirely from its media all objectivity—much less dissent."
  -Gore Vidal, novelist and critic

"Washing one's hands of the conflict between the powerful and the powerless means to side with the powerful, not to be neutral."
 -Paulo Freire, educator (1921-1997)

"Who of us does not recognize that the life we live, however larded with brave talk about values and thought and ideals, is not actually a life dedicated to immersion in the endless torrent of images, songs, sounds and stories?"
 -Todd Gitlin, in a talk at the Commonwealth Club, February, 2002

"The first casualty of War is Truth."
 -Variously attributed to US Senator Hiram Johnson, Arthur Ponsonby, Samuel Johnson, and Aeschylus. But mostly Hiram Johnson.

"Thus in an age of specialization, of social fragmentation, the library, like the communication system of which it is a part, can become a great cohesive force at a time when social cohesion is most vital. But unlike the mass media of communication it need not be an instrument for the achievement of conformity. It is, and should remain, the stronghold of individualism. Whereas the mass media, the newspaper, radio, television, are declaratory, the library is interrogative. To the library men come seeking truth, each in his own way for his own ends. In the library the patron is not told what to think or when to think it, but in his search each must discover for himself the thoughts and opinions of others and try to understand them, to appreciate them for what they are, even though he may not share them. The library, then, must be a force for understanding, for cohesion, in a world of antagonisms, conflict, and specialization, but it must be a unifying, not a homogenizing force. The social role of the library is a very complex role and the responsibilities which society, often quite unwittingly, has placed upon it are very heavy. Certainly there is no one library form that can achieve them all; there must be many types of libraries to assume so varied a burden. But there is a unity in the library process as an agent of communication. In the character of that unity lies the key to the dilemma which the library faces today."
 -Jesse Shera, *The Foundations of Education for Librarianship*, (1972: John Wiley and Sons), p. 108.

"There is more to life than increasing it's speed."
-Mohandas K. Ghandi

"To make a contented slave it is necessary to make a thoughtless one. It is necessary to darken his moral and mental vision, and, as far as possible, to annihilate the power of reason."
-Frederick Douglass, quoted in Carl Sagan's *The Demon-Haunted World: Science as a Candle in the Dark.* (New York: Ballantine Books, 1997), p. 355.

"The library is not an institution which exists removed from our increasingly interdependent and politicized world. The professionals who control America's information institutions ... cannot retreat into those institutions and ignore the larger society. The result of this sort of myopic professionalism is to support intellectual freedom for those who have power while denying it to those who are powerless."
-Jane Robbins, *Library Journal,* January 1973. Quoted in Mark Alfino and Linda Pierce, *Information Ethics for Librarians* (Jefferson, NC: McFarland, 1997)

"The phrase, 'the free marketplace of ideas' does not refer to the market value of each idea. On the contrary, what it means is that ideas should have a chance to be put to the public, to be expressed and argued fully, and not in soundbites."
-Andre Schiffrin, *The Business of Books,* (Verso, 2001), pp. 103-4.

"It seems to me that libraries stand, above all, for the enlightened and rational notion that human beings are improved by the acquisition of knowledge and information and that no bar should be placed in their way. We stand for the individual human being pursuing whatever avenues of enquiry she or he wishes. We also stand for rationalism as the basis for all of our policies and procedures in libraries. Librarianship is a supremely rational profession and should resist the forces of irrationalism both external and internal."
-Michael Gorman, "The value and values of libraries"

"You don't have to burn books to destroy a culture. Just get people to stop reading them."
 -Ray Douglas Bradbury

"In truth, American libraries and the profession of librarianship are confronted with a structural transformation in the overall economy. It is nothing less than thorough privatization of the information function. The production, processing, storing and transmission of information have been scooped up into private, for-profit hands. Social sources and repositories of information have been taken over for commercial use and benefit. It is not because American libraries and library schools have fallen behind in the mastery of the new information technology that their existence increasingly is called into question. It is their bedrock principles and long-term practices that collide with the realities of today's corporate-centered and market-driven economy. The extent to which librarians insist on free and untrammeled access to information, 'unrestricted by administrative barriers, geography, ability to pay or format,' they will be treated by the privatizers as backward-looking, if not obsolete, irrelevant, and unrealistic. The technology issue, therefore, is merely a screen behind which a far-reaching and socially regressive institutional change has occurred. The focus on technology also serves to delude many, librarians included, that the new means to achieve status and respect is to concentrate on the machinery of information, production, and transmission. When and if this focus turns regidly exclusive, wittingly or not, the social basis of the profession and the needs of the majority of people are left unattended."
 -Herbert Schiller, *Information Inequality: The Deepening Social Crisis in America*, p. 36. (Routledge, 1996)

"For aesthetics is the mother of ethics... Were we to choose our leaders on the basis of their reading experience and not their political programs, there would be much less grief on earth. I believe-not empirically, alas, but only theoretically-that for someone who has read a lot of Dickens to shoot his like in the name of an idea is harder than for someone who has read no Dickens."
 -Joseph Brodsky (b. 1940), Russian-born American poet

"How could our precious nation have become so uncharacteristically vulnerable to such an effective use of fear to manipulate our politics? What happened? For one thing there's been a dramatic change in the nature of what the philosopher Jürgen Habermas has described as the structure of the public forum—the way our political discourse takes place. It no longer operates as it once did. It is simply no longer as accessible to the vigorous and free exchange of ideas from individuals in the way those ideas were freely and vigorously exchanged during the period of our founding."
 -Al Gore, speaking at a conference at The New School in early February, 2004, on "The Uses and Misuses of Fear," quoted by Eric Alterman in his column in *The Nation*, March 1, 2004, p. 12.

"In the beginning was the press, and then the world appeared."
 -Karl Kraus

"It would seem impossible in a year such as the past year has been with its overturnings and upheavals, not only of material things but of ideals and of what had seemed moral certainties, that we should spend the time of our annual meeting in the discussion of small or esoteric questions. These crises in life show us the littleness of little things, the subserviency of technique; make us feel through the pull of events our connection with the rest of the world, and even with the universe; take us out of our professional selves and make us conscious of more inclusive selves. And they make us see, as perhaps even we have not seen before, that our profession has a not insignificant part to play in world matters. Hence we have chosen as our general theme for the conference, "THE PUBLIC LIBRARY AND DEMOCRACY.""
 -Mary Wright Plummer in her "President's Address: The Public Library and the Pursuit of Truth," delivered at the ALA Annual Conference in Asbury Park, New Jersey, 1916.

"What a sad want I am in of libraries, of books to gather facts from! Why is there not a Majesty's library in every town? There is a Majesty's jail and gallows in every one."
 -Thomas Carlyle, in his journal while on his farm in Craigenputtock, quoted in *History of Public Libraries in Great Britain*, 1845-1965.

"Libraries are the face of government as it existed before we started
hating government and, therefore, ourselves."
-Jennifer Vogel, in "Can the Public Library (and Democracy) Survive?," *The Rake*,
February 2005.

"The third question, freedom, may be the most fundamental of the
questions raised by the information explosion. Can man be free when his
encounters with the media are dominated by the engineered response? Can
he be free when his culture becomes a kind of propaganda system, when
values and concepts are flashed at him so frequently that they are
inescapable? Can he become free when the alternatives for his life are
shown in increasingly limited ways, so that from childhood he is encouraged
to think only in certain terms about what is possible and which routes can
be followed successfully? Freedom may be God's greatest gift to man; it is
also something that man achieves, rather than begins with. Obviously, there
are different kinds of freedom; the option to choose between brands of
cereal at the store is different from the freedom to challenge someone in a
ticklish, possible threatening situation. The freedom to believe in what you
choose to believe in, to select and fight for a cause, emerges only from
mature minds and emotions which allow us to recognize the difference
between true and false freedoms."
-William Kuhns, *The Information Explosion* (1971: Thomas Nelson, Inc.), p. 82-83.

"The demand for 'relevance' by the Social Responsibilities Round Table,
and related movements in the ALA, can be traced back to the nineteenth-
century faith in the public library as a social force that would, through the
promotion of reading, save mankind from poverty, crime, vice, alcoholism,
and almost every other evil to which flesh is heir. But a more striking
parallel to the present day unrest is to be found in the pleas of the young
librarians for social action during the 1930s, for ferment was also taking
place in the profession during that decade. The storms of crisis that battered
the American economy during the last years of the Hoover Administration
and the first years of Roosevelt's promoted an awareness that the library
had sociological roots, and that the librarian should have a vigorous and
vocal social consciousness."
-Jesse Shera, *The Foundations for education in librarianship.* 1972, Becker and Hayes,
Inc. (John Wiley & Sons, Inc.)

"There are those who, clinging to the idea that the library profession should be politically neutral, would contend that contributing to social projects is not an appropriate activity for librarians. However, without a clear and vital set of philosophical and political ideals acting as a guiding beacon, the library profession will not remain neutral, but will drift aimlessly with the currents of power and privilege. "Librarians must forcefully articulate their commitment to serving the information needs of all segments of society. They must rededicate themselves to assuring the widest and most equitable access to information by opposing fees for services and the commercialization of knowledge. Furthermore, librarians must be willing to enter the political arena and advocate for these principles."
-Henry Blanke, in "Librarianship & Political Values: Neutrality or Commitment," *Library Journal*, July 1989, pp. 39-42.

"The press, which is mostly controlled by vested interests, has an excessive influence on public opinion."
-Albert Einstein, from an interview for the *Nieuwe Rotterdamsche Courant*, 1921; also quoted in *Berliner Tageblatt*, July 7 1921; Reprinted in *The Quotable Einstein* (Princeton University Press, 1996)

"As the circuit supplants the printed page, and as more and more of our communications involve us in network processes—which of their nature plant us in a perpetual present—our perception of history will inevitably alter. Changes in information storage and access are bound to impinge on our historical memory. The depth of field that is our sense of the past is not only a linguistic construct, but is in some essential way represented by the book and the physical accumulation of books in library spaces. In the contemplation of the single volume, or mass of volumes, we form a picture of time past as a growing deposit of sediment; we capture a sense of its depth and dimensionality. Moreover, we meet the past as much in the presentation of words in books of specific vintage as we do in any isolated fact or statistic. The database, useful as it is, expunges this context, this sense of chronology, and admits us to a weightless order in which all information is equally accessible."
-Sven Birkerts, *The Gutenberg Elegies*, p. 129. (Faber & Faber, 1994)

"The old idea of the intellectual as the one who speaks truth to power is still an idea worth holding on to. Tyrants fear the truth of books because it's a truth that's in hock to nobody, it's a single artist's unfettered vision of the world. They fear it even more because it's incomplete, because the act of reading completes it, so that the book's truth is slightly different in each reader's different inner world, and these are the true revolutions of literature, these invisible, intimate communions of strangers, these tiny revolutions inside each reader's imagination, and the enemies of the imagination, politburos, ayatollahs, all the different goon squads of gods and power, want to shut these revolutions down, and can't. Not even the author of a book can know exactly what effect his book will have, but good books do have effects, and some of these effects are powerful, and all of them, thank goodness, are impossible to predict in advance.

-Salman Rushdie, in "The power of love: Salman Rushdie on how literature can transform information into gold," *The Guardian* (UK), April 23, 2005.

Suggested Paper Topics

By Rory Litwin
Published in an earlier form in *Library Juice* 6:5, March 6, 2003

The following is a collection of paper topics designed to provide library students with research projects that are stimulating and that encourage some deep investigation into those core topics that make librarianship so fascinating.

Discuss the debate over whether to call library users "users," "patrons," "customers," "clients," or by some other name, with reference to appropriate concepts in sociolinguistics and other relevant disciplines e.g. symbolic interactionism, etc.

There has been some talk about "metadata" replacing MARC. Explain what is really meant by this and provide your own prediction of the future of cataloging, carefully justifying your view.

Library of Congress Subject Headings are slow to be updated to reflect changes in language and reality, and no good system exists to propagate updates into existing catalogs. Improvements in search engine technolgies and a growth in the amount of text available for keyword searching have resulted in a decline in use of subject access tools in general. Budget cuts in libraries have resulted in shrinking cataloging departments. In light of these challenges, is there a possible future for *LCSH*? What changes would LC and the library community need to put in place to overcome the trends leading away from the use of subject access, and how can the advantages of subject access be maximized in the electronic environment?

Discuss the implications of international trade agreements such as GATS and FTAA for public libraries. Evaluate the arguments of critics of these agreements in the library community and those in the community who do not see the same degree of threat.

Critical Theorists such as Jurgen Habermas as Theodore Adorno have said the Public Sphere is dead or dying, having been replaced by consumerist relations between individuals and society as a whole. Using the framework of Habermas' *The structural transformation of the public sphere* (1989), discuss how libraries and their role in society (as part of the public sphere) have changed during the period discussed. Try to develop some strategies for preserving in libraries, and in society through libraries, those aspects of the public sphere that are essential for democracy and a good society and have some hope of preservation.

In his 1950 paper, "Classification as the Basis of Bibliographic Organization," Jesse Shera wrote, "(T)here can no longer be any doubt that library classification has failed, and failed lamentably, to accomplish what it was designed to do," and called contemporary methods of library classification obsolete. Why did he make this statement? What might Shera say on the subject a half century later? ("Classification as the Basis of Bibliographic Organization." In Jesse Shera and Margaret Egan, eds., *Bibliographic Organization*, University of Chicago Press, 1951.)

Discuss the historical foundations of the common-sense distinction used in information literacy training between fact and opinion in an information source. Is the distinction between fact and opinion as clear as it first seems? Are there cases where the status of an information source as fact or opinion is unclear? What are the implications of your findings for information literacy education?

Assess the "Berninghausen debate," about intellectual freedom and the social responsibilities movement in American libraries. What is the history of the debate, including its continued life up to the present? Refer to the relevant literature. Express and defend your opinion on the issue.

Is the value of the public library measured as a part of the Gross Domestic Product? Should it be? Discuss possible methods for measuring the economic value of library services?

In a 1983 essay, Jesse Shera wrote, "Twenty years ago, I thought of what is now called information science as providing the intellectual and theoretical foundations of librarianship, but I am now convinced that I was wrong." Why did Shera say this? What is your assessment of the relationship between librarianship and information science? Include definitions of the two terms and justify those definitions with reference to the literature. ("Librarianship and Information Science," in *The study of information: interdisciplinary messages*, Fritz Machlup and Una Mansfield, eds. John Wiley and Sons, 1983.)

Current community information, often in the form of brochures and flyers from local non-profit organizations or other community groups, is usually uncontrolled, uncatalogued, and likely to be missed in public libraries. What are some reasons for this? What are some possibilities for improving access to this type of community information? What types of community information might have a place in the library but usually aren't found there? What systems exist in libraries for providing access to community information, and how would you improve upon them?

Examine the problem of 'library anxiety,' particularly anxiety of patrons in approaching reference librarians. Are reference librarians aware of these patrons or are they invisible in the reference context? What contributing factors to library anxiety can you find in the literature? Can you think of any other contributing factors? Is gender a factor in library anxiety?

What are the historical origins of the UNESCO Public Library Manifesto ("Missions of the Public Library")? What is its application in real terms, in the United States and elsewhere? Does it have any effect? How? What were/are the implications of the US leaving UNESCO and its recent return for US, global, and other national cultural and educational institutions?

Read the article "Epistemological Positions and Library and Information Science," by Archie L. Dick, in *Library Quarterly*, vol. 69 no. 3. In light of this article, consider the question of "Creation Science" literature in your library, in terms of collection development, reference service, and cataloging.

Read the short essay, "Neutrality, Objectivity and the Political Center," in this book. What are your own views on the subject? Explain your differences with Litwin's ideas, making your arguments carefully and completely.

Explain what "intellectual freedom" would mean in an absolute sense. What are some of the various types of limitations to intellectual freedom that librarians routinely apply? What are some hypothetical situations where intellectual freedom might be limited by other concerns even for the strongest believers in the ethic? Feel free to disagree with the premises of the question, but discuss the limits or potential limits to intellectual freedom as a practical value.

Media critics refer to "market censorship" as the weeding out of challenging ideas in mainstream media as a consequence of the media's ownership by larger and larger companies that have more and more ties to other industries. How do trends in the publishing industry related to market censorship affect book selection in libraries according to standard methods, and what are some possible ways of countering market censorship in libraries? Is market censorship an intellectual freedom issue?

In *Prejudices and Antipathies* and later writings over the years, Sanford Berman raised a series of strong criticisms of Library of Congress Subject Headings. Analyze these criticisms in terms of their basis. Do they fall into identifiable categories according to the principles that Berman applied to the problem of subject headings? How did Berman himself express these principles? Are these principles ever in conflict? To what extent do you agree or disagree with Berman's ideas about subject headings and their application? Carefully defend your ideas.

Part 1: Summarize the current controversies surrounding recent and proposed changes to copyright law. Part 2: Compare the current state of copyright law to the agreements in the Berne Conventions of 1887 and 1889. Part 3: Offer some innovative (or not so innovative) strategies that the library community should pursue in order to preserve in libraries the freedom to read in the face of these changes. (Be practical, considering the political realities with which policy makers have to contend.)

Much has been written about the "death of the book" in the electronic age, now that the potential exists to distribute, manage and read texts in electronic media. Are we rather beginning to see the "death of reading," as electronic communication has sped up processes of work and communication to the point that people feel too impatient with paragraphs to spend the time required to understand and contend with fully-formed thoughts? What are the implications for libraries of the quickened pace of life in the information age?

Of what knowledge does Library and Information Science consist? What disciplines does it overlap, and what are the defining elements and boundaries of the discipline? What areas of research are purely "Library and Information Science?" Describe the body of knowledge that has been collected via research in the field, evaluating the progress that has been made in each area. Based on what you find, in what areas has research been most lacking, and where is the greatest potential for progress in the field?

Read "Libraries, Librarians, and the Discourse of Fear," by Gary and Marie Radford, *Library Quarterly*, Vol. 71 Issue 3 (July 2001), pp. 299-330. Critically assess their findings. To the extent that their uncovering of the public's negative images of libraries and librarians is accurate, what are its implications for the efforts of younger librarians to "update" the image of the profession? What unexamined possibilities exist for overcoming negative aspects of the image of libraries? What changes would these require in the actuality of libraries and in professional practice?

Self-identified radical or progressive librarians (organized in groups such as SRRT and PLG, or floating freely on the anarchist librarians listserv), especially in the younger generation, are often seen as insurgents in the profession, threatening to the professional culture in some way. By contrast, these individuals usually see themselves as keepers of the professional flame. Examine the issues surrounding this discontinuity of perception and make the case for each opposing view. Extra points for applying relevent sociological concepts.

What does "agribusiness versus farming" offer as an analogy to commodified versus community-based information and communication?

Describe some of the alternatives to hierarchical organizational schemes (as in indexing) that have been suggested. Are they truly non-hierarchical forms of organization or are they merely non-hierarchical representations of hierarchical structures? To what extent do they truly offer something new? For each organizational scheme that you examine, identify potential advantages, likely problems and suggest solutions to those problems.

Some Books for Progressive Librarians

Libraries and philosophy

Alfino, Mark and Linda Pierce, *Information Ethics for Librarians*. (McFarland, 1997).

Budd, John M., *Knowledge and Knowing in Library and Information Science: A Philosophical Framework*. (Scarecrow Press, 2001).

Frankfurt, Harry G., *On Bullshit*. (Princeton University Press, 2005).

Gramsci, Antonio, *Selections from the Prison Notebooks*. (Lawrence and Wishart, 1971).

Jameson, Fredric, *Postmodernism, or, The Cultural Logic of Late Capitalism*. (Duke University Press, 1992).

Shera, Jesse, *The Foundations of Education for Librarianship*. (John Wiley and Sons, 1972).

The present situation of libraries

Birdsall, William F., *The Myth of the Electronic Library: Librarianship and Social Change in America*. (Greenwood Press, 1994).

Buschman, John E., *Dismantling the Public Sphere: Situating and Sustaining Librarianship in the Age of the New Public Philosophy*. (Libraries Unlimited, 2003).

Crawford, Walt and Michael Gorman, *Future Libraries: Dreams, Madness, & Reality*. (American Library Association, 1995).

D'Angelo, Ed, *Barbarians at the Gates of the Public Library: How Postmodern Consumer Capitalism Threatens Democracy, Civil Education and the Public Good*. (Library Juice Press, 2006).

Harris, Michael H., Stan A. Hannah, and Pamela C. Harris, *Inventing the Future: The Foundations of Library and Information Services in the Post-Industrial Era, Second Edition.* (Ablex, 1998).

Harris, Roma, *Librarianship: The Erosion of a Woman's Profession.* (Ablex, 1992).

Machlup, Fritz and Una Mansfield (eds.), *The Study of Information: Interdisciplinary Messages.* (Wiley, 1983).

Rikowski, Ruth, *Globalisation, Information And Libraries: The Implications of the World Trade Organisation's GATS And TRIPS Agreements.* (Chandos Publishing, 2005).

Postindustrial capitalism and communication

Bagdikian, Ben, *The New Media Monopoly.* (Beacon Press, 2004).

Chomsky, Noam and Edward S. Herman, *Manufacturing Consent: The Political Economy of the Mass Media.* (Pantheon, 2002).

Gandy, Oscar H. Jr. *The Panoptic Sort: A Political Economy of Personal Information.* (Westview Press, 1993).

Gandy, Oscar H. Jr. *Communication and Race. A Structural Perspective.* (Edward Arnold and Oxford University Press, 1998).

Klein, Naomi, *No Logo: Taking Aim at the Brand Bullies.* (Picador, 1999).

McChesney, Robert W., Ellen Meiksins Wood, and John Bellamy Foster, (eds.) *Capitalism and the Information Age: The Political Economy of the Global Communication Revolution.* (Monthly Review Press, 1998).

Mosco, Vincent and Janet Wasko, *Political Economy of Information.* (University of Wisconsin Press, 1988).

Schiffrin, André, *The Business of Books.* (Verso, 2001).

Schiller, Dan, *Digital Capitalism: Networking the Global Market System.* (MIT Press, 1999).

Schiller, Herbert I. *Information Inequality*. (Routledge, 1996).

Sinclair, Upton, *The Brass Check: A Study of American Journalism*. (University of Illinois Press, 2003).

Soley, Lawrence, *Censorship, Inc.* (Monthly Review Press, 2002).

Stauber, John and Sheldon Rampton, *Toxic Sludge is Good For You : Lies, Damn Lies and the Public Relations Industry*. (Common Courage Press, 1995).

Vaidhyanathan, Siva, *Copyrights And Copywrongs: The Rise Of Intellectual Property And How It Threatens Creativity*. (New York University Press, 2001).

The information age and cultural change

Birkerts, Sven, *The Gutenberg Elegies: The Fate of Reading in an Electronic Age*. (Faber and Faber, 1994).

Borsook, Paulina, *Cyberselfish: A Critical Romp Through the Terribly Libertarian Culture of High Tech*. (Public Affairs, 2000).

McLuhan, Marshall, *Understanding Media: The Extensions of Man (critical edition)*. (Ginkgo Press, 2003).

Ong, Walter J. *Orality and Literacy: The Technologizing of the Word*. (Routledge, 2002).

Orr, David, *Ecological Literacy: Education and the Transition to a Postmodern World*. (State University of New York Press, 1992).

Perelman, Michael, *Class Warfare in the Information Age*. (Macmillan, 1998).

Postman, Neil, *Amusing Ourselves to Death*. (Viking Penguin, 1985).

Postman, Neil, *Technopoly: The Surrender of Culture to Technology*. (Vintage Books, 1992).

Roszak, Theodore, *The Cult of Information: A Neo-Luddite Treatise on High-Tech, Artificial Intelligence, and the True Art of Thinking*. (University of California Press, 1994).

Urgo, Joseph, *In the Age of Distraction*. (University of Mississippi Press, 2000).

Progressive library history, biography, and memoirs

Bundy, Mary Lee and Frederick J. Stielow (eds.), *Activism in American Librarianship, 1962-1973*. (Greenwood Press, 1987).

Du Mont, Rosemary Ruhig, *Reform and Reaction: The Big City Public Library in American Life*. (Greenwood Press, 1977).

Hildenbrand, Suzanne, *Reclaiming the American Library Past: Writing the Women In*. (Ablex, 1996).

Horn, Zoia, *Zoia!: Memoirs of Zoia Horn, Battler for People's Right to Know*. (McFarland, 1995).

Josey, E.J., *The Black Librarian in America*. (Scarecrow Press, 1970).

Kister, Kenneth, *Eric Moon: The Life and Library Times*. (McFarland, 2002).

Litwin, Rory (ed.), *Library Daylight: Tracings of Modern Librarianship, 1874-1922*. (Library Juice Press, 2006).

Raber, Douglas, *Librarianship and Legitimacy: The Ideology of the Public Library Inquiry*. (Greenwood Press, 1997).

Robbins, Louise, *Censorship and the American Library: The American Library Association's Response to Threats to Intellectual Freedom, 1939-1969*. (Greenwood Press, 1997).

Robbins, Louise, *The Dismissal of Miss Ruth Brown: Civil Rights, Censorship, and the American Library*. (University of Oklahoma Press, 2000).

Samek, Toni, *Intellectual Freedom and Social Responsibility in American Librarianship, 1967-1974*. (McFarland, 2001).

Thomison, Dennis, *A History of the American Library Association, 1876-1972*. (American Library Association, 1978).

Tucker, John Mark, *Untold Stories: Civil Rights, Libraries and Black Librarianship.* (University of Illinois, Urbana-Champaign: Graduate School of Library and Information Science, 1998).

Issues in Libraries

Atton, Chris, *Alternative Literature: A Practical Guide for Librarians.* (Gower, 1996).

Baker, Nicholson, *Double Fold: Libraries and the Assault on Paper.* (Vintage Books, 2002).

Berman, Sanford, *Prejudices and Antipathies: A Tract on the LC Subject Heads Concerning People.* (McFarland, 1993).

Castillo-Speed, Lillian, ed., *The power of language : selected papers from the Second REFORMA National Conference: El poder de la palabra.* (Libraries Unlimited, 2001).

Danky, James, *Alternative Materials in Libraries.* (Scarecrow Press, 1982).

Luévano-Molina, Susan, *Immigrant Politics and the Public Library.* (Greenwood Press, 2001).

McCook, Kathleen de la Peña, *A Place at the Table: Participating in Community Building.* (American Library Association, 2000).

McCook, Kathleen de la Peña, *Introduction to Public Librarianship.* (Neal-Schuman, 2003).

Nauratil, Marcia J., *Public Libraries and Non-traditional Clienteles: The Politics of Special Services.* (Greenwood Press, 1985).

Venturella, Karen (ed.), *Poor People and Library Services.* (McFarland, 1997).

About the Contributors

Luis Acosta

Luis M. Acosta is a Legal Information Analyst in the Public Services Division of the Law Library of Congress. He received a B.A. in sociology from the University of Florida, a J.D. degree from the George Washington University Law School, and an M.S.L.S. from the Catholic University School of Library and Information Science. He practiced law in Washington, D.C. prior to becoming a librarian. He became a reference librarian at Howard University Law Library in July 2000, and has worked in the Law Library of Congress since August 2002.

Chuck D'Adamo

Politicized in 1968, Charles D'Adamo was a re-founder of the Alternative Press Center in 1974. D'Adamo is co-editor of the *Alternative Press Index*, co-author of *Annotations: A Guide to the Independent Critical Press*, and editorial collective member of Baltimore Indymedia and its newspaper the *Indypendent Reader*.

Doug Horne

Doug Horne has been a librarian for 15 years, most of that time in the academic library environment at the University of Guelph where he is currently the Head, Academic Liaison. Although being precoccupied with the day to day work of being a senior manager, he devotes as much time and energy as possible to pondering and developing information technology services. This work has included developing an early CD-Rom network, web design, and the development of a web-based system for delivering numerical data.

Mark Hudson

Mark Hudson has worked in public and academic libraries and is currently Adult Services Librarian at the Monroeville Public Library in suburban Pittsburgh. He is a member of the Progressive Librarians Guild and the American Library Association's Social Responsibilities Round Table, and a longtime activist in movements for peace and global justice.

Margaret Myers

Margaret Myers is former director of the ALA Office for Library Personnel Resources (now ALA Human Resource Development and Recruitment). After working at ALA she served in the Peace Corps in Botswana. She also served as Assistant Professor and Placement Director at Rutgers University School of Communication, Information and Library Studies (her alma mater). She is presently retired.

Rhonda Neugebauer

Rhonda L. Neugebauer is Bibliographer for Latin American Studies and Interim Assistant University Librarian for Collections at the University of California, Riverside Libraries. She has organized several delegations of US librarians to visit Cuban libraries and librarians written about her research in Cuba and encouraged the collaboration of US and Cuban librarians.

Larry Oberg

Larry R. Oberg is university librarian emeritus, Willamette University, Salem, Oregon. He is a Phi Beta Kappa graduate of the University of California, Berkeley. His career interests include library administration, library staffing, new models of reference service, and Cuban librarianship. He now lives in Quebec City and publishes in French as well as English. His biography appears in Who's Who in America.

Tami Oliphant

Tami Oliphant is currently working toward a PhD in Library and Information studies at the University of Western Ontario. Her research interests include publishing, historical and philosophical foundations of librarianship, information behaviour, reference services, and collection development.

Carol Reid

Carol Reid is a cataloger at the New York State Library. She has edited numerous library publications, including NYLA's Intellectual Freedom Round Table newsletter *Pressure Point* and ALA's *SRRT Newsletter*. She has written extensively on the subject of censorship and was the 1991 recipient of the NYLA/SIRS Intellectual Freedom Award. Carol is also a fan of children's books and recently curated an exhibit at the Albany Institute of History & Art about Louis Slobodkin.

Mark Rosenzweig

Mark Rosenzweig was a founder of the Progressive Librarians Guild and of the journal *Progressive Librarian*. He has been active in the American Library Association as an elected Councilor-at-large and as a member of the Social Responsibilities Round Table/Action Council. Mark lives in New York City.

Ann Sparanese

Ann Sparanese, MLS, is the Head of Adult & Young Adult Services at the Englewood (NJ) Public Library. She is a two term elected member of ALA Council, and has served on many ALA committees, as well as the SRRT Action Council, during her 15 years of membership in ALA. She received both a New York Times Librarian Award and ALA's Elizabeth Futas Catalyst for Change Award in 2003. Sparanese speaks and writes on library activism, libraries and labor, and other issues. She has been a frequent traveler to Cuba since her first trip there in 1972 as a member of the Venceremos Brigades.

Barbara Tillett

Dr. Tillett is Chief of the Cataloging Policy and Support Office (CPSO) at the Library of Congress and Acting Chief of the Cataloging Distribution Service. She has been active in the American Library Association throughout her 36 years as a librarian, including founding the Authority Control Interest Group in 1984 and chairing the ALCTS Cataloging and Classification Section. She has served on the editorial committees of *ACRL Publications in Librarianship*, *Advances in Librarianship*, and continues for *Cataloging & Classification Quarterly*, and was a reviewer for *Library Resources & Technical Services* and *College & Research Libraries*. Her many publications have focused on cataloging theory and practice, authority control, bibliographic relationships, conceptual modeling, and library automation. Her dissertation on bibliographic relationships has been a source for conceptual designs of computer-based systems for bibliographic control.

Jessamyn West

Jessamyn West is a community technology educator in central Vermont, where she works with public librarians and seniors, helping them use technology to solve problems. Her first technology education position was in 1994, training journalists in Bucharest, Romania how to use pine and gopher. She started her website *jessamyn.com* in 1995; she is also the editor of the weblog, *librarian.net*, where she examines the intersection of libraries, technology, and politics. She is a moderator of the online community metafilter.com. She can teach anyone how to use a computer, and still types letters to friends on an Underwood-Olivetti Lettera 22. She will send you a letter if you send her a postcard.

About Rory Litwin

Rory Litwin grew up in a small house in a redwood grove in Larkspur, California, just north of San Francisco. He came to library school in 1996 with a background that included studies in philosophy and art, political activism, and an "eclectic and colorful" work history. After a period of intense self-reflection and a sense ennui that resulted from a surfeit of options, like many in his generation, he discovered the profession of librarianship as a much-needed path to a meaningful life.

Litwin lived four blocks from the San Jose State University campus while attending graduate school there. He read widely and deeply in library studies and related fields, formed important connections with LIS faculty and librarians locally and nationally, began his professional contributions to the American Library Association and the Progressive Librarians Guild, began publishing the e-zine *Library Juice,* and established the Libr.org Web domain, which is the site of numerous progressive projects. Despite his zealous approach to librarianship ("zealot" is the word to describe him in these days), he found his coursework at SJSU mind-numbingly dull and intellectually vapid, and earned mediocre grades. He is not a member of Beta Phi Mu.

Since graduating Litwin has worked in public, corporate, government and academic libraries, and is presently happy as a reference and collection development librarian with responsibilities in humanities and the arts at the University of Minnesota, Duluth. He has served as a member of the Action Council of the ALA Social Responsibilities Round Table since 2001 and as a member of ALA Council since 2005. He is a member of the editorial board of *Progressive Librarian* and has served on the Coordinating Committee of the Progressive Librarians Guild since 2003.

Litwin's viewpoint on contemporary library issues is shaped in part by the Frankfurt School of critical theory, but also by certain existentialist and spiritual concerns that he encountered in his studies in philosophy.

Rory Litwin lives alone with his cat, Marjorie (Margie for short), in an old house a short walk from the shore of Lake Superior. He finds the quietness of Duluth conducive to productive thinking and the various projects he pursues in his free time. Fine food and live jazz, however, two things he loves, are somewhat scarce.

Index

International Federation of Library
   Associations, 159, 163, 171-172
   Free Access to Information and
   Freedom of Expression Committee,
   171-172
Internet, 67, 119-131, 142, 150
Iraq war, 94, 119-131
   See also Gulf War 1 and Gulf War 2
Iraqi Resistance, 125
Iraqi retreat from Kuwait, 120

J

Jameson, Frederic, 7-8
Jessamyn.com, 152
Jews, 81-82
Jim Pattison Group, 97
Johns Hopkins University, 69
Johnson, Hiram, 206
Jose Marti National Library [Cuba], 155
   See Biblioteca Nácional "Jose Marti

K

Kant, Immanuel, 37-38
Kautsky, Karl, 38
Kent, Robert, 163-173
Kerry, John, 30
Kraus, Karl, 209
Kropotkin, Peter Alexeyevich, 140
Kuhns, William, 210

L

"L" word (Library), 71
LCSH, 75-83, 142
LC subject heading reform, 75-83
Labadie collection, University of
   Michigan, 140
Labor movement, 90
Lacey, Mike, 111
Last.fm, 70
Latin American solidarity, 110
Law Librarians Society, Washington,
   D.C., 49
Law Library of Congress, 54

Lesbian alternative literature, 109

Lee, Dennis, 107
Left (political), 113-115, 141
LISnews.com, 10
Librarian.net, 140, 151
Librarians
   Academic, 21
   'Content' people, 19-20
   Facilitator of dialogue and
   interpretation, 34-35
   Militant, 197
   Mission, 199
   New generation, 135
   Relevance of, 22
   Salaries, 41-57
   Social activists, 115, 210, 211
   Social consciousness, 210,211
   Stereotypes, 59-60, 135-136
   Techie, 25-27
   Triumphant, 197
   vs. "information professionals," 15-23
   Wake-up call, 129
   Web-centric, 71

Librarianship, 8, 208
   Altruism of, 43-44
   Anarchist, 139-145
   Beginnings, 141
   Contradistinction to commercialized
   information, 70
   Deluded, 208
   Democratic ideas of, 49,209
   Derivative, 198
   Education, 51
   Fascism, no true l. under, 35
   Humanistic approach, 33-38
   Information science, 214
   Lure of the machine, 202
   Not an information profession 15-23
   Philosophical foundation, 33-38
   Privacy, 71-74
   Rational, 207
   Role, 202
   Salaries, 41-57
   Social good of, 44
   Socialism, 145
   Status, 41-57
   Synthetic, 198
   Unifying force, 198

Printed in the United States
104197LV00006B/146/A

9 780977 861736